THE HUMANE ECONOMY

NORMAN POLLACK

THE HUMANE ECONOMY

POPULISM, CAPITALISM, AND DEMOCRACY

RUTGERS UNIVERSITY PRESS
NEW BRUNSWICK AND LONDON

Library of Congress Cataloging-in-Publication Data

Pollack, Norman.
The humane economy : populism, capitalism, and democracy
Norman Pollack.
p. cm.
Includes bibliographical references.
ISBN 0-8135-1599-8
1. Capitalism—United States—Moral and ethical aspects.
2. Populism—United States—History. 3. Democracy—History.
4. Liberty—History. 5. Industry and state—United States—History.
I. Title.
HB501.P638 1990
330.12′2—dc20 90-31078
CIP

British Cataloging-in-Publication information available

Copyright © 1990 by Norman Pollack
All Rights Reserved
Manufactured in the United States of America

For dearest Mom

Ninety years
in God's light
devoted to truth, simplicity, nature
Inner peace
courage
a life of goodness

Contents

Preface

This book explores the Populist movement in order to identify the economic and political correlates of a democratic society. I am drawn to Populism because of its substantive concerns, its moral clarity, and its intellectual complexity. I also find it fascinating because it occupied an ambiguous and, as I shall try to explain, a historically untenable position within the context of American capitalist development. Studying Populism is a means of ascertaining the limits of democracy in America. These can be seen in both the grievances that constituted its acute indictment of American industrial development on moral, economic, and political grounds and the repression of Populist ideas and protest. Yet the limits of American democracy are also revealed in Populist thought itself. When critics mute their own criticism, this may indicate internal restraint, limitation of awareness, and self-pacification, all of which require explanation and understanding.

In this work, I am looking *at* Populism as a self-contained scholarly enterprise. My primary interest is the elucidation of Populist ideas as they were applied to the conception and practice of democracy. However, I am also looking *through* Populism to understand the meaning of America. The latter aim is my subtext, and because specialists in the field of American history are sometimes unconcerned with problems of subtext, I am addressing a different kind of reader as well. These hypothetical readers may care little about Populism; perhaps they are approaching it for the first time in a serious way. But they care deeply about the concept of democracy and, in practical terms, the relationship between democracy and capitalism in the American setting. Yet whoever the readers are, it is important that they set aside all preconceived notions about what is proper to a definition of American democracy.

Ideological blinders, from whatever source, will only prevent comprehension of the topic. Thus, the historian should set out neither to fault the Populist movement nor to use it merely as a vehicle by which to pronounce with certainty the only acceptable definition of democracy. Particularly at the level of subtext, the inquiry has to be open-ended. Perhaps it should be initiated by this question: When Populism is viewed in the harsh light of the contemporary economic and cultural setting, can it be said that the movement contributed to a social vision of human welfare? Populism was not a utopian projection from the philosopher's desk. Undoubtedly, this will disappoint some, who hold transcendence of social systems as the only satisfactory test of democratic thought. Populism was not a fully conceived or self-proclaimed socialist movement. This will displease others, who reject on *a priori* grounds any real or potential connection between capitalism and democracy. Populism did not give unqualified sanction to capitalism; it even proposed significant modifications of the property right. This will probably disillusion others, who demand the strict equation of capitalism and human freedom. In other words, the charm of Populism is that it pleases almost no one of orthodox persuasion. Conversely, the unorthodox investigator, who searches beneath ideology to determine the human factors in social thought, might profit most from the study of the movement. Finally, some may doubt the value of ideas per se as a useful guide to the analysis of historical experience; yet I find that with age I grow closer to a philosophy of Idealism (the American Jamesian, rather than German Hegelian, variety).

In my recent book, *The Just Polity*, I presented the constitutional, legal, and moral features of Populist thought that contributed to the movement's formulation and expression of a democratic faith. As part of their ideological mission, Populists identified several critical areas as essential to a public philosophy of democracy. These included the nature and location of sovereignty and the whole relation of the political order to an expanding system of capitalism; the characteristics of, and requirements for, a democratic state, and the permissible scope of its powers; the role of moral values in giving the social structure human purpose; and lastly, the meaning of individual rights and the balance to be struck between the individual and the community that would ensure the protection of rights to both these spheres. Many Populists believed that these concerns were derived from a common source—a monopolistic encroachment on the traditional framework of liberty in America.

The present book marks the transition from a political to an economic frame of reference. Here I look specifically at the Populists' construction of democratic capitalism. I examine the economic implications of their political analysis, and because they themselves would not have accepted the artificial distinction between the economic and political realms of thought, I also examine their public philosophy of democracy for the provisions that complete their discussion of social organization. Society is more than government or a conception of justice, however important both government and justice were to the Populist conception of a humanly fulfilling economy.

This is not to suggest that economic thought was the movement's intellectual culmination, the point toward which all political currents flowed. Quite the contrary, Populists regarded economics, at best, as the dependent variable in society. Economic deprivation had resulted in a loss of *political* liberties. Populist political discourse was always primarily about power relations and the foundations of authority, and only secondarily (or when the context was appropriate) about the electoral process and politics. Yet, because the political and economic realms were inseparable, Populists saw an order of priorities: Until the society returned to its constitutional principles and respected the rule of law, no form of democratic economic arrangements would have lasting effect. I felt it essential to begin, in the preceding volume, with the theme of constitutionalism and related ideas of a political nature. I have not abandoned them here, but I now reapproach the body of evidence from a different angle. I want to determine more directly the attitude of Populists toward elements in capitalism that they thought should be changed as well as those that they believed worth conserving.

In this second work, I move from the idea of a just polity to an analysis of Populist thought as it pertains to modernization. This shift in emphasis introduces a range of concerns that makes clear the industrial specificity of the Populist argument on behalf of individual rights and the democratic state. The term "modernization" connotes a broad historical process, and Populists appear to have fully understood this, although they used other words to describe the advent of modern times. It is therefore necessary to indicate the separate components of the process as Populists used them in their analysis of American society. Significantly, they did not construe modernization solely in terms of technological advancement divorced from issues of political economy.

The rise of industrialism was the most visible factor defining the modern era, and this was uniquely the province of technological forces. But in addition, industrialism meant the economic organization (and the capitalist appropriation) of industry and technology. Populists were concerned about the power of this organization to shape class structure and control the lives of working people.

They then proceeded to a wider context of meaning. Modernization became identified with the idea of a social transformation. Populists' focus in this case was on the political determinants of an industrial society. Implicitly, they raised the fundamental question of the relationship between capitalism and government and its bearing on achieving political democracy. They were asking what alterations would be required in these respective spheres of power—capitalism and government—if the principle of individual freedom was to be safeguarded. And their usage of modernization was bound up with their awareness of historical development itself. To a surprising degree, Populists grasped the main features of the capitalistic formations that preceded, and developed in, their own period. In this book, I attempt to define the Populist variant of capitalism. Populists affirmed a particular framework of economy, but they also spoke independently and rejected major parts of the laissez-faire and prevailing modes of capitalism.

Throughout the course of my discussion, it is apparent that an economic analysis of Populist social theory emphasizes the movement's political philosophy. Populists conceived moral questions concerning democracy, justice, and equity as inseparable from the functioning of the economic system, and they considered government the medium through which these moral and economic factors operated. One can speak of a moral economy of capitalism in describing the specifically economic factors of their argument, but even this falls short of a full statement of their position because the moral economy could only be built on the foundations of political democracy. This book, therefore, is concerned with not only Populism's view of capitalism but also its understanding of the democratic state; here economic theory and political theory become indivisible, reflecting the Populists' own unwillingness to divide the structure of contemporary society.

My previous work called attention to the role of law, constitutionalism, and traditional premises of liberty as shaping forces in the movement's political and moral thought. I now want to provide a more formal treatment of the macroeconomic plane in order to locate Populism's ideological position within a capitalist spectrum. This approach further helps to identify the importance of government to the Populist variant of capitalism; indeed, the independent state was its differentiating feature. The independent state, in contradistinction to a structural partnership of business and government, would have supervisory powers over the business system; but moreover, it would possess extensible powers because its sovereignty would be derived from the people, who are the source of final authority in a democratic society. The idea of extensible powers frequently appears in this study; in addition, to describe the contours of the Populist variant of capitalism with greater preciseness, I have made a fairly detailed comparison between it, the Smithian mode of capitalism, and the contemporary mode. Comparative analysis helps one to appreciate the varieties of capitalism. Capitalism is not everywhere and at all times the same.

In this book, I use historical evidence in two ways. First, I provide sufficient primary materials so that the reader can see the sources I draw on for my analysis of Populism. There is no hard and fast correspondence between the body of evidence and the resulting theory. No single document matches a specific aspect of theory; instead, the evidence taken as a whole constitutes a unified field from which reasonable projections can be made. In a variety of documents, one finds an acceptance of private property, a quest for structural relevance or political legitimation, and an idealization of America and its heritage of democratic rights. What does it all add up to? The task of theory is to make sense of disparate elements, hitherto overlooked fragments of thought, or incompletely expressed ideas. One takes one's bearings, asking what has been learned about the facts in the course of the investigation. I also use historical evidence in this book to convey a sense of the Populist experience, its universe of discourse, mental rhythms, speech patterns—in fine, the interior dimension of the movement with its crosscurrents of doubt, ambiguity, and profound conviction—so that the reader will have a better sense of what Populism represented.

Roughly speaking, evidence precedes theory in my account, and theory becomes progressively more speculative toward the close of the analysis, when I compare the Populist formation of capitalism with other modes of capitalism. The first two chapters provide the general themes of Populism relating to capitalism, industrial repression, the nature of humanity, the democratic state, and political sovereignty. In furnishing the basic documentation for the theoretical study, I give only the gist of the evidence from the previous book; I have reorganized my findings to ascertain their specifically economic implications. The remainder of this book consists of theoretical analysis. These chapters discuss sequentially the Populist framework of capitalism. They examine Populism in relation to modernity, laissez-faire, and contemporary capitalism. Here I condense the earlier material still further and add brief extracts from other sources, such as Henry D. Lloyd's *Wealth Against Commonwealth*. Combining evidence with theory provides firmer guidance to the reader.

In addition to the editors of the Topeka *Advocate* and the Lincoln *Farmers' Alliance*, I have included the following Populists, listed here in the order of their appearance in the text, in my account: William A. Peffer, a Populist U.S. senator, lawyer, and newspaper editor, from Kansas; James B. Weaver, the Populist presidential candidate in 1892, former congressman, and Greenback-Labor party activist, from Iowa; W. Scott Morgan, a newspaper editor, organizer of the National Reform Press Association, and popular reform voice of the Southwest, from Arkansas; James H. Davis, a lawyer, publicist, and outstanding party orator, from Texas; Lorenzo D. Lewelling, a Populist governor and compassionate spokesman for the unemployed, from Kansas; Frank Doster, a jurist, philosophical humanist, and party theoretician, from Kansas; Tom Watson, an Alliance congressman, active political campaigner, major figure in southern Populism, and newspaper editor, from Georgia; Ignatius Donnelly, a reform author, state party leader, and popular tribune on behalf of antimonopolism, from Minnesota; and Thomas L. Nugent, a jurist, religious mystic, student of monetary questions, and twice candidate for governor, from Texas. This group reflects a diversity of ideological and political positions within Populism and represents both principal regions of the movement's strength.

In *The Just Polity* I attempted to determine whether Populism constituted an alternative pattern of modernization in American history, despite its acceptance of the property right and its other ideological restraints. This question has a more positive answer in the light of the preponderant trends of capitalist development. Yet I would argue that Populism remained a movement of reform, not radicalism. In what follows, I present a succinct account of the Populist synthesis of economics and ethics to form a democratic polity that was outside the mainstream of the American historical experience.

This book benefited immensely from Jeanine Rosenberg's skillful editing of my tangled prose. Anne Albers patiently transcribed my microscopic writing into typescript and cheerfully presided over seemingly endless revisions. Lisa Nowak Jerry superbly copyedited the manuscript for the press. For sustaining me in my work, I am grateful to many teachers, colleagues, and students, particularly Frank Freidel, Gordon Stewart, Stanley Vittoz, and Ronald Edsforth. Because of their creative vitality, Gerhard Magnus and James Adley inspire me to remain sensitive to aesthetic values. I owe my deepest obligation, for their love and companionship, to my wife, Nancy, and my son, Peter. They define my life, nourish my heart, and, in the warmth of our mutual trust, return me to elemental truths.

"Plain song"
February 1990

THE HUMANE ECONOMY

Introduction

I provide the background for my theory in a brief sketch of Populism. I simply cover the traditional ground of Populist economic grievances to familiarize nonspecialists with basics necessary for them to follow more closely the ensuing analysis of political and economic ideas. But in reality I also address scholars of Populism. I suggest to them that the traditional ground conceals as much as it reveals the substance of Populist thought. However exhaustive one's coverage, the tacit equation of historical location and economic grievances fails to take into account the movement's noneconomic and nonagricultural dimensions, or to be exact, its wider critique of the prevailing industrial society. In the introduction I discuss the essentially commonplace; in the body of the text, I seek new avenues of discussion.

Populism was a movement of social protest in the western and southern United States at the close of the nineteenth century. It expressed agricultural discontent in the face of widespread structural and political change that was rooted in the development of industrial capitalism. Populists accepted both industrialism and capitalism; they rejected the specific form of modernization, which, they believed, resulted in an organized structure of corporate power that was leading to the economic, social, and political dominance of business throughout American culture and society. According to Populists, modernity should neither limit nor destroy democracy, but the consolidation of wealth, in their view, menaced the continued existence of free institutions of government. They envisioned a social order in which the democratic control of industry would be possible; they were searching for a moral basis for capitalism and an autonomous government that would be devoted to the public interest.

Populists' agrarianism took in fundamental issues extending beyond the problems in the countryside. Part of the reason for their atypical social perspective lay in the way their agrarianism had actually developed. It grew with the movement, and it was based on decentralized organization that encouraged the development of political consciousness and articulation of political ideals, as well as a sense of community among members. In this phase of Populism, identified chiefly with the Farmers' Alliance in the South and parts of the West, farmers created an ostensibly nonpolitical mechanism for education, discussion, and social and economic cooperation. They were able to achieve a broad and coherent ideology that prepared them for further action. Technically these years, about 1887 to 1892, constituted the prepolitical period of agitation, which witnessed the merger of farm organizations, massive recruitment, proliferation of a reform press, purportedly national reform conferences, and the endorsement of candidates thought sympathetic to the purposes of the movement. Populists had begun a process of self-education that could generate sustained inquiry and would call more and more of the existing society into question. This process also raised the likelihood of direct political action, in the form of an independent or third party, if the farmers' organization either experienced a decline of strength or was thwarted in its efforts.

The political phase of Populism, during which the national People's party and its various state organizations were formed, began in 1892 as the result of a reform conference at St. Louis in February and a nominating convention at Omaha in early July. The movement's overt politicization subtly altered the complexion and purposes of Populism. The People's party was the ideological and social product of mobilizing farmers' discontent. It was a fully crystallized political force; it had a mature set of ideas and was conscious of its identity and the direction of its protest. This degree of awareness would have been unthinkable without the prior stage of preparation, and it helps to account for the clarity of thought in Populist argumentation and the focusing of demands in the movement's central document, the Omaha Platform. Yet if the People's party owed much to the previous stage, it differentiated itself from the Alliance experience by formalizing its political independence. Populism was no longer an appendage of the established political order: This was especially significant in the South, where the Democratic party had become synonymous with political power and cultural loyalty; for this reason, the transition from the Farmers' Alliance to the People's party involved selective recruitment. The fainthearted or insufficiently committed individuals dropped away.

This was not presumptive evidence of greater radicalism in the members of the later formation; perhaps neither phase of Populism was radical, but it was evidence of their greater determination to act in a political way. Populism changed from an interest-group orientation to one that acknowledged latent principles of class feeling and confronted the structure and realities of power. The character of Populism also changed because the avowed spirit of confrontation entailed deliberate economic and political reorganization; the movement had previously taken an amorphous form. To act politically was to accept responsibility for transforming the social order, and this deepened and widened the purposes of the movement. Populists were agrarians who inhabited and were now coming to terms with an industrial world.

As farmers, Populists had identified three broad areas of economic discontent in the prepolitical as well as political phases of their protest: the familiar Populist trinity of demands contained in the Omaha Platform of 1892—transportation, money, and land. These demands conveniently define the genesis of the movement's protest, particularly because they were critical to what Populists viewed as a forcible process of modernization that sacrificed agriculture to the presumed imperatives of a rationalized industrial order. Their cumulative effect was greater than the sum of their separate consequences, and this led Populists to generalize specific economic grievances in their political analysis and indictment of a system that resulted in the loss of human liberties. Populists protested against the extension of the mechanisms of power of an advanced capitalist economy into the more settled institutions of the countryside. The agrarian economy was also capitalistic, but it was unable to counter the superior industrial, financial, and commercial pressures that fostered a closed market in agriculture and made the conditions of farming onerous. The burden of conducting agricultural operations, and perhaps even of maintaining a particular way of life (not necessarily pastoral, but founded on the aspiration for, or in many cases the reality of, economic and political independence), motivated Populists to enlarge the basis of their criticism. They were not only agrarians who confronted the industrial structure, but they were also political democrats who sought the realization of constitutional principles. These principles were applicable to both industry and agriculture, and they would confirm the sovereignty of government, acting on behalf of the people, over the total modern economy. If capitalism was to have a moral basis, its political foundations must sustain equitable social and economic relations: The people's welfare must become the standard of public authority. That alone would reduce the power of consolidated wealth and preserve a democratic social order.

The transportation question probably most clearly represented the common grievances of farmers in both regions because their other grievances were specific to landed practices and financial conditions in the West and the South. When Populists criticized the railroads, they were criticizing considerably more than freight rates as such. These discriminatory charges provided the railroads with a stable source of profit that offset the rebates granted to, or extracted by, powerful corporate shippers, and to this extent agriculture helped to underwrite the stability of the transportation system. Agriculture's dependent position in the industrial economy had a more exact meaning as well: High freight charges, which by the late 1880s were becoming confiscatory because of fixed or increasing costs of production, were widely interpreted as creating the very closed market about which farmers strongly complained. This relation between freight rates and access to the market focused attention on further aspects of market closure. Populists discerned a pattern of interlocking controls among the railroads, commission merchants, and processors that not only determined shipping routes, storage charges, and grading practices but also artificially depressed the prices of agricultural commodities. And they also viewed as fundamentally constraining the necessity of purchasing tariff-protected manufactured goods while farmers were compelled to sell their crops on the open market, or worse still, on what purported to be an open market.

The problem of the railroads introduced a more serious grievance: the power of the corporate structure to define its own rules and stand outside the law in the conduct of business. According to Populists, railroads were a microcosm of private government. They were a corrupting force that engaged in abusive practices, and they could continue these practices through their political dominance at the state and local levels of government. The open and covert bribery of public officials and the control of elections were merely the surface manifestations of deeper abuses, although Populists saw these falsifications of democracy as instances of the closed world in which they (and the remainder of Americans) were compelled to live. The People's party would open the political process to, and legitimate the concerns of, dissident groups, just as it would remove the restrictions placed on economic activity by a monopolistic framework and encourage widespread participation in the process of capitalistic development. Because the railroads influenced the bar, the bench, the executive branch, the legislature, and probably even the local constabulary, they constituted an inner, if informal, government that ensured their ultimate protection against unacceptable forms of regulation. (This dominance, particularly as it applied to the national government, nullified the constitutional powers inherent in the commerce clause and was, for Populists, a telling argument on behalf of public ownership of railroads.) But in addition to warding off threats of regulation, the railroads' influence and control enabled them, sometimes in partnership with investment syndicates, to engross large tracts of land for the purposes of speculation; to acquire valuable mineral concessions, exclusive leasing rights in the field of other natural resources, and choice manufacturing sites; to receive preferential treatment in the payment of taxes (they refused, in most cases, to assume a share of the tax burden on their lands and in the states and the communities in which they operated); and finally, to threaten towns with economic isolation, so that they would issue bonds to finance the actual construction of the lines.

Populists ascribed to the monetary and banking systems the same overall features that they perceived in transportation. Indispensable functions of economic life—pertinent to facilitating exchanges, creating a vital market framework, and safeguarding individuals' livelihood—had fallen under private control. Here, however, private government, characteristic of the corporate structure and policies in general, made a more direct inroad into the sovereign powers of government. Populists sought scientific management of the currency, but their debates on the entire range of issues associated with the financial question reflected the prior consideration that money was uniquely subject to the legitimate authority of the nation. Even for a capitalistic society, this standard was the conventional test of sovereignty, and in fact the public control over money, as they frequently implied, endowed capitalism with its democratic possibilities. Populist nationalism, as a secondary attribute of the movement's ideology, drew much of its inspiration from the idea that supremacy in the financial structure of society was the constitutional prerogative of the people. By voluntarily abrogating or relinquishing its powers in this area, as it did under the National Banking Act and existing monetary practice, government had violated a sacred trust; it also had acted unconstitutionally, to the detriment of public well-being and the rule of law.

In recognizing analogies between the transportation and financial sectors, Populists saw that the dominance of private government had practical as well as legal and constitutional implications. The power of railroads may have constituted a less urgent test of sovereignty than the control of money; in theory, railroads could be left in private hands when neither subject to monopolism nor given to abuses, but money as such was essential to the economic and political integration of the nation. However, abuses by railroads raised issues about the public principle in the same way the financial system did. The ordering of social priorities that placed the authority of the people before the workings of the contemporary political economy was integral to political democracy. The fundamental law had an enduring quality; business practices did not. Populists believed that law and business were often at variance, always so when monopolism created a rival authority to government. Yet the practical side of private power more clearly defined the common features of finance and transportation. As in the case of the railroads, the financial system helped to shape the contours of economic society and, more particularly, the relations between the less advanced sectors of capitalism and the dominant industrial sector. This resulted in the general subordination of agriculture. Populists regarded the financial system as having discriminated against farming as an occupation because it restricted the availability of credit to agriculture at the same time that it partially underwrote the expansion of industry. In a sense, freight rates and interest rates appeared to Populists to be symbolically and structurally connected because both were discriminatory charges that affected their livelihood and lives. And they saw a further similarity between finance and transportation: The movement of prices and the movement of crops were synchronized at harvest time. A closed market was created for agricultural products. This mutually reinforcing development, on its financial side, meant being denied impartial access to the resources of capital.

Populists examined the financial system in detail; they also made adjustments for their specific region and pattern of land tenure. The financial question was more deeply felt in the South, where there was a shortage of capital, credit, and banking institutions, than in the West. In addition, cotton was in a weakened position as compared to wheat and corn in the respective one-crop regional economies. The fortunes of cotton affected the whole of southern life in a way that would not be possible where there was greater diversification of agricultural production. Moreover, southern farmers were not permitted to supply products for internal consumption, and cotton was inelastically bound to the extension of credit and the international market structure. The South was a cash-and-credit starved area, rendered still more vulnerable to the operations of the financial system by the seemingly inexhaustible capital needs of cotton production; therefore, it was understandably preoccupied with the money question as a solution to the farmers' discontent.

In more specific terms, Populists in both regions argued that private bankers' management of the currency resulted in a contraction of the money supply; and they further held that such management, combined with the commanding role of bankers in determining monetary policy, resulted in a specie-backed currency system and the operational acceptance of the gold standard. In their numerous monetary histories of the United States, Populists cited legislative chapter and verse for these practices; and, particularly for the gold standard, they identified the relevant Treasury policies and the secretary's discretionary powers to promote the bankers' and creditors' interests. Here, as in the decision to maintain a fixed gold reserve (which eventuated in the issuance of lucrative, gold-bearing bonds to the influential banking houses), the abrogation of the government's sovereign powers was most apparent. Populists contended that currency contraction, a specie basis, and the gold standard were all responsible for a long-term decline in agricultural commodity prices. The decline was greater than that in industrial prices, and this was nowhere more evident than in the prices of the principal crops—cotton, wheat, and corn.

Commodity price levels were symptomatic of agriculture's declining state. While high freight charges were making farming unprofitable, the steady fall in agricultural prices was having a catastrophic effect on the farmers' debt repayment. Exacerbating the experience of deprivation and actual want was the perception that declining prices were artificially caused rather than the product of impersonal market forces. Although the suffering of farmers would have been the same in either case, Populists, having identified the problem as artificial rather than inevitable, were encouraged to find their solutions in the internal features of the financial system, notably, the issuance and distribution of currency, as well as the optimal criteria for regulating the money supply. Populists did not feel betrayed by the ineffectuality of market forces, nor were they propounding a conspiracy theory to explain the role of private bankers; instead, they made provision for government authority as the decisive force in controlling the financial system.

Price declines, then, were an important stimulus for articulating criticisms. Farmers could not meet their set obligations, which were contracted when the monetary value of the dollar was lower. Even to keep pace with these obligations required two or three times the original scale of production. Moreover, according to Populists, the deflationary economic trends that occurred after the close of the Civil War and continued through their own time not only favored creditors over debtors but also led to an endemic condition of underconsumption and prevented the lower strata from participating in the exchanges of a capitalist society. Deflation hampered the activation of economic life. Extreme fluctuations of the business cycle and even periodic depressions were now the rule. Furthermore, Populists saw increasing disparities in wealth between social classes, between regions, and between sectors of the economy. In each case, the degree of wealth depended to some extent on the favorable or unfavorable relation to the institutional flow of capital and credit. The example they frequently cited, that currency was contracted at the time of greatest pressure, particularly when agricultural products were being moved to market, meant that the financial system was inadequate to society's business needs and that its benefits were selectively applied.

Entrepreneurs, if able to accumulate capital, prospered in the hard times. Their dollar, an appreciating dollar, was worth more; hard times were ideal times for expanding investment in plants and equipment. The appreciating dollar also permitted employers to pursue a low-wages policy, and this was made possible, in part, by the already low cost of food. In this way, agriculture had become an important source of primary accumulation for industrial capitalism. Finally, the invidious application of deflationary trends was apparent in the nation's export trade. Again, agriculture was subsidizing industry, and its cheap foreign exports (this production still accounted for four-fifths of America's export trade in the early 1890s) offset the inflow of capital and materials necessary to development of manufacturing.

Paradoxically, the militant ideology directed against banking and transportation was not extended to the land question. Even though Populism was primarily an agricultural movement, the structure of economic and social relations in the countryside does not seem to have been directly subject to alteration. Populists did not articulate a clear or critical position specifically addressed to problems on the land because they instinctively realized that to do so might endanger the property right. They were most conservative where one might expect them to be most radical.

Actually, there was no paradox in their seeming neglect of this issue; they simply chose not to be as bold on the land question as on the others. They reasoned that because transportation, money, and land were interrelated concerns, agricultural grievances had their origin in the industrial sectors of the economy. This was not implausible, particularly given the Populist emphasis on comparative economic power within a single system. A closed market, monetary contraction, and high freight charges undoubtedly had adverse effects on agriculture as a whole. Yet as one looks closer, it appears that Populists wanted to improve agriculture as such, rather than to democratize its central arrangements. By avoiding a systemic perspective on the land question, they could propose remedies of general material and social betterment that would correct a wide range of abuses, some of which were clearly structural in character, but these remedies would not directly modify patterns of land tenure and class relations in agriculture.

Populist solutions to the land question were primarily conceived, as if by a special form of political bookkeeping, at one or two removes from agriculture. This meant that there was a national focus on regional or local problems. Populists' agricultural policy did not incorporate antimonopolist and collectivist principles in the way that their national industrial and financial policies did. Thus, only indirect benefits accrued to the countryside. Public ownership of railroads would ensure an accessibility to markets, freer commercial dealings between farmers and processors, and considerably lower overall costs of production. But while agriculture would be made more profitable and individual farmers would benefit from significantly lower costs of operation and be relieved from a degree of hardship, the consequence of public ownership in this realm would not be to redistribute farm income, raise the status of the lower social classes, or otherwise rearrange internal economic and class relationships. Indeed, because transportation uniquely pertains to the market framework, farmers who were in a sufficiently independent economic position to be able to dispose of their crops—in practice, the landholders and, in the South, those not trapped by the crop-lien system—would gain special advantages, thereby conceivably widening the disparities of wealth and class within agriculture. In a similar fashion, public control of the monetary and banking systems would raise agricultural commodity prices, reduce the pressure on interest rates, and even make credit directly available to the farmer through the Alliance-sponsored subtreasury plan.

But to the extent that monetarist correctives were to be applied to the problems of agriculture, this would provide, in effect, a structural safety valve or external set of solutions that made unnecessary a direct tampering with power relations on the land. Not only would landholders again benefit, but the more entrepreneurial among them would benefit most because of their specific market orientation and relative freedom of operation. In both cases, the political bookkeeping consisted in transferring basic ledger entries, which were properly land issues, to transportation and financial issues. Direct solutions to the latter afforded only indirect solutions to the problems of the countryside. Tenants, sharecroppers, and farm laborers were mere onlookers as the hoped-for national economic improvements slowly produced benefits for the existent structure of agriculture.

The national orientation proved invaluable in criticizing the broader structure of power. Populists invoked the concept of public sovereignty, which implicitly sought the alteration of capitalism in the decisive sectors of finance and transportation. What had been transposed to agriculture, however, was very different. The land question had been divorced from the alteration of capitalism. When Populists looked for national solutions to agricultural problems, they were adapting potentially far-reaching measures, which had full integrity in their specific areas of application, to the narrower scope of a market framework. But they would not persist in exploring the agricultural sector separately.

In the West, the problem of mortgage indebtedness was seen as a part of the financial question, and this reinforced the grievances against the contraction of the currency and the shortage of credit. But the social consequences of mortgage indebtedness were relegated to the sphere of personal anguish because they were not permitted to form the basis for a deeper criticism of capitalism or a reexamination of landed arrangements. The heart of the land question should have been agricultural expropriation. In the West there was a pervasive fear of dispossession of land and in many cases the actual loss of farms. There was also increased tenantry and the heartbreaking forced migration of displaced persons to marginal lands, industrial centers, or Canada. Populists had not satisfactorily integrated their trinity of demands from the Omaha Platform. As a solution to tenantry and human displacement, they could only advocate for a miscellany that included the reclaiming by actual settlers of surplus corporate land and, to prevent speculation, antifutures legislation. Similarly, in the South, the crop-lien system was placed in the category of finance, made subject to the remedies of an expanded currency and abundant credit, and denied explicit political and structural meaning.

Here the central issue should have been the system of sharecropping that affected the members of both races, rather than a subtreasury plan that was a method of implementing the financial demands and in practice only applied to the minority of farmers who remained independent.

Expropriation and sharecropping were realities of farm life. Despite their overall record of advanced substantive demands, Populists could not face those realities. The land question shows us an important element in the genesis of Populists' protest, and for this reason—whatever their limitations on this account—it forms part of the background of the conditions they confronted. If there were no land question, broadly conceived as the endemic state of economic and social misery, there would probably have been no Populism. Yet this question did not produce outrage; it was not a source of discontent that would create advanced doctrines of social democracy on the land. The countryside would remain capitalistic in both structure and spirit; in Populist ideology, it had been separated from the industrial economy, where structural modification was allowable. Populists were not hypocrites in this matter. Their dual standard was meant to conserve capitalism. They introduced alterations that increased in magnitude as they approached society's private monopolistic epicenter, but the land epitomized the dream of democratic capitalism.

The land question became a source of affirmation, not outrage. It provided the basis for an ideology that contained mixed, and sometimes conflicting, concepts of political economy and structural change. The land itself was the Populists' social and psychological sheet anchor. It was a conservative—yet seemingly radical—source of identity that would put both their capitalistic and American credentials beyond question and thus allow them to offer a penetrating critique of the wider economy and society. But the land was an emotional and ideological constant; its institutions were essentially immune from criticism, and it gave Populists a secure base from which to venture forth into the larger political world. It had tremendous emotive power in Populist thought and discourse, not only as the source of the property right but also as the expression of general natural rights theory. The land was the symbol of independence; in a political democracy, it differentiated the free person from the medieval serf, although it only incompletely differentiated the free person from the sharecropper chained to the land through a system of debt peonage. The affirmation of the property right attested to the movement's essential moderation. Still, because the land led to a defense of human freedom in the face of corporate power, it contributed to Populism's adversary role in late nineteenth-century American society.

In the study that follows, Populists are presented not merely as farmers whose concerns were restricted to economic grievances. They emerge as citizen-democrats who sought rectification of overall conditions and a more humane political and social order. These goals were not inconsistent with a primary identification with agriculture, and they hardly deserve the label of antimodernism. Populists were endeavoring to shape the future definition of America.

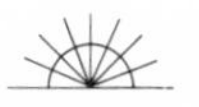

ONE

Foundations of Social Degradation

Populists approached the contemporary system of capitalism in a critical spirit. Their primary concern was the idea of the free individual, whose independence, security, and rights appeared to be endangered by an emergent structure of economic monopolism, political absolutism, and cultural materialism. Monopolism embodied a new system of power that varied completely with traditional constitutional principles of a sovereign people and the autonomous individual who comprised its basic unit. Human freedom was not entrepreneurial license; their definition of freedom owed more to their conception of American democracy than to their conception of capitalism, whether as a system of economy or way of life. Populists therefore insisted on the separation between America and what was perhaps its most pronounced structural characteristic. The separation was fraught with ambiguity the moment they attempted to address the problems of the current social order.

Yet in practical terms, Populists experienced little difficulty in distinguishing between society and economy because they believed that the latter's transformation had partially disqualified it as a true representative of American political institutions and the democratic heritage. Corporate economic dominance portended the loss of all liberties and the reduction of the less-propertied as well as laboring classes to a dependent position in society. Corporate wealth was taking the form of a private sovereignty that rivaled the power, authority, and legitimacy of government. Not only was capitalism no longer fully entitled to the emotive sanctions of democracy, but also, in its prevailing manifestation as monopolism, it had become antithetical in purpose and operations to the American heritage.

In response to this condition, Populists articulated a theory of the democratic state that would make the people sovereign in fact as well as in name, so that they would become the ultimate source of government and law in a free society. They conceived the state as independent from, and exercising power over, the business system. To arrive at this understanding, Populists relied on constitutionalism both to sanction the rule of law and to define the correct relation between public and private power. Government, as an extension of the people's will, should testify to the rational capacity of the enlightened individual to shape the economic and political development of society. Its mandate was to achieve human welfare.

Individuals, however, found their capacities for rational thought and democratic participation in human affairs stifled by the consolidating trends of the economic system, which gave rise to a particular formation of the state, class relationships, social ideas and attitudes, and institutional means for organizing and extending power. Together these features of the economic system created a hostile environment for the expression of specifically human, as opposed to materialistic and power-oriented, aspirations. Because the individual's plight in relation to the organized structures of society was central to their criticism of industrial capitalism, Populists implicitly identified what would later be termed the human condition—the loss of power and meaning facing mankind in contemporary society. But their perception of the problem was perhaps more acute than that of succeeding generations, who lived during periods when the sources of human alienation were less readily detected.

Populists were quick to point out the diminution of human values throughout economic, political, and cultural life. Yet rather than ascribe this situation to a supposedly impersonal process of industrial development, they rooted it in a corporate system, the center of social power, which knew no moral or legal restraints on its policies and conduct. It was as if humanity had entered a state of decline precisely as the organized structures of society grew more powerful. For Populists, the powerless condition of the individual was not fated; rather, it was a product of economic concentration, and, more specifically, the creation of a polarized society whose purpose was to cheapen the lives of working people. They believed that class relationships, based on the inequitable distribution of wealth, were taking a permanent form. Furthermore, class relationships depended on the control of government by private forces. They defined not only the common forms of industrial and agricultural exploitation but also political usurpation that challenged the existence of a sovereign people. The Populist concern about the individual almost necessarily led to the examination of the causes of economic and political deprivation, and from there to the importance of the rule of law in remedying a basic imbalance between the private and public spheres in the American polity. From these introductory statements, it is plain that the Populist interpretation of capitalism included a faith in constitutionalism and the democratic state as prerequisites of a morally satisfying, and economically and politically just, capitalistic system.

Individual Rights and the Corporate System

William A. Peffer quite typically began his analysis of current grievances by calling attention to a basic discrepancy in American society between the potential for an abundant life and the reality of deepening social misery. As society increased in wealth, it increased in poverty. The argument supposed a tremendous pride in, and appreciation of, the factors contributing to the nation's material achievements; these contributions ranged from vast natural wealth and the growth of technology to an earnest, hard-working laboring class in industry and agriculture. Yet this objective potential for widespread social welfare had been used to create a society that withheld its economic and social benefits from its own people. Peffer's implicit point is that impoverishment was unnecessary; it was cruel and arbitrary and the product of human activity. Moreover, it directly denied a democratic system of government. He stated that despite unparalleled material advances "the men and women who [did] the manual work [were] growing relatively poorer," subjected to the arbitrary and capricious rule "as if they were foot-balls or dice" of upper social groups.[1] They were becoming a submerged class, but equally important they no longer controlled their own lives.

Peffer was describing a class relationship as part of a still more fundamental political relationship: the denial of rights, power, and place in society to laboring people. Although his analysis was mainly concerned with agriculture, he considered it pertinent to his discussion because of the implications for a democratic society that farmers and workers were becoming similarly disadvantaged and deprived of an independent position in society: "The wealth of the country is fast passing into the hands of a few rich persons, while the number of impoverished grows alarmingly larger every year."[2] This polarization of the class structure and its logical corollary, the formation of a new ruling stratum, contradicted America's equalitarian political values. The realities of power prevented the conditions that could provide opportunity for, and develop the individuality of, all the members of society. It was perhaps even more significant to Peffer that this alteration of the social structure contradicted the ideal of human dignity, which anteceded political democracy itself. He posed a basic question having a biblical derivation and long familiar to the history of social struggles: "Is not the workman worthy of his hire?"[3]

The concept of the laborer's worthiness, as the practical basis of human dignity, had been effectively denied by the productive system. Here as elsewhere in Populist writings, this concept defined the individual not simply as a laborer but as a total person. A fair remuneration was only one aspect of equitable treatment; working men and women were worthy of their hire for the essential reason that they were human beings. Peffer had in mind moral entitlements as well as wage rates when he posed the question, and he also had in mind the social independence and personal security that underpinned the dignity of the individual. To express his thought, he freely combined an attack on corporate wealth and the imagery of propertied independence: "We are in the hands of a merciless power; the people's homes are at stake."[4] The loss of a home, according to Lockean premises, implied a forfeiture of rights and independent status. However, Peffer was more interested in the direct connection between the productive system and the individual's economic and social subordination: "We are steadily becoming a nation of hired men."[5]

The haunting phrase, "a nation of hired men," summarized the inversion of American democracy. Peffer did not envision a paradise of the lesser capitalist: There would still be workers; there would still be farmers living in all grades and conditions. But the term "hired men" again emphasized the moral dimensions of the Populist argument: Whether or not individuals were self-employed, they should not be at the mercy of another person, a specific firm, or the general system of enterprise. They should not be rendered powerless through the institutional life of society. They should still be whole persons. By viewing farmers and workers as unified, as having experienced hardship and subordination arising from common sources, Peffer could move beyond the problems of agriculture to examine the wider structure of society. The prevailing framework of modernization was deficient in human meaning.

Specifically, the power exercised by the corporate system to enforce a work discipline had led to a pervasive condition of depersonalization in which "the individuality of the separate workers [was] virtually lost." This process of depersonalizing the individual predicated the very subordination that Peffer saw in advancing monopolism; it formed an important part of the unfolding class relationship. Corporate power gave "to the employer a practical ownership of his work-people." In this strict sense one individual became dependent on another, a legitimated coercion that had less to do with industrial growth than with the broader social context in which industrialism operated. Peffer implied that repression far exceeded the requirements for organizing the industrial system; such repression destroyed human independence. Peffer regarded the worker as the social archetype of a newly dependent person: "He is becoming merged into the business of his employer; practically he is out of view."[6]

James B. Weaver recognized this same diminution of human values in the organized structures of society. He believed the lost independence of laboring people resulted from the fundamental imbalance of private and public forces in the contemporary system of capitalism. Weaver thought that the preponderant influence of business in political life defined the nature of the imbalance of forces, and, perhaps more emphatically than other Populists, he assigned the responsibility to government for allowing this influence to occur. The relationship between corporate power and the state threatened "the overthrow of free institutions."[7] If Peffer's criticism centered on the economic and social dependence of the individual, Weaver's criticism centered on the political and moral dereliction of government in failing to fulfill its constitutional mandate to safeguard the public welfare. Nevertheless, his attack on business was unsparing; business and government were interpenetrated, and he would permit neither partner to escape censure.

The ascendancy of monopolism depended upon a compliant government. Weaver saw the product of this relationship as an increasing deterioration of the social order. The plight of the individual was also becoming the plight of the nation: lost identity, rights, and social purpose. He asserted that the prerogatives of government had "been leased to associated speculators," the corporation "through evolution in crime" had replaced the pirate, and a ruling class had "usurped the Government and [was] using it as a policeman to enforce its insolent decrees." Without a public directing force the nation was being given over to its worst and most disreputable social elements. A system of private hegemony, bent on mere spoliation and destructiveness, had taken command, and the government was hardly an innocent bystander to this process: "The public domain has been squandered, our coal fields bartered away, our forests denuded, our people impoverished, and we are attempting to build a prosperous commonwealth among people who are being robbed of their homes—a task as futile and impossible as it would be to attempt to cultivate a thrifty forest without soil to sustain it." In reality, the national soil had been depleted, leaving a society barren of democratic institutions. The polity was fast becoming a wasteland; it was questionable whether it was still a polity at all, because corporate power was seeking to construct a society based on the impoverishment of its own people. The focus of sovereignty shifted to business, extending even to the corporate appropriation, through hired mercenaries, of "police duties which clearly belong to the State."[8]

Throughout his work, Weaver used the term "corporation usurpers" to designate not only the corporation's challenge to lawful authority and the broader sense in which business had taken on a political character but also the resistance to democratization. Modernization occurred within a static ideological and class system. Weaver believed that industrialism had not realized its potential for altering the social structure to make it more equitable. "Their Juggernaut must move and the car of progress stand still."[9] The imbalance of private and public forces created a new configuration of power that threatened greater economic and political inequity: "The corporation has submerged the whole country and swept everything before it." Business was remaking the total society in its own image. This was a retrograde change because it endangered the existence of the rule of law and political democracy: "The corporation glacier is now sweeping over this country and lifting out of place the solid granite of our Judiciary and threatening to carry away the very pillars of the Republic."[10] It was as if a new Ice Age were bringing about a full-scale demolition of the legal and political foundations of the polity.

While corporate usurpation implied the collaboration of business and government in promoting the growth of capitalism, Weaver's more immediate concern was that its undermining of fundamental legal processes had made difficult a peaceful resolution of grievances along constitutional lines: "The pirate plunders by violence. The burglar enters your house prepared to take life if he cannot otherwise escape. But the corporation plunders by the permission or through the agency of the State, and to cut off all hope of redress they seize upon the courts, which constitute the only hope and refuge of an oppressed people this side of revolution."[11] In itself this fear of revolution indicated that Populism would not go beyond reformist boundaries, but perhaps the basic concept in the passage is Weaver's attack on government-business interpenetration as being a provocation for revolution. Weaver advocated for restoring the structural balance, and with it the supremacy of law, by affirming the state's autonomous powers. This solution was not antimodern because "the great battle for industrial emancipation" defined the context of social protest.[12]

The Democratic Basis of Property

Populists developed a unified conception of liberty in which economic restraints took on a political character. A popular theme in other Populist writings is that the monopolistic system endangered political liberties specifically by creating a closed market that denied an equitable return for labor and prevented the operation of freely competing units. This aspect of their critique of corporate capitalism, centered on the economic and social restrictions of a closed market, tended to equate property with individual rights. Yet their intention was not to sanction the unlimited accumulation of wealth, which only reinforced the trends toward corporate usurpation, but to enlarge the base of economic participation, which provided the lower and middle strata of society with a more secure and independent existence. Private aggregations of power, Populists reasoned, had no place in an open-market framework because they would control the market mechanism and constitute a rival to the state. The decentralization of economic power was a prerequisite of economic opportunity, but it would also verify that basic institutional processes had not been abrogated through the rise of the corporation. In Populist thought, the right to own property was compatible with human freedom because it pertained to the guarantees to the person as well as to his livelihood; political and economic concepts were fused because fundamental rights could not be realized in a context of economic dependence.

Populists accordingly maintained that a well-ordered polity was necessary to the protection of property; only in such a political framework could the standard of public interest be raised to ward off threats, which they perceived to originate in a monopolistic system, to personal holdings and the fair remuneration of labor. "Usurpation" and related terms connoted the illegal seizure of property and labor-created value by corporate enterprise. This expropriation of the lesser capitalist and laborer signified the breakdown of the legitimate authority that alone was capable of enforcing general-welfare principles in the regulation of society. When W. Scott Morgan stated that "a trust is a conspiracy against legitimate trade," that "it is against the interests of the people and the welfare of the public," and that "it is demoralizing in its influence, inconsistent with free institutions and dangerous to our liberties,"[13] he simultaneously affirmed a free-market economy, invoked a public standard for the protection of property, and presented a case for government as the necessary guardian of individual rights.

Populists frequently did not specifically define property; they did not distinguish between concrete holdings and the remuneration for work in their loosely reasoned labor theory of value. Yet the more basic point is that in their definition of property, they shifted the emphasis from capital per se to a conception of just entitlement. Property had a more vital meaning in Populism than in the larger society. It was a means of livelihood rather than domination; it was a safe anchorage in a world that was in upheaval and sought to deny the autonomy of the individual. Property, moreover, formed the basis of the family, which, as a microcosm of the polity, suggested the relations of equity and mutuality to be extended to all society. For Populists, this meaning of property implied a principle that included, but went beyond, individual possessions and possessory rights: It was essential to the political and social creation of a free citizenry. For all these reasons, the Populist usage of property could support an antimonopolist construction. Property was chiefly menaced by monopolism. The defense of property, as a basis for human independence, necessitated an opposition to its consolidated form. On the same grounds, the Populist definition of property could also support a doctrine of public ownership, which would eliminate the constraints of monopolism on the economic activity, political rights, and social independence of those of smaller means.

Morgan's writing contained the foregoing ideas. He viewed with concern the effect of a closed market on the farmers: "Monopoly names the price of what they have to sell, and charges them what it pleases for what they are compelled to buy." In human terms, productive labor was to no avail in improving their condition; this heightened the sense of being totally and illegally controlled: "Individual effort is fruitless. The relentless, remorseless and unyielding grasp of monopoly is upon every avenue of trade and commerce."[14] The stark juxtaposition of individual rights and corporate power indicated widespread coercion. He spoke of "extortion" and, translating economic abuse into political terms, asked if it was surprising "that the law of self-preservation [was] forcing him [the farmer] to unite with his fellow sufferers to repel these encroachments upon his rights?" Monopolism was likened to an "invader." This justified the agrarian challenge on what was possibly the most general political ground: "The organization of farmers is the outgrowth of an invasion of their natural rights."[15] The defense of property had shifted from an economic to a political struggle, suggesting that the property right was itself a natural right. Morgan extended the sanction of nature to his labor theory of value when he stated that "the natural law of labor is, that the laborer is entitled to all the fruits of his toil." Although he qualified the application of his theory by making room for the separate contribution of capital in determining a fair remuneration, he clearly viewed the protection of earnings as a right that had been violated: Massive wealth "is but the accumulated labor of millions who have received but a part of a just reward for their services."[16]

When Morgan spoke of a "just reward," he was analyzing monopolism through an ethical criterion. He now added to this perspective a more specifically political criticism. Monopolism had denied individuals mastery of themselves. Tracing the pattern of monopolistic coercion, he saw the depersonalization of the worker as symptomatic of a broader dependence: "The individual laborer is not the master of his own actions. He must work or suffer and is therefore compelled to submit to the exactions of his employer who is also his master."[17] Not only the laborer but also society itself had been reduced to a condition of dependence through the dynamics of monopolistic growth. Here Morgan elaborated the theme of expropriation. In its operations, the corporation had appropriated to itself the property held in the remainder of the social order. The corporate siphoning of wealth from the small holder and worker, in this case by means of a cheapening of labor, had ignored "the inevitable degradation of the community, and its peril to the estate of those who are fortunate enough to accumulate anything, and to the future of the Republic."[18]

This plaintive statement wove together the security of the small property-holder and the destiny of democratic society. It seemed obvious to Morgan that the right of property and the loss of liberty were the two sides of the pending social question: What shall be the place of corporate power in a political democracy? The confluence of these issues was dramatized by the way railroads, as the prototype of monopolistic power, had "set at defiance the laws of the land and . . . trampled upon individual and public rights and liberties," as they meanwhile undermined "internal commerce," engaged in numerous corrupt schemes, and enlarged the framework of dependence to include the nation. "This power," Morgan concluded, "is used against the interests of the people. This despotism in common with that of other monopolies threatens them in every relation of their national life."[19] Perhaps inevitably, although he did not question the property right, his strong political denunciation of monopolistic "despotism" and his inclination to accept the public ownership of railroads led him to enunciate a principle that would have seriously restricted the application of that right: "Any system that is not for the public good—that is detrimental to the public welfare—is and of right ought to be subject to public control."[20]

James H. Davis informally accepted this principle of the public interest. But he combined the theory of government intervention in the economy with parallel doctrines of classical liberalism; as a result he suggested that the principle of the public interest would also serve the needs of an invigorated market economy. Public ownership of railroads, although plainly anti-monopolist, had a limited objective: "The government being in charge of the great highways, all men would be on an equal footing in the distribution of their wares, products or merchandise." This measure would therefore assure to all producers an equal access to the market. Davis carried the discussion in several directions, always returning to the renewal of opportunity as the logical corollary of preventing monopolism. Thus, when a "monopoly in the coinage and distribution of money" had been destroyed, "all men would be in a manner equal before the law in the privilege to secure a home as well as in production and distribution of wealth."[21] The recurrent imagery of the home in Populist writings conveyed the idea of propertied independence that here, because of associations with the marketplace, had a clearer Lockean meaning.

Nevertheless, Davis's contribution to Populist analysis was to extend the powers of government by a literalistic construction of the Constitution, including an emphasis on the principles of the preamble and the "necessary and proper" clause. This extension of governmental power would not contradict a free-market economy in his paradigm of capitalism; it would make the free market practicable by removing the obstacles to competition. He maintained that Congress, in executing its mandate, had to implement fully and uniformly its enumerated powers, particularly in the areas of the regulation of commerce and the coinage of money. This full and uniform implementation of its constitutional powers would signify the government's acceptance of primary responsibility for the public welfare. It would also preclude a system of government-business interpenetration. Despite his laissez-faire overtones, in this area of vitalizing public powers Davis shared the structural views of Weaver and other Populists. The powers of the state could not be effective without the national control of transportation and banking. But a more basic principle was that the government could protect the public interest only if it did not share or delegate its power. Davis insisted that government had to act "*directly on the people and for the people,* and not through the States, counties or any other subdivisions of government, *much less through corporations or syndicates.*"[22]

Davis was not dealing in exquisite legal distinctions, but in the hard realities of conflict between competing structures of power and, to an even greater extent, competing principles of social organization. As Populists saw it, the public interest was to be directly protected by a government for its people; no supervening force could perform this function. Specifically, capitalist intermediaries such as railroads and banks could not be safely entrusted with the powers of government. In actuality, "Congress allows, yea even charters, licenses a lot of cold, faithless, soulless, heartless, merciless corporations, to stand between the government and the people," thus denying its own responsibility for the public welfare.[23] In Davis's mind, the issue here was that of power and its responsible use in a constitutional democracy. For government "to 'farm out' or delegate its powers to anyone is to betray the trust of the people," but even more it is to place major sectors of the economy under private governments, such as traffic and banking associations, which tax and regulate the lives of the people without their consent.[24]

These critical areas of the economy were not only public in nature because they affected the whole of society, but they were also generally the source of the greatest economic profit. In addition, there was the political deduction from the constitutional argument: Corporate power had created a private taxation without representation. The corporation ("cold, faithless, soulless, heartless") had transcended the bounds of accountability. To allow the private arrogation of sovereign power merely legitimized the usurpation by the corporate system. A self-willed monopolism, "with almost unlimited power over lands, highways, and money, and under no oath of office, obligation or bond to the people," had resulted in an amoral, monolithic structure that Davis styled a "communism of capital" because it concentrated wealth in "a despotism of aristocracy" that knew no restraints on its conduct.[25]

Despite Davis's animus toward corporations and his consequent reliance on public ownership, he had not overlooked the goal of reconciling the public and private spheres of the polity. He sought to correct the structural imbalance of forces through the liberation of the entrepreneurial energies of the smaller capitalist. A reconciliation of these spheres would enlarge the field of opportunity. One could be vigorously antimonopolist and vigorously capitalistic at the same time. Indeed, Davis was saying that the two positions were integrated and mutually reinforcing. In his own description of a two-tiered structure, defining the public and private spheres of activity, he presented a clear relationship between means and ends, in which the public realm would promote the widespread distribution of property: "The object of our platform is . . . to establish a system of laws and regulations that will prevent all kinds of monopoly and all kinds of aristocracy of wealth, and at the same time encourage individual industry in the acquisition of property and the enjoyment of the same; establishing an aristocracy of industry, merit and honor, instead of an aristocracy of wealth, arrogance and idleness."[26] Within this apparently radical critique of capitalism was the plea for acquiring property, an important component of Populist thought that practically assured the movement's reform identity.

The Structural Character of Human Misery

Yet even when Populists affirmed, or at least did not repudiate, the property right, there could be subtle differences over how far the democratization of society would be encouraged. Davis was fairly representative of southern Populists in emphasizing wider opportunities, a market economy, and the acquisition of property. These goals implicitly defined the relationship between the public and private spheres of activity because the former would support the latter's essentially individualistic purposes. However, Kansas Populists frequently shifted the priorities of the analysis. They did not abandon the property right, but they gave it a social application, which included a standard of community. Their two-tiered economic structure achieved a more nearly perfect balance between its public and private forces and defined more exactly the purposes each sphere of activity would serve. These Populists argued that government and property each had to be respected and that each sphere had a proper and distinctive contribution to make to a democratic society. In fact, they talked less about capitalism than about democracy itself; and, unlike the majority of southern Populist thinkers, they laid great stress on industrialism and the structural causes of impoverishment. This shared position of the public and private spheres meant that public ownership and government power would no longer be dependent variables; they would not be the means of supporting the goals of the private sphere. Instead, they would represent the democratic possibilities of the social control of industry. If antimonopolism still conserved the property right, it was also based on social and ethical premises that suggested a collective orientation and the public responsibilities of government.

Lorenzo D. Lewelling took strong exception to the prevailing emphasis in contemporary values: "The trouble has been, we have so much regard for the rights of property that we have forgotten the liberties of the individual." This implicit dichotomy between human rights and property rights had far-reaching significance. Not only was the property right somewhat antagonistic to individual liberty, but also individual liberty itself depended for its fulfillment on the state's playing an active protective role. His thought was a response to the reality of pervasive human misery; individual liberty pertained less to property than the sustainment of life. Lewelling, in his reference to individual liberty, was addressing the question of human survival under corporate capitalism: "I claim it is the business of the Government to make it possible for me to live and sustain the life of my family." The doctrine of liberty refuted social Darwinism: "I say now, it is the duty of government to protect the weak, because the strong are able to protect themselves." But it was more than a refutation of current values; it positively obligated government to achieve societal welfare. If government failed to act, the result would be "a state of barbarism" in which the poor would be left defenseless, preparing the way for "industrial slavery."[27] This "state of barbarism" was suspiciously close to a laissez-faire polity of unrestrained aggressiveness culminating in a winner-take-all monopolism.

Conditions in Kansas were not worse than in other areas of Populist strength, such as the South, but Lewelling and other Populists were less encumbered by wider cultural associations in their approach to issues of property, government, and welfare. They could move to the center of the discussion of a democratic society, which in Lewelling's case meant a humanly organized economy that afforded personal security and mental and spiritual growth to the individual. Elsewhere he demonstrated the democratic potential of a literalistic construction of the nation's founding principles. Traditional rights in the modern setting were predicated on enlarging the role of government as an agent of social welfare. His active reading of the Declaration of Independence supposed precisely the democratic control of industry: "Government is a voluntary union for the common good. It guarantees to the individual life, liberty, and the pursuit of happiness. The government then must make it possible for the citizen to enjoy liberty and pursue happiness." By fixing this positive injunction within the framework of a social compact, Lewelling underscored the seriousness of the obligation he placed on government: "If the government fails of these things, it fails in its mission, it ceases to be of advantage to the citizen; he is absolved from his allegiance and is no longer held to the civil compact." When he characterized the current struggle as "a contest for the protection of home, humanity, and the dignity of labor," he subtly altered the meaning of the equation of property and freedom so that both factors had a clearer social content. Individual possessory rights appeared less important than the advancement of society and, more particularly, its working people. The term "humanity" took on the meaning of a people's government, a standard both of popular rights and political sovereignty that anteceded a narrow doctrine of property rights: "The people are greater than the law or the statutes, and when a nation sets its heart on doing a great and good thing it can find a legal way to do it."[28] The nation became a people acting on its own behalf; this required the use of government. The passage also sanctioned government's potentially extensible powers because power emanated from the people, the ultimate source of authority. In the process, the natural rights' argument for property in its exclusive form was qualified.

Frank Doster enriched Lewelling's theory of political obligation and his criticism of social Darwinism, through a more inclusive definition of the social welfare goals of the state: "It is the business of government to discover and enforce those laws of harmony which raise man above the barbarous antagonisms of the natural state into relationships of social unity and fraternity." Here the active role of government has been supplemented with an implied pattern of evolutionism. It is as if Doster advocated moving society from laissez-faire to socialism (or at least a definite form of cooperation), skipping the stage of contemporary capitalism altogether. He, too, made provision for private property in his social framework, but it is clear that such notions as "social unity" and "fraternity" qualified strict individualism. The task of government was "no other than the equality of human brotherhood." The effect, while not a denial of the importance of property, was certainly a diminishing of its value: "I know that humanity is above property, and that profit making on the bread of poverty is an abomination in the sight of the Lord."[29]

Doster sought to limit capitalism's application to society. He used the concept of a two-tiered structure, reserving the public realm for all economic activity affecting the general interest. But his primary concern, as can be seen from the preceding statement, was the overall moral purpose of the political economy, which cut across particular spheres of activity. Whether or not he implied a form of socialism in these passages, he emphatically endorsed a standard of community rights in relation to property rights. In fact, Doster had no quarrel with the capital that he viewed as productive, but he carefully distinguished between capital that had come to live "with us" and capital that had come to live "off of us." He rejected the latter as mobile, impersonal, and parasitic, or in other words, as recognizing no obligation to the community. "It is that capital which locates nowhere, and identifies itself with no community but which comes to abide temporarily, while it advantages itself upon the necessities of the people, which is the curse of the industrial world."[30] Like Lewelling, he saw the necessities of the people as a prior claim on government.

Perhaps Doster's most compelling statement was a far-reaching declaration of public welfare specifically in response to the problem of monopolism. In his view, monopolism was the most evident expression of irresponsible wealth. It was the antithesis of community rights and public welfare. From the standpoint of political thought, the importance he ascribed to the people as the source of final authority gave cogency to his analysis. The "only means" of checking monopolism was "to utilize the power of the combined whole, to bring the power of the social mass to bear upon the rebellious individuals who thus menace the peace and safety of the state." The standard of a people's government once more logically followed from the Populist theory of political democracy. It was reinforced here by the implied charge of monopolistic usurpation. Doster extended the idea of a people's government to include its economic as well as political functions. In this case he claimed for the public the natural sources of energy, vital to all social production, that had come under the control of monopolies. But his formulation had still wider application: The People's party maintained "that the subjects of those monopolies and trusts are public in their nature, and that the powers exercised through them are in reality the functions and agencies of government itself." Only government had jurisdiction in the public realm; the community's welfare should not be the object of private profit. Hence "it would have the government, that is, the people, assert their rightful dominion over the same," which suggested, as a principle of Populism, "that the industrial system of a nation, like its political system, should be a government of and for and by the people alone."[31] This paraphrase of Lincoln was not inconsistent with asserting traditional rights; nevertheless, it is equally significant that these rights were specifically transposed to the modern setting.

Doster had presented an informal conception of industrial democracy; this conception was strengthened by such terms as "the social mass" and "rightful dominion" to indicate, respectively, the integral relation of industrial democracy to political democracy and its ethical basis in the sovereign authority of the people. The idea of industrial democracy contributed to a broader social vision of government responsibility and power. It added to the standard of a people's government the criterion of socially determined needs in sanctioning the role of the state. Stephen McLallin, editor of the

Topeka *Advocate,* used exactly this criterion. He identified "this 'modern condition'" of widespread misery and the displacement of labor through "this monopoly of machinery and other means of production and distribution." He then contrasted it with "what might be attained by a proper use of the instrumentalities of modern production and distribution."

Like most Populists, McLallin denied the inevitability of poverty. But he was more precise than many Populists in defining the welfare of society as the frame of reference for political action. He used the capitalist appropriation of machinery as a prime example of the failure to meet this standard of society's welfare. The example implied a deeper level of criticism because it raised a systemic question: "Has society, as a whole, derived the benefits from the use of labor-saving machinery that it might have done under a different system? We think not. Under the prevailing system the capitalist has been the chief beneficiary." The case for the fundamental alteration of the social system was made from following the logic of McLallin's question. This was possible initially because his discussion had an industrial specificity that allowed him to address capitalism in structural terms. The issue was no longer machinery but the system in which it operated. In addition, his term "proper use" suggested both the existence of an alternative system and the necessity of an ethical basis for organizing any economy. Finally, his emphasis on society as the rightful beneficiary of technology made clear how benefits should be distributed. He argued throughout for limiting mere entrepreneurial rights: "When a labor-saving machine is invented, instead of using it to displace men, it should have been used to reduce the hours of labor, thereby continuing the opportunities of all to provide the comforts and luxuries of life for every member of society."[32]

McLallin conveyed the idea of a purposeful, cohesive, and humanly organized society. Such a society would have a clear direction; the property right—private control over the uses of machinery—would be subordinated to the welfare of the community. More interesting, though, is his positive vision of an alternative system that would be based on universal participation in the workings of the economy. This system had noncapitalistic connotations. Ordinarily in Populist discussion, inclusive participation meant simply the active involvement of the middle and lower strata of society; this involvement would attest to the vitality of a market economy. But here the literalistic usage of "all" and "every member" posed a test of performance that a market economy was not intended to meet. It implied a democratization of the social base that would make each individual in society a meaningful economic actor. Only structural alterations of both the system of power and the system of business enterprise could make this possible. The goal of benefiting "every member" shifted attention from equal access to the market to equitable distribution of wealth. It raised the idea of socially determined needs, now supplemented, however, by a further standard: the rational allocation of the productive factors to achieve benefits to the wider society. If the term "proper use" suggested an ethical guideline for the operation of industry, it also was a more technical reference to economic and political rationality, implying that monopolism was an irrational as well as illegal force. The "instrumentalities of modern production and distribution" required regulation external to both the market mechanism and monopolism to reduce workers' hours, keep labor from being displaced, and meet a criterion that placed society foremost.

McLallin's conclusion fused the ethical and rational elements in his analysis of the productive system: "Work should be so distributed that each should do his share and receive the reward of his labor. Work enough should be done to supply the demand of the whole people for every comfort and luxury of life; and the time not required for such production should be devoted to rest, to mental culture, to social intercourse and recreation."[33] What he termed the "modern condition" was a human nightmare of atrophied lives. He called for an equally modern industrial system, but one that respected the worth of the individual. Production was not an end in itself. This passage demands a measured process of economic growth and, its corollary, the promotion of the multidimensional human being. These goals entailed a stronger government role in the economy, if not in fact a degree of public planning.

It is not surprising that when McLallin focused on public ownership, he purged it of any traces of classical liberalism. Its purpose would be to advance the welfare of society rather than simply to liberate economic energies in general or the small producer in particular. The doctrine of public ownership had an implicit political as well as economic content. If it referred to nationalization and antimonopolism, it also supposed a concept of the people acting in a collective capacity, a people that had sovereign rights in the public realm: "We propose that the people shall own and operate the railroads, telegraphs and telephones for their own interest and benefit; and that private corporations shall cease to monopolize these public functions for purposes of public plunder." The term "public" effectively resolved the question of benefits from the operation of the economy, not only between the people and monopolism, but also between the people as a distinct political entity and the sum of producers acting in their individual capacities. Then, in strictly economic terms, McLallin went further; the existence of monopolies was a sufficient ground for the change to public ownership: "We propose that every monopoly, as soon as established, shall be seized by the people and used for the public good, instead of, as now, for private gain."[34] In McLallin's usage, the people had become identified with the public sphere of activity; this emphasized the distinction between collective and individual concepts of the public good.

The standard of socially determined needs as a rationale for government power could be seen even in McLallin's discussion of municipal ownership. This area of public intervention has been traditionally regarded as more moderate than the nationalization of major economic sectors, and it attracted the interest of the middle classes and the advocates for good government. In McLallin's discussion, however, it had the same public and collective associations as broader statements about public ownership. He stated that municipal ownership of public utilities provided an effective service "by which serious abuses are corrected and great benefits secured to the public," once more suggesting the removal of the lesser capitalist from the center of the discussion. What made his position significant was his use of municipal ownership as a basis for generalizing to all of government activity. Here McLallin gave a modified socialist construction to public ownership at every level; this was an essentially Fabian interpretation of the public principle, but it was tailored to America: "The best features of our government to-day, national, state and municipal, are those which are purely socialistic. We would refer especially to our public school system and our postal system." Despite the choice of examples, his literalistic reading of the national experience differed from that of James H. Davis and many other Populists, particularly in the South, because he did not impose a fixed limit on the scope of government power. His conception of governmental possibilities was open-ended, reflecting belief in public welfare and the people's ultimate sovereignty. He rejected arbitrary limits to the application of the public interest principle, and, consequently, did not fear enlarged powers of the state. After he had discussed municipal ownership, McLallin further stated that "observing and studious Populists with such examples before them, have come to believe that a still wider extension of socialistic doctrines and practices would be beneficial to mankind."[35]

McLallin approached the issue of government power in a nondoctrinaire spirit. His approach to socialism was improvisatory and pragmatic. He would accept public ownership to the extent that it proved workable; he was not bound by theoretical restraints, such as a commitment or disposition to laissez-faire, or equally theoretical imperatives of development, such as a deterministic view of capitalist breakdown and socialist triumph. Socialism, in his usage, was merely a more intense form of public ownership and a people's government. But his view was moral as well as pragmatic; socialism, and government power in general, also had to prove "beneficial to mankind." Although the phrase "beneficial to mankind" might invite widely differing interpretations, even among Populists, the meaning intended by

McLallin is reasonably clear: The creation of a human economy and society would not be sacrificed to the needs of a monopolistic system.

His words "a still wider extension of socialistic doctrines" suggest the potentially extensible powers of government; and the specificity of his argument is especially noteworthy. The power of government would be directed against monopolism, which, in its pursuit of profit, could not be considered beneficial to humanity: "Looking about them they see nearly every industry monopolized by a corporation; and they are conscious of the robbery practiced upon them for private gain." McLallin returned the analysis to its ethical basis and to its implicit standard of rationality: "They have come to believe that many of the abuses to which they are subject might be remedied, and their condition be bettered by a proper exercise of the power of the government." In a later editorial calling for the public ownership of railroads and "all other utilities now monopolized or susceptible of being monopolized for private gain at the expense of the people," he added the final element of the political obligation of the state: "it is therefore the *duty* of the government in execution of the constitutional obligation to provide for the public welfare to *assume* the ownership and management of all such utilities and monopolies in the interest of the public."[36]

The Corporation and Public Welfare

The Lincoln *Farmers' Alliance* also took an advanced position on the mandate of government to serve the public welfare. Its continuous advocacy of public ownership and, even more, its careful reporting of the succession of labor disturbances at the time of Populism led this newspaper to accept the enlarged powers of the state as a political and structural corrective to the imbalance of private and public forces. It shared with the Kansas Populists a universe of economic, legal, and political discourse in which corporate power represented a threat to democratic institutions. Both viewed government intervention in the economy as necessary to achieving the rational and ethical control of industry. In Populist discussion, modernity was not merely the sum of the changes associated with industrialization; it was also the political context that could shape these social and technological forces for the public welfare. The *Farmers' Alliance* used the organization and betterment of working people as a test of the human purposes of modernization. Although it did not accept the idea of class struggle, it charged that the degradation of laborers by monopoly capitalism was responsible for precipitating such a struggle.

Yet the views of the Lincoln paper subtly differed from those of the Kansas Populists in the importance it attached to the small propertyholder when it presented its case for public ownership. Davis and, to a lesser extent, Morgan emphasized the equal access to the market and a market economy as such, but the *Farmers' Alliance* was concerned about preserving the capitalistic system as the basis for extending government power. When the *Farmers' Alliance* fused the elements of private property and state action, it did not diminish the importance of the public factor in contemporary society, nor implicitly or explicitly support laissez-faire. Its strong disapproval of corporate capitalism prevented this and reinforced its conviction that antimonopolism preserved both the public and private spheres of activity. In succinct language, the newspaper summarized its position: "To use the power of government in doing something which it is dangerous to permit a few individuals to do is wise statesmanship. In fact that is the only final protection the people have against the oppressions and extortions of monopoly."[37]

The *Farmers' Alliance* saw corporate policies toward labor, including the hiring of Pinkertons to engage in outright suppression, as expressions of the growth of arbitrary private power in American society. Monopolism endangered not only the rights of labor but also the rule of law. Implicitly, the paper held that the interpenetration of business and government had formed a structure through which a compliant state permitted economic lawlessness to occur: "The most notable and alarming feature of the business is the indifference of all local authorities to the glaring violation of law and infringement of all sound constitutional principles involved in the employment of this force; or worse, the subserviency of the authorities to the corporations which employ it." The contending powers, capital and labor, were grossly unequal, but the transfer of public sovereignty to the private sector was also to be deplored: An "overgrown corporate power" prevented workers from organizing as it meanwhile "arrogate[d] to itself all dominion and functions which belong to the people."[38] Again, one finds the combination of economic and political grievances in which the overriding issue was the loss of liberties.

In a related editorial, the *Farmers' Alliance* defined the ideal of a responsive government as one that accepted responsibility for the public welfare: While strikes were "unfortunate," the case at hand, the New York Central strike of 1890, was "justifiable and in fact necessary" because until "labor and its interests form the first care and duty of the government, as it properly should and some day will," labor must defend itself "with the only weapon it has at hand." The newspaper was reluctant to support strikes; this attitude indicated its general vision of social stability, but all such matters were outweighed by the undemocratic implications and consequences of corporate economic dominance. The railroad, "worth hundreds of millions, sharing the sovereignty of the state in its right of eminent domain, granted the franchise of a public highway in perpetuity, organized industrially in the most perfect manner," was a microcosm of "the most complete, the most tyrannical and the most powerful force known to modern society." It stood opposed to "a multitude of atoms," having "no rights the corporation is bound to respect," even though "the atoms are the ones who produce the wealth" and thus "who have created the capital" that ownership had turned "into an engine of oppression."[39] In describing the situation at Homestead, the newspaper saw the forcible atomization of working people through the deliberate destruction of their union: "Once this is broken up, the capitalist will only have the individual laborers to deal with. He can then use the laborers to beat down their own wages through competition for employment."[40]

The *Farmers' Alliance* had developed the concept of the reserve army of labor; self-pacification of the working class had occurred as a result of the pressure of competition. The *Alliance* perceived that this process was made possible by the power of corporations to structure the operations of the labor market. In the context of corporate dominance, "the number unemployed is made to grow constantly greater and wages less by the pressure of poverty," thus resulting in a "pauper-manufacturing system." In paraphrasing a Marxian critique of classical economics, the editor showed disdain for the idea that laissez-faire could achieve equitable social relations of production. Whether or not he had actually read Marx, the argument was consistent with Populist themes of class polarization, corporate power, and the discrepancy between society's potential wealth and actual misery: "The beautiful economic law of the competitive system reduces wages by an iron rule to the lowest level (at last) on which the workers can live and rear children to recruit their ranks. Observe, by this law the profit to the idle capitalist is made to increase with the increase of the number unemployed. His wealth depends upon their destitution; his fortune grows relatively as the poverty of the poor makes them powerless." Like McLallin, the editor invoked a standard of rationality, implying that a remedy had to be sought in the state: "Why is all this necessary? It is not necessary. By the aid of invention, machinery and free motive power the work of the world can be performed in about half the time, with less than half the labor that was formerly necessary." Although the editor had not laid the basis for, and possibly did not intend, such a ringing assertion, he nonetheless concluded that the "means of production must be placed in possession of the people."[41]

All the editorials expressed the feeling that corporate capitalism offered a clear provocation to the remainder of society. Yet this perception of the injustice of organized wealth did not preclude, although it tended to obscure, the editors' identification with the lesser capitalist and the aspiration for property. In a separate editorial in the same issue, the *Farmers' Alliance* launched an equally strong attack on monopolism, but it also said of the People's party: "It demands equal opportunities and exact justice in business for each individual, and proposes to abolish all monopolistic privileges and power." These goals could be seen as congruent with each other. The former provides the incentive for the latter; the latter provides the ratifying condition for the former. Despite its reference specifically to "*industrial* freedom" and a "people's government," the editorial made provision for the private sphere of activity in the midst of a passage excoriating capital and praising the People's party: "It is a grand new party which shall bind together the people for mutual help as well as defense, a party organized to dethrone the money kings, the monopolist despots, the ruling class; and which shall make of this nation an industrial democracy in which each citizen shall have an equal interest, and his own home secured."[42]

The motifs supporting property ownership and the lesser capitalist were also developed elsewhere, here as part of the wider concern over the expropriation of the individual: "Now what is life and so-called liberty if the means of subsistence are monopolized? Hunger-scourged, the dependent laborers must accept the wages that independent employers choose to offer, and the wages are made so low that the dependent cannot become independent. More are reduced to dependence than rise to independence." This process of impoverishment involved not only the worker but also the holder of property: "The army begging work is every year increasing, the small capitalist is being crowded down into the ranks of the wage earners by bigger, richer business rivals, and capital is concentrating and drawing to itself all power."[43] This issue of corporate power, however, relegated the paper's allegiance to property to a secondary position. During a summer of intense labor suppression, the paper observed: "In the condition of the labor market today, the laborer without an organization is at the mercy of an organized capital that knows no mercy."[44]

But perhaps the *Farmers' Alliance* criticized corporate power most decisively on political grounds: The corporation, by usurping public authority, had become the basis for reorganizing society under a private system of government. This development of monopolistic economic and political control was given philosophical and emotional assistance through the role played by individualism in the American democratic heritage. According to the editor, individualism had been aligned with democracy in the formative period of the nation, but with the rise of the corporation individualism had outgrown and then falsified its original meaning. It was joined to the corporate form itself, endowing monopolism with the sanctity of personal liberties. The editorial therefore approached a sensitive area; although individualism was highly valued in Populist thought, its distortion in contemporary usage necessitated a reevaluation of its meaning.

Clearly, the editor had mixed feelings, as if the dedication to the property right had hidden costs: "The plutocracy of to-day is the logical result of the individual freedom which we have always considered the pride of our system." In reality, individualism promoted economic activity; it was not a puristic principle of human rights: "The theory of our government has been and is that the individual should possess the very greatest degree of liberty consistent, not with the greatest good of the greatest number, but with the very least legal restraint compatible with law and order. Individual enterprise was allowed unlimited scope." The results of "individual enterprise" had "excelled the most extravagant dreams," forcing the process of capital accumulation beyond the single individual to the "accretions of other individuals," namely, "an artificial individual" that "was named the corporation."

From this baseline, the editor could state the case against corporate power, which was a new formation marking the institutional change from the rule of law to a self-ruled capitalist structure. But more, he implicitly acknowledged that liberty had been used to destroy liberty and hence that the corporate transformation of society endangered the political tenets of a democratic order: "This individual, the creation of the law, soon began to bend to its uses the forms and powers of the law. While in its nature and development it is only the original and cherished principle of individual liberty, it has absorbed the liberties of the community and usurped the power of the agency that created it." The progression from individualism to monopolism further implied that classical liberalism had no effective means of preventing the concentration of wealth: "Individualism incorporated has gone wild." The editor did not wish to discard individual liberty. He sought to redefine its meaning to make it consistent with the ethical standard of community. It would be brought to fruition through cooperative principles: "The corporation has absorbed the community. The community must now absorb the corporation—must merge itself into it. Society must enlarge itself to the breadth of humanity." There would be no conflict between the individual and the community: "A stage must be reached in which each will be for all and all for each. The welfare of the individual must be the object and end of all effort."[45]

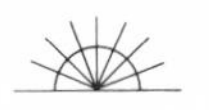

TWO

The Vision of a Sovereign People

The concept of public welfare, especially when it emphasized respect for the individual, supposed a complex relationship between traditional liberties, the powers of government, and the ability of a sovereign people to bring about social change. Traditional liberties would set economic and political boundaries to individual rights, in the case of Populist thought preserving a general capitalistic orientation, but they would not oppose the social coherence and extension of these rights as an affirmation of community. The community could have a capitalistic or simply neutral structure, but in Populist thought community was the higher embodiment of the individual's moral, economic, and political development. It was an indispensable, if usually implied, factor in most of the preceding writings. Yet the idea of community, when given the specificity of a political ethos, not merely cooperative buying and selling, failed to make significant headway among the majority of southern Populists. Morgan's formulation of "the public good" expressed it well; Davis's statement about a vitalized market economy barely tapped its possibilities. Southern Populists may have found it difficult to embrace the idea of community in its modern economic and political dimensions because it required a spirit of social mutuality that was inimical to the purposes of the southern racial system.

The concept of public welfare, as other than a dutifully endorsed abstract goal, entailed several challenges to southern Populists' cultural and historical understanding of the polity. The term "public welfare" bore the political and moral connotations of an inclusive social order and the inclusive application of benefits within that order. It was manifestly incompatible with racialism, even when the issue of race was not raised. Implementation of a policy promoting the public welfare would require political and structural changes, including more extensive government power; and potentially extensible government power tended to raise the specter, even in the minds of southern Populists, of national interference with local self-government and customary ways. Again, the racial system did not have to be mentioned; localism, partly derived from the experience of maintaining first a system of plantation slavery and then a system of racial separation, ran so deeply through southern culture that any exhibition or concentration of national power, or perhaps even power as such, was intuitively mistrusted.

In addition, the idea of public welfare questioned other regional characteristics. It disconcerted southern Populists because the challenge was directed to intangible, although quite real, considerations: an instinctive belief in the hierarchical ordering of society; an acceptance of customs of social deference; an inclination to view the classes as ultimately reconciled in an organic social framework. The implied structural and cultural equalitarianism in the concept of public welfare cut across and undermined these interrelated structural features and mental attitudes. The ideal of endowing the people with full sovereign rights, of remaking society according to their moral and social vision, was the final stumbling block to an acceptance of the public welfare, for although the people could be honored in principle, the prospect of unmediated social change would presumably throw the society off its established course.

A Divergent View of Public Welfare

Tom Watson's thought exemplified the southern Populist attitudes outlined in this brief sketch. He was probably the most agile and, in the racial area, complex thinker in the southern branch of the movement. But he was essentially a product of, and bound by, the regional political culture, an intellectual context that antedated Populism and would continue long after it. His Populism was an adaptation of his southernism. This meant that he was not fully engaged in broader reform thought and that he lacked the incipient class and industrial consciousness that would have made him receptive to government power. Watson approached contemporary society from prior cultural categories of social and structural understanding. His orientation toward social change was not necessarily retrogressive, but it was preservative, moderate, and, one might say, Burkean. This characterization stands in contrast to his sometimes incendiary rhetoric, politically flamboyant style, and uncontrolled anger, all of which translate as a vigor that the unwary mistake for radicalism; but surface political signs cannot be allowed to hide a measured, conservative variant of Populism.

In contrast to the Populists I have already discussed, with the possible exception of Davis, Watson failed to develop an expansive role for government in the ethical and structural reorganization of society. One finds in Watson's theory a perfunctory acceptance of public ownership, largely for the purposes of an open market; nowhere is there evidence of a unified conception of the democratic state. He separated specific programs of Populism from broader principles. He saw the world as requiring order—not the order of corporate capitalism, which flatly asserted the conservation of property in all situations, but nonetheless an ideal of order based on fixed notions of race, hierarchy, organic social relations, and paternalism. Watson's ingrained elitism was badly matched with any meaningful conception of public welfare. Finally, he confined his criticism of the contemporary system to the unfair political and economic advantages (that is, special privileges) conferred by class legislation. This was an unexceptionable point in Populist discourse, but he failed to go on to address the specifically capitalistic sources of corporate dominance, the implications of monopolism for creating private sovereignty, or the constitutional and ethical premises for enlarging the power of the state.

In fact, Watson feared the enlargement of state power and the reorganization of society that it implied. He possessed little vision of community, except in its patriarchal form, and perhaps still less vision of human possibilities. Such terms as "humanity" and "mankind" did not come readily to him. It is not that he disliked abstractions (his speeches and writings contain the richly associative concepts of the South), but the referents to which these particular abstractions applied included a social tranformation that could bring about mutual bonds and human equity. Rather than increased government power and structural reorganization, Watson favored overall harmony in political and economic arrangements and in racial relations. His support of hierarchical principles in the social order were mixed with a somewhat contradictory disposition to laissez-faire in the economic order. However, laissez-faire and social hierarchy had in common the presumed laws of harmony that he so highly valued. Watson was sophisticated and brilliant, but he lacked both a systematic and systemic mode of analysis. He was not a disciplined thinker; his political and economic discussion tended to be fragmentary, and he seldom sustained a focus on substantive content. Conceivably, he avoided close reasoning and a systemic approach to social problems as a way of reaffirming a regional perspective that would preclude the disturbing questions of class, industrialism, and public welfare.

Watson assured an audience of working people that "capital is the child of labor." But his labor theory of value was qualified to make "due allowance for material and the use of the capital," and his critical tone, once he had mentioned human misery, underwent an abrupt change: "Don't understand me to be making war upon capital as such. I am but denouncing that capital which is used tyrannically. I recognize the fact that without capital there can be no progress. If labor consumed its products day by day, and there was no surplus collected anywhere, advance would be an impossibility." This undifferentiated notion of "surplus," on which he claimed the advancement of civilization depended, was in reality the private accumulation of capital. Watson used a classic Lockean legitimation of wealth to place the existence of capitalism as a total system beyond criticism. The "surplus" would lead to "a leisure class" devoted to scientific, artistic, and legal achievements; it also, when "accumulated in the hands of some citizen," would enable society to advance beyond "the simplest manual labor" into a world of factories, railroads, merchants, and bankers.

Through a doctrine of "just harmony," Watson provided an organic model of the class and productive systems. In this model, he abandoned his labor theory of value, implied the compatibility of, and necessary collaboration between, capital and labor, and sanctioned capitalistic institutions and practices that other Populists viewed critically and sought to change. In the process, he made the capitalist the prime benefactor of society:

> The healthy, happy prosperous community is not that which consists either of capitalists alone, or of laborers alone. Neither can do without the other. The truly prosperous community is that in which a just harmony is preserved between the two, and they become allies instead of enemies. Every class has its legitimate work and cannot be dispensed with. The banker is as natural a part of the business system as the borrower. In fighting an abuse in the banking system I do not wage war on banking itself—for some poor man will always want to use the surplus of the rich one, and if he can do so on equitable terms, both are benefited.

Each class had its assigned place. The structure was fundamentally sound; only excesses, such as usury, could be deplored. Other Populists were more reserved in their praise of banking and interest taking, and they might have been shocked if they followed closely Watson's further tribute to the manufacturer: "I do not for a moment forget that his prosperity is absolutely essential to national welfare." It was as if the logical corollary of an organic society were a trickle-down theory of wealth.

Then he lectured his labor audience on the virtues of social peace. This theme provides a superb example of encouraging what is popularly meant by a state of false consciousness or, more aptly, the plea for class reconciliation: "I hope to see all ranks meet the difficulty [the labor question] in a spirit of fairness and conciliation. You are a laborer. Remember that it is possible you may be a capitalist tomorrow. You are a capitalist. Remember you may be a laborer tomorrow. This is the spirit in which serious issues should be adjusted." If laborers avoided class appeals, they could look forward to the trickling down of the economic surplus: "The time will surely come when the producers of wealth must share equally its benefits, when the bounteous results of your toil will not all turn in at the gates of the palace, but a portion thereof will pass on down to the cottage and lift that humble tenement into dignity, comfort and happiness of a home."[1]

Watson would humanize poverty rather than transform the society that produced it. There is a sense of detachment about the preceding speech and, in his word choice, a not quite veiled condescension. Despite his oratorical powers and remarkable imagination, he was able neither to identify with the laborer or the sharecropper of either race nor to appreciate fully the fictive nature of the equality between the "palace" and the "cottage"; instead, he preferred to let rich and poor remain as fixed social categories, bound together by common feelings of respect. Watson's doctrine of "just harmony" was invoked precisely to avoid social antagonism. Fundamental social questions were subject to adjustment; they would not be determined forthrightly on behalf of the lower social orders. The doctrine of "just harmony" limited social protest. It left intact the regnant economic and social categories of a class society; it encouraged "a spirit of fairness," which is to say, a spirit of accommodation on the part of working people; and it premised basic social relations on the mutual trust of capital and labor. Furthermore, this doctrine supposed as a structural principle an equilibrium of social forces that would control the pace and direction of social change. Change would be gradual, as befitted a society that was both sound and organic; but even more, its purpose would be to move the social order toward the middle range of property.

Watson would not sacrifice his principles of hierarchy, in either his value system or the social structure. He envisioned a propertied society of the middle range that would incorporate necessary class differences and at the same time purge itself of socially disruptive elements. An equilibrium of forces would be brought about by the purification, rather than the democratization, of the existing structure. For Watson, this meant that while capital and labor would remain intact as categories, the sybaritic rich and the despondent poor had to be removed from society if social harmony was to be preserved. He had an abhorrence of extremes, and yet, when he discussed capital, he questioned not the existence of upper groups or the structure of wealth, but the irresponsibility of elites: a "Shoddy Aristocracy based on Commercial Spoils."[2] This criticism was consistent with his well-defined sense of paternalism and propriety. When he discussed labor, he tended to see the laboring poor as a permanent feature of society, and he objected only to destitution because it was the breeding ground of crime, militance, and social upheaval.

Watson's middle-class polity would normalize the capital accumulation process and make it legitimate, widen the influence of property consciousness, circumscribe the boundaries of economic deprivation, and eliminate special privileges, which were created by law. It would not directly raise the propertyless class. Even when Watson introduced an anti-Pinkerton resolution in Congress, he emphasized most the conservation of order; militant labor, though only a hypothetical force, and armed strikebreakers were alike undesirable: "I am as much opposed to laborers having a standing army as I am to capitalists having it. I believe in law; I believe in order; I believe that when there is civil disturbance the peace should be preserved by an impartial magistracy, not by the armed belligerents on either side." His attempt to force an investigation of the Pinkerton system clearly demonstrated that he did not have a class perspective: "Let us see whether there is not an evil which deserves to be restrained or corrected in the interest, not of the laborer, merely as a laborer, not of the striker, merely as a striker, but in the interest of the citizen, whether he is a laborer or a capitalist—in the interest of the good order, the peace, and the dignity of society."[3] If capitalism was normalized, the labor struggle was, to the same degree, neutralized.

Watson's moderate position was best revealed in his reputed call for revolution. Within Populism he was unsurpassed in depicting social misery: "Millions were wasted on feasts while gaunt starvation walked the streets. . . . The Sheriff's hammer is never idle, and with every minute which passes the light of some home goes out forever."[4] He also conveyed a semblance of radicalism in the pithy warnings he issued: "It is only when Tyranny sees danger that it hears reason. . . . The sword of Damocles never hung by a slenderer thread than does the false system of to-day."[5] In a passage expressing his support of free trade, he even criticized the organic model of society he had applauded elsewhere: "Labor is robbed under the baptismal designation of Protection and it is very seldom that the laborers themselves do not assist. They are entrapped, misled, deluded, defrauded, rifled and jugulated in the name of Arcadian Friendship."[6] But already, because his concern was about dissipation in upper circles of wealth rather than about capitalist structure, one is prepared for a discrepancy between the causes of revolt and the promise of change: "Belshazzar is repeated at every epoch and wherever the mad King reaches his last evening on earth his feast is certain to be had. . . . The pampered Aristocrats will listen to no warning, until Daniel strides into the Hall and the laugh of the voluptuary freezes on the lips of the quaking coward."[7] His discussion steered away from systemic problems and placed blame on a vaguely defined elite that itself had no clear connection with the operations of capitalism.

More specifically, if Watson's statement of revolution was melodramatic, it did not transcend the bounds of order: "As the Nobleman said to the King, the night the Bastille fell, 'No sire, it is not a Revolt, it is a Revolution.' So it is. Peaceful, bloodless, unstained by crime, but as resistless as destiny." The passage in which his call for revolution occurs is astonishingly mild; it has nothing to do with revolution and very little to do with substantive reform. Instead, Watson would abolish special privilege because it had vitiated the normal course of society, and he would do this in the name of law and order: "We do not blindly seek to tear down. We offer the good Law for each bad Law; the sound rail for every rotten rail. We work in no spirit of hate to individuals. We hate only the wrongs and the abuses, and the special privileges which oppress us. We call on good men and good women everywhere to aid us. We call on God above to aid us. For in the revolution we seek to accomplish, there shall be Law and order preserved in-violate."

As he continues, it is apparent that his objectives are modest—preservation of order and internal purification. Poverty would continue; even crime and suffering would continue. Watson's revolution would attack only their legally created forms. In a profound way, the law had become a scapegoat for the workings of capitalism, and at any rate the ills of society would remain, if in a somewhat less severe form. Under these circumstances, individuals would be thrown back on their own resources in true laissez-faire fashion:

> We do not assert that poverty will disappear. We do not assert that the Law itself shall make no more of it. We do not assert that there will be no more crime; we do say that vicious Legislation shall cease to produce it. We do not say that there will be no more suffering; but we do aver that hereafter and forever the statutes shall not empty the homes of the people, turn their children into the streets and fill the hospitals and the alleys and the gutters with the distracted victims of the Law.

Even "the strong man" would continue "to have the advantage of the weak one," though no longer through the aid of the law.[8]

Then Watson came to the foundations of his middle-class polity. First, he condemned the social extremes of wealth and poverty, viewing them as interrelated threats to the good order of society. When these extremes were removed, the revolution would be complete, and no further changes would be necessary: "The hot-beds of crime and vice to-day are at the two extremes of Society. One is among the class who will have all the work and no money; the other is with the class who have all the money and no work. The one class is driven to crime and vice by hardships, despair, desperation. The other class chooses crime and vice because of their surplus of money, their lack of purpose, their capacity to live in idleness and gratify sensual pleasures."[9] In his analysis, despair and sensuality assumed the same importance. He responded by condemning both; opposition to one did not breed compassion for the other. Yet more striking is Watson's making "crime" and "vice" central problems of America; this view trivialized the entire Populist criticism of monopolism and corporate power. His use of crime and vice fused the identity of the two classes; and, by projecting their objectionable features to the fringes of society, he defined as centrist, normal, and legitimate the complete institutional life of society that fell between the extremes.

Watson did not exonerate monopolism, nor was this his intent. But he affirmed a stable social order that by definition was based on the structure and culture of capitalism. The term "middle class" here becomes deceptive in one respect: it hides the features of the social structure that are not middle class, including responsible upper groups and the respectable laboring poor. In Watson's view, the polity should be established on propertied lines; Watson assigned primary value to what numerous other Populists accepted only secondarily and as part of a broader configuration of rights: "The great Middle Class is the mainstay of life. It is the judicious mixture of work and leisure which makes the complete man; the useful man; the God-fearing, law-abiding man." If Watson had to choose between the two social extremes, he would choose the upper groups. He appeared to fear lower groups more because of their potential militance: "Any system which increases the Moneyed Class where there is all money and no work, debauches Society. Any System which increases the class where there is all work and no money debauches and endangers Society." But debauchery itself is hardly adequate to characterize the economic, political, and social consequences of inequitably distributed wealth and power.

His call for revolution was deeply antirevolutionary in conception. It posited the middle-class basis of society as a moral and structural goal, and he also saw this goal as the mission of Populism: "Any system which will add to the great Middle Class where there is reasonable work and fair reward, secures to Society the best results of which humanity is capable. Every principle advocated by the People's Party seeks that end and logically leads to it." Finally, purification also had a literal meaning that concerned not monopolism but intemperance and the gratification of sensual pleasure. Watson's revolutionary bang was reduced to the whimper of middle-class purity: "When this System comes, (and it is bound to come) the Revolution will be complete. The dens of vice will loose their feeders. The supply-trains of crime will be cut off. The Bar-room will disappear and the gambling hell sink to its larger namesake. The attendant train of evils which the present system carries with it will vanish with the system itself."[10]

The Expansion of Government Power

Ignatius Donnelly shared with Watson a gift for popular oratory and colorful writing, a colossal and largely unfulfilled ego, remarkable intelligence, traces of a Manichaean outlook, and a thirst for political advancement. Both men were visionaries, social and political dreamers who were not quite at home in their surroundings. Both were in flight, spiritual and intellectual, from the present and, to an extent, from their contemporaries. Despite their enormous energy, activity, and visibility, both men also sought the seclusion of their studies. They came from different generations (Watson was considerably younger) and drew on very different traditions in their politically formative years—traditions centered on the meaning and outcome of the Civil War as it applied to racial freedom and national power. But the personal similarities of the two men are useful to recall because they heighten the substantive differences between them. As talented scholar politicians, Donnelly and Watson chose a common mode of self-expression to reach almost opposite conclusions on the nature of the political universe. The essence of their difference, affecting their views of the human being and the social order alike, was the framework each employed: Donnelly's system of thought was open-ended; Watson's was closed. The issue was the potentiality of human and societal achievement.

Watson's social vision had its inspiration in the past, a lost world of patriarchal order that could be regained through strengthening the material base of an autonomous South. Without slavery or overt economic coercion, a vitalized regional culture and society could overcome the South's political and structural backwardness, which was imposed by the commercial penetration of the North. A measure of internal improvement could occur without destroying the southern racial system and political values. Watson was not an enemy of modernity. But he opposed with equal fervor the South's dependence on the contemporary system of capitalism and the rapid industrialization of southern society itself because these interrelated forms of modernity would place insupportable strains on the basic institutions and culture of the South.

The social structure based on racial separation was only the most prominent characteristic he had in mind when he spoke of the conservation of southern institutions. A deeper, almost instinctive set of attitudes and allegiances included the conception of time, law, custom, family, and place; emphasized the importance of status, lineage, and habits of deference; and embraced a totally harmonious setting. Harmony was not at odds with the principle of social hierarchy; it would make the hierarchy work more smoothly and, by Watson's lights, more equitably. For Watson, human freedom would be made possible by the refinement of order, a slow evolution of tried and proven mores, rather than a fundamental departure from, or transcendence of, the organic processes that kept social classes and races bound together on the terms of the dominant political culture. Humanity was not infinitely perfectible; society, for its own best interests, could not advance beyond its painfully constructed foundation of paternalistic welfare. The system of thought was closed. It rested on the supposed perfection of a primordial, if temporarily declining, way of life that had the capacity for resolving its inner tensions and regenerating its central values.

However, Donnelly's flight, despite a brief return to the American Revolutionary past, was toward the future. In part, his discontent with the present was due to horrendous social conditions both leading to the utmost degradation of working people and for that reason, he believed, threatening a revolutionary upheaval that would destroy the achievements of civilization. But he was also impatient with contemporary society because it had not fulfilled the promise of welfare and justice inherent in its moral teachings and technological development. If Watson would modernize paternalism, Donnelly would democratize modernity. He drew upon the American Revolution and, less explicitly, the Constitution to state the principles of political democracy, but his orientation toward the future (Donnelly undoubtedly had the most restless mind among the leading Populists) led him primarily in the direction of industrial democracy.

For him, industrial democracy was a cultural as much as a political and structural question. He spoke of civilization with greater frequency than other Populists, and indeed throughout his political writings ran a theme that human freedom had to be measured by the quality of life of society. The elusive phrase "quality of life" implied nonmaterial indices of human welfare. There had to be equitable economic and political arrangements, but equity in economic matters would be a consequence of the ethical valuing of social bonds. Donnelly invoked public spirit as necessary to human welfare and promoted a secular religion based on the principle of the limitless possibilities of human and social development.

In the present context, one finds that Donnelly and Watson harnessed their considerable gifts to very different ends. Donnelly's thought was fresh and spontaneous, a lively contrast to Watson's pursuit of a conventionally respectable social order. Donnelly blended the fantast and moralist, but he was always critical of the existing structure. In Watson's usage, virtue was a way of keeping order; it had no meaning beyond maintaining "a just harmony" of interests, thus perpetuating the class structure. For Donnelly, virtue took on the character of a civic religion. It was an attribute of the socially cooperative person, part of a dynamic creed in which individuals could realize their growth in a context of mutual welfare: a total attitude of society with government serving as its vehicle.

Watson's treatment of government was curiously passive, for although Populist ideology had necessarily assigned it extended powers in such areas as transportation and banking, he would not credit its protective functions in actively shielding the individual from abuses or eliminating them at their source. By removing legally created privilege, Watson gave the remaining inequalities an appearance of normality. Even the economic surplus was merely a datum of the contemporary scene, not a social product to be used for upgrading the whole of society. Donnelly, however, made government an intimate part of everyday life; it was infused in the social structure and testified to the human capacity for effecting rational changes in the political and economic realms. His references to universal human possibilities had no counterpart in Watson's political lexicon, nor did his vital fusion of human and divine purpose find an equivalent in Watson's invocation of God. Watson called upon a stern Diety who was completely separated from humanity, rather than a loving presence mystically penetrable by all people through a gospel of deep human bonds and good works. The "God-fearing, law-abiding man" was replaced in Donnelly's writings by individuals who freely consented to the law because the law emanated from their inner needs and basic intelligence and who worshiped God just as freely because this reverence confirmed their obligation to others. Finally, Watson's grasp of social misery appears to have begun with the individual, singly or aggregated, while Donnelly saw social misery in the masses as one body. The collective impoverishment took on an order of magnitude that questioned the quality of the whole contemporary society.

In stating that the world now clamored "for love, not intellect," Donnelly was protesting sharper class divisions, which were symptomatic, he believed, of a general decline of life in modern society. "Who is it that is satisfied with the present unhappy condition of society? It is conceded that life is a dark and wretched failure for the great mass of mankind."[11] Industrialism had bred a callousness to human problems, resulting in the widespread feelings of ennui that eventuated in suicide for increasing numbers of people: "From a mere weariness of feeling that they are nothing, they become nothing."[12] Despite its outward success, the society had become "so hollow and rotten at the core" that "all above is cruelty, craft and destruction, and all below is suffering, wretchedness, sin and shame." The working people walked a "narrow, gloomy, high-walled pathway, out of which they could never climb," knowing that "to-morrow could bring them nothing better than to-day—the same shameful, pitiable, contemptible, sordid struggle for a mere existence."[13] Donnelly's novel, *Caesar's Column,* warned against the catastrophe that would occur if existing tendencies were allowed to continue for another century. Yet, despite its use of a future setting, the novel was directed to the salient features of his own time, including the senseless discrepancy between a high state of technology, which could have made it possible to overcome impoverishment through rationally distributing productive increases, and the dire circumstances of laborers, who were given "the least sum that will maintain life and muscular strength" consistent with ensuring that "the world's work should not end with the death of one starved generation."[14]

If preventing a destructive revolution was a motivating factor in writing, Donnelly envisioned a positive solution as his paramount goal: the replenishment of the human spirit through affirming humanity's abilities to control the course of political development. He did not blindly rely on government as an agency of change; rather, its efficacy depended on the human factor that was essential to providing its direction: "Government is only a machine to insure justice and help the people, and we have not yet developed half its powers." Donnelly also had an unbounded faith in experimentation: "And we are under no more necessity to limit ourselves to the governmental precedents of our ancestors than we are to confine ourselves to the narrow boundaries of their knowledge, or their inventive skill, or their theological beliefs." Perhaps only by stripping the state of any intrinsic worth could Donnelly return the focus to humanity as both the ultimate source of creativity and the standard for governmental action: "The trouble is that so many seem to regard government as a divine something which has fallen down upon us out of heaven, and therefore not to be improved upon or even criticised; while the truth is, it is simply a human device to secure human happiness, and in itself has no more sacredness than a wheelbarrow or a cooking-pot. The end of everything earthly is the good of man; and there is nothing sacred on earth but man, because he alone shares the Divine conscience."[15] When he added, in the same vein, that "government—national, state and municipal—is the key to the future of the human race," he was extending a defense of a state whose foremost concern would be the elevation of humanity. This could be accomplished through principles of social cooperation: "We have but to expand the powers of government to solve the enigma of the world. Man separated is man savage; man gregarious is man civilized. A higher development in society requires that this instrumentality of co-operation shall be heightened in its powers."[16]

Donnelly believed that unalloyed individualism had given rise to a combative mentality, which was directly antithetical to the aim of civilization: to provide the institutional context for human fulfillment. Individuals when acting alone were not discharged from the moral obligation to enhance the welfare of others. This sentiment was expressed in *Doctor Huguet,* which criticized the persecution of blacks and made a more general statement about human worth: "If we can plainly perceive in the progress of humanity the movement of a great Benevolence, every year adding to the comfort and happiness of mankind, why should we not, to the extent of our little powers, aid Him in His tremendous work? How divine a thought is it that we are participating in the purposes and work of the Almighty One!"[17] In this novel, Donnelly's ethical principles served as a guide to action, although they tended to blur class lines in the process: "I shall labor to enlighten minds, to enkindle souls, to sweeten tempers, and to lift both races out of the slough of bigotry and intolerance. I shall preach mercy and good will and peace on earth to men, for the great Gospel of Brotherly Love is the true solvent in which must melt away forever the hates of races and the contentions of castes."[18]

In *The Golden Bottle* he summarized the categorical imperative of his social Christianity: "Men worshipped God by helping their fellows."[19] But this later work also made it clear that individual effort had to be multiplied and given tangible form through the use of government if ethical principles were to have a binding effect. Donnelly was adamant about the human-centered nature of the polity: "Statutes, ordinances, customs; banks, bonds, money; beliefs, theories, religions; philosophies, dogmas, and doctrines, are only valuable as they conserve the happiness of mankind. Whenever they conflict with it, they must fall to the ground."[20] Strictly speaking, humanity anteceded property in value; this concept went beyond the limitations imposed by Locke on the functions of the state: To preserve the property right was no longer an exclusive charge on government.

In fact, only when one comes to see how closely Donnelly sought to integrate human purpose and government power does his legitimation of an expanding state appear intelligible. Government was indispensable for advancing civilization, which was itself synonymous with improving the human condition: "The poor man is, at first, like the new-born child, he is perfectly powerless; he needs protection, if he would advance to the full stature of manhood. He has now fought his own way, by organization, a long distance; government must come to his help for the remainder of the path of progress he is to travel over."[21] Donnelly had in mind a government that was not only broadly paternal but also capable of removing impediments to economic activity and stimulating self-help. He created an antimonopolist paradigm with collective features of social and economic organization that would result in a mixed economy. His model town was a microcosm of a planned society; it had a humanly proportioned environment, public centers for cultural activities, health care and other services, and such programs as profit sharing in industry. Significantly, he named his model town "Cooperation."[22]

Through a series of questions, Donnelly reasoned that there could be a progression from contemporary needs to conditions in which humanity would be liberated and realize its moral nature: "Why should not government expand its powers with the necessities of its surroundings? Has government any higher function than the relief of the human estate? And does not earthly power seem likest God's when it lifts up man and makes him contented, virtuous, and happy?"[23] Virtue was inseparable from a strengthening of social bonds. Significantly, Donnelly's conception of law began where Watson's left off: "Law can prevent crime and insure justice, but it has its limitations. It deals not with thoughts, but acts. It can regulate the opening and shutting of the doors of the temple of the soul, but it cannot enter in and purify the polluted chambers. Only that which connects man with the vast spiritual brotherhood around him can do that mighty work." Donnelly's concept of purification reveals his vision of a higher stage of society, in which structural and political change would rest on ethical foundations: "No reform of legislation is complete which is based on a beast-world, without conscience. Besides a fair division of the rights and goods of the world there must be a something vaster and profounder—man's love for his fellow—not merely a willingness to give him a fair show and a fair divide, but an *affection* for him, reaching from heart to heart."[24]

The Principle of Sovereignty

One notes that even the more specifically constitutional arguments for the expansion of government powers, found chiefly in the writings of William A. Peffer and James B. Weaver, supposed a moral climate in which the public welfare was an object of supreme regard. With disarming simplicity, Peffer observed: "The people of the United States constitute a nation."[25] They possessed a capacity to act and a charter of fundamental rights that was meant to be acted upon—an agenda, sanctioned by democratic tradition and American history, that was constantly evolving in response to changing needs. Upper social groups, who believed themselves to be "specially commissioned to prey upon the people" and who could "rake in a railroad, a state, or a nation with equal complacency," were "fast undermining the liberties of the people."[26] Just such economic and political circumstances required a restoration of lawful authority, an assertion of state power (as in regulating commerce and levying taxes): "All of these things are the prerogatives of sovereignty." Together the three branches of government become "an agent of the people for the purpose of executing the popular will."[27]

Peffer's treatment of the right of eminent domain as an example of sovereign power led to the sweeping statement that the regulation of commerce *and* all specific means to its achievement had, alike, been invested with a public character. A literalistic construction of the Constitution mandated the nationalization of American railroads: "If, then, Congress is authorized to regulate *commerce* among the several States, it is also authorized to regulate the *instruments* of commerce. . . . The same power which authorizes the Government to open and maintain highways, post roads, and the like authorizes it to build roads for the people without the intervention of any corporation whatever; to build the roads, to own them, to manage them in the interest of the people; and this right to regulate commerce includes necessarily—not only impliedly, but *necessarily*—every function essential to the work."[28] Holding that money also *"is a necessary instrument of commerce,"*[29] Peffer itemized the provisions of monetary and banking policy that would be defined as public functions in executing the government's power and responsibility in this area. Government, in its sovereign capacity, could "do for the people directly what it is now doing for them indirectly through banking institutions, and permitting the banks to charge a very high percentage for their services."[30] By prohibiting corporate intervention in the issuance of currency, interest rates, and the availability of credit, he sought to fuse popular self-governance and a doctrine of public rights, thus bringing about "the inauguration and management of a system by which the people can control their own financial affairs in their own way."[31] Throughout his analysis, he implicitly rejected the idea of the interpenetration of business and government.

Weaver proposed a still more far-reaching statement of sovereign power in which the state would have inclusive and undisputed authority to act in the political and economic spheres, insofar as its prerogative of regulation was warranted by the Constitution. Indeed, he was so concerned that the state might abdicate its sovereignty to private groups (in this case to banking interests on which the payment of the national debt depended) that he issued a blanket pronouncement which ignored even constitutional sanctions: "The Nation is supreme and rules over the whole body as an individual controls his own person. It commands and every member, the head, the eye, the ear, the tongue, the hands, the feet—the whole organic structure must obey. No member of the body politic can become so great as to rise above, none so insignificant as to fall below the control of the Sovereign will." Weaver, however, was not making a case for absolutism; for in defining the principle of sovereignty, he was contrasting the relative powerlessness of individuals to "direct [their] own actions" and the ability of "an independent and powerful Nation, if wisely governed" to avoid "such limitations and vicissitudes."[32] In brief, the concept of nationhood entailed the powers of self-direction. Moreover, his claim of universal jurisdiction brought the "great" and the "insignificant" alike within the administration of the law, primarily as a way of preventing usurpation by "a horde of artificial persons, who are void of the feelings of pity and the compunctions of conscience" in the conduct of business.[33]

Notwithstanding these motivations, Weaver was hardly restrained in his conception of government power; in fact, he gave the property right only a conditional status: "If circumstances warrant, the Sovereign hand can be laid upon the persons, the property, the commerce, and even the lives of its subjects." He saw the need of limitations, and yet his basic position was that the state had a protective role to perform in fulfilling its constitutional obligation; not to utilize its powers was a dereliction of political responsibility: "That power so vast should be exercised with prudence and caution none will gainsay. But Government was created to meet and master emergencies with which individual powers and capacities are inadequate to cope. Each individual member of society consented to the full exercise of this power when his citizenship began, and this consent can neither be withdrawn nor ignored; neither can the primal functions of Government ever be rightfully surrendered." The irrevocable nature of political consent placed an equally heavy burden on government, as a constant and permanent constitutional standard, to act where it was empowered to do so: "What moral right have the rulers and lawmakers of a Sovereign and Independant [*sic*] Nation to refuse to exercises the legitimate powers entrusted to their care?"[34] To surrender control of fiscal and monetary policy to private bankers reduced government to the weakened state of the individual, a displacement of "the sovereignty of the people" which "is rarely ever regained—never except by upheavals which convulse society from center to circumference."[35]

The Moral Sources of Authority

This brief survey of Populist economic and political ideas reveals the interplay of individual and collective elements in shaping a distinctive notion of public welfare. Nominally, what unified these Populist writings was a common hostility to monopolism and, more particularly, its restrictions on economic security and personal independence. Yet Populists shared a wider political discourse in which the opposition to monopolism was only the most prominent feature. Not excepting Watson, they appreciated traditional democratic values that emphasized the individual's worth; Watson's racial attitudes and regional perspective restricted the range of their application, but he did not reject the values themselves. Populists looked to a doctrine of constitutionalism as the means through which to preserve, implement, and, when necessary, extend these values. They interpreted differently the meaning of individualism and individual rights, centered on the emphasis to the property right or, alternatively, the social character of human identity, just as they differed over the meaning and possibilities of constitutionalism as an affirmation of sovereign power. However, if a profession of the democratic faith was not exceptional in the American political culture, Populists were set apart from their contemporaries and could integrate their diverse views because they placed this faith into direct opposition with the existing system of capitalism. They broke the simple connection in American ideology between capitalism and democracy. They might differ on the latitude accorded the concept of public welfare, but they agreed that there should be such a concept. That concept implied reconciling the needs of the individual and the community. This exceeded mere reconciliation of property and society because the individual was already viewed as having fused human rights and property rights, and the community, unlike society, was invested with the noncapitalistic ideals of mutual social bonds. In addition, the concept of public welfare became inseparable from the idea of a sovereign people as the foundation of legitimate government.

The Populists examined here, in one way or another, stepped outside the contemporary context of capitalism. Their individual lines of advancement represented intellectual forays in numerous directions. Some Populists emphasized the sacredness of the human person, others a modified political collectivism, and still others an apparently reversional stage of political economy through methods hardly sanctioned by classical economics. But a diversity of views can be a strength rather than a weakness. In the case of Populism, it enriched the underlying purpose of the movement: to provide an alternative mode of human freedom in refutation of the economic, political, and cultural dominance of the expanding corporate system. The final case study, that of Thomas L. Nugent, also had a unique contribution to make to the Populist configuration of thought. Nugent's moral emphasis elevated antimonopolism to a powerful statement of social Christianity, and he combined this with a biting critique of the inner decay of contemporary institutional forms. Conversely, he came the closest among these Populists to making an unabashed appeal for laissez-faire.

Nugent did not endorse Weaver's view of the "primal functions" of government. Instead, he conceived its essential role as rejuvenating the economy through stipulated monetary changes, particularly inconvertible paper and the abolition of bankers' control of the money supply. He did not believe that government should be an overriding presence that could reconstruct or transform the social order. The state, even when he accorded it some powers assigned to it by other Populists, was nevertheless inextricably bound up in his thought with the spirit and purposes of a laissez-faire framework. His treatment of government had an antiseptic quality because he studiously avoided the correlative issues of constitutional obligation, public sovereignty, and welfare, emphasizing instead the state's ancillary position in relation to the presumably more effective sources of reform, such as ethics and the natural processes of the economy. He accepted and even enlarged Donnelly's ethical context; however, he partly divested this context of its supporting governmental structure, and hence he was inclined toward Watson's polity of the "great Middle Class." In Nugent's thought, antimonopolism should attack the privileges and restrictions that derived from concentrated wealth, but he warned "against every measure calculated to break down the security which the laws afford to private property,"[36] and he also wished "to restore to the commercial and social world the lost ideas of equity and justice, thus to untrammel legitimate industries and skill and leave them to pursue in freedom the beneficent work of producing wealth."[37] In both cases, he diminished the positive force of a state more oriented toward collective goals.

Nugent's undoubted complexity lay in his synthesis of these characteristics: He had a deeply moral sensibility, which had the potential for, and practically demanded, some form of transcendence of existing society; moreover, this dissatisfaction with the prevailing order was reinforced by an equally clear animus toward corporate power. But he reduced this almost visionary level of thought to commonplace demands that showed an affinity with classical liberalism. There was "poverty for the millions, vast, unearned wealth for the very few,"[38] and yet, in response to admittedly horrendous conditions, he proclaimed the need to "disembarrass trade of arbitrary legal interference, give free play to competition within the proper sphere of individual effort and investment, and steadily oppose those extreme socialistic schemes which seek by the outside pressure of mere enactments or systems, to accomplish what can only come from the free activities of men."[39] As a whole, this was a coded refutation of government intervention, a strong endorsement of a market economy, and a denial of the systemic character of economic and social problems.

In fact, when Nugent turned to the labor question proper, he observed with sympathy that "the laboring classes live constantly under the apprehension both of wage reduction and the loss of jobs," but he also continued his criticism of the protective function of the state, confining public policy basically to the stimulation of economic growth:

> The demand which labor makes is, not that it be fed by the charity of government or individuals, but that it be given fair opportunities to exert itself; that social and economic conditions be so adjusted that every laboring man will find, not a job artificially created for him by a makeshift of legislation, but employment freely coming to him from the liberated, enlarged and revivified productive forces—coming to him in fact under such beneficient changes in our laws and public policies that he can hold in his firm and honest grasp all the fruits of his labor.[40]

If Nugent implied the need to curtail monopolistic power, he manifestly rejected social confrontation or the active questioning of the main features of a class society. He wanted "real, genuine and lasting reforms which labor and capital equally need."[41] And he carried his theme of class reconciliation quite far when he stated, "Let us cultivate the duty of submission to lawful authority, and in times of civil commotion, be first to give it support in its conflicts with the lawless." He avoided all forms of class violence; moreover, he severely confined the method of social change to politically acceptable channels: "An intelligent ballot is the only refuge of justice and liberty."[42] The willingness to accept the electoral process was itself meant as a tribute to the efficacy of the democratic heritage.

In the moral dimension of his analysis, Nugent sought to infuse antimonopolism with a puristic Swedenborgian Christianity. He returned to the historical personage of Christ, whose teachings had not yet been influenced by the bureaucratic rigidities of later church organization, in order to call for unsublimated feelings of human concern and social love. He saw in Christ's teachings the supreme ethical challenge to the callousness and the excessive structuralization of economic and social life. He also believed these teachings would be an antidote to the spirit of opportunism that characterized the major political parties. More immediate was Nugent's desire to heighten political consciousness among Populists themselves; he looked to the ethical realm and called for a basic rethinking of first moral principles and the meaning of reform. Despite his moderate economic position, this general moral enterprise posed a challenge to contemporary patterns of thought and conveyed the possibilities of greater social and political militance. In Christ he had summoned an unimpeachable source—to which Jefferson was added—for attacking corporate wealth and power. Populism's methodology of literal construction had now been pressed back nearly two millenniums!

Christ was to be a vital political force in contemporary society, particularly among the lower classes: "The spirit of humanity which Christ left in the world has not departed, although periodically subjected to partial suppressions. It is here in this wonderful country of ours and among our wonderful people. But it is kindling the fires of reform, not among the socially or politically wise and mighty, but among the untutored masses."[43] It was as if latent discontent had prepared the ground for a mass political awakening. Christ would present a symbolic rallying point because modern culture and institutions had become lifeless, corrupt, and uncaring. For Nugent, Christ represented "the ideal reformer, the one single, complete and symmetrical character of human history," who upheld "the rule of absolute right in the face of an age given over to superstitious veneration for dead forms and whose highest ideals never rose above the level of the merely technical or legal."[44] The loss of human feeling characterized Nugent's age as well, and he believed that reformers, however much they were in earnest, had not then, nor at any time in history, "been able to transcend their external environments" and instead had "run in grooves worn by existing social and political systems." Unwittingly, they too had become technicians of the established order. But his broader point was that human thought was constrained by institutions that had lost their original vitality and purpose. This mental and cultural inertia illustrated "the tendency of institutions to perpetuate themselves by means of the veneration in which they are held and the dread which they inspire."[45]

Institutional and cultural rigidity was historically exemplified through the way major religious systems reproduced, in slightly altered form, the previous intolerance they had sought to remove. In Nugent's own period, political parties also lacked a mystical basis, which would have been impervious to both opportunism and a fear of dissolution, and could have supported the search for truth, a search unhampered by powerful economic forces, the desire for personal advancement, or the leaders' own "lust for dominion." Parties were merely another example of ossified institutions. But again, even reformers, protesting against unresponsiveness to the problems of society, did not raise their own criticism to a higher plane. Few reformers, he contended, "have ever penetrated beyond the mere physical basis of existence." Nugent wanted to inform politics with a transcendent purpose, the reanimation of the "spirit of humanity" that he identified with Christ's teachings. This goal implied the need for a moral and political epistemology that would allow individuals to discern and act on primordial principles. Truth stands revealed "only to men who win her as a bride"; the desire to find the truth must be an "unquenchable" longing that draws its inspiration from Christ as the archetypal reformer: "'He sleeps in God who wakes and toils with men,' says the rarest of modern reformers. Here is the lesson—the rule—and he who works out the rule in practical life will know truth by an interior recognition far more convincing than any process of human reasoning."[46]

Like Donnelly, Nugent communicated a forceful vision of humanity's God-like character; but by quickly invoking Jefferson, he also demonstrated that such a vision would still impose conventional limits on reform: "The transformations already effected and which yet impend are largely due to the fundamental, political truths taught by Jefferson." Although these founding ideals had become distorted, they could be retrieved for the future, and Jefferson would remain a principal source for defining Populism's ideological universe: "A crude generation appropriated them only to the demands of an extreme, selfish individualism, but the opening epoch will appropriate them to the demands of social and political justice."[47] What had begun as the plea for complete intellectual and spiritual emancipation was limited to a finite economic and political context that sanctioned a classically defined version of antimonopolism.

In construing Jefferson as a modern day exemplar of Christ's teachings, Nugent gave moral legitimation to a particular formation of capitalism and a generally circumscribed framework of state power. However emotionally satisfying he was as a political symbol, Jefferson served, especially among southern Populists, as the incarnation of a pristine Democratic party, and Jeffersonianism became the code word for anticollective public welfare. If only the Democratic party could be restored to its Jeffersonian-Jacksonian purity, then presumably there would be no further need for Populism. In this case, to define Populism's ideological universe was to limit its freely developing goals. Political consciousness would be activated and yet confined to a moral course that tended toward individual rather than structural change. Nugent's interpretation of Jefferson confirmed the macroeconomic decision: Populism would be linked to capitalism as the only acceptable form of political economy. This was not a surprising conclusion for Populists to reach, but here it became slightly tarnished because of Nugent's profession of total openness.

The formation of capitalism that Nugent favored equated individual enterprise with human freedom; the obligation of government was to prevent artificial restraints on opportunity and sustained economic growth. This position might be termed an antimonopolism of laissez-faire, except for the provision for the regulatory powers of government. In this regard, Nugent was rigorously consistent in countering the specific challenges to a liberal social order as it was classically defined.

The acceptance of private property did not mean a corresponding endorsement of the corporate structure. He said of the Pullman strike, as an example of increasingly prevalent "industrial paroxysms," that "the spirit of plutocratic capitalism is the dominating force in our organized social and industrial life." Like Peffer and many other Populists, he saw a pattern of widespread economic restriction and social devastation. He was especially incensed by the abridgement of the liberty implicit in a divinely bestowed right to occupy the land and by the deformation of social values and human character under the spell of monetary success:

> Yes, it gathers the fruits of industry and divides them at its will. It controls and manipulates with almost unbridled power and license, every function of trade and finance. Its speculative lust finds opportunities of gain in the tolls levied upon the right to occupy the earth. It denies to the people the heritage which the Creator gave them "without money and without price." It gathers into its storehouse the bounties which nature designed for the common use of all. . . . Thus it wipes out as with a sponge the distinction between right and wrong, makes merchandise of the noblest ideals, sets gain before the world as the highest end of life, and converts men into predatory human animals.[48]

Nugent, in his inclination toward laissez-faire, made no concession to the contemporary structure of capitalism.

He identified the powers of expropriation inherent in a monopolistic situation: "Give to a few individuals organized into a corporation the right to dispense for a price services of a necessary and public character—services essential to the existence and well-being of organized society—and you arm them with the power to levy tribute upon the whole community, and acquire wealth almost without limit." Although he had a clear understanding of structural bottlenecks, which provided a strategic advantage by which to absorb wealth from "all the productive industry of the country,"[49] this basic insight did not alter his preference for a classical orthodoxy: "Wealth acquired in legitimate ways, by the exercise of the industry and skill and the investment of capital, cannot hurt either its possessor or the community." The operant distinction was between capitalism itself and monopolism as its aberrant form: "It is the spirit of gain run to riot in monopolies, that poisons and corrupts the fountains of individual and social life: and against this spirit must the efforts of populists be directed."[50]

THREE

Tensions: Conservation and Transformation

Populists had a selective attitude toward capitalism. They approved its basic features—the property right, a system of wage labor, and a market framework of exchange—provided that these features were applied to a non-monopolistic system of economy. Populists did not criticize the capitalist formation as such. They took for granted the historical association between its earlier stages of development, during which there had presumably been equitable social and economic relations, and the prevalence of democratic political institutions. Even in the context of contemporary society, the ideas that underlay the private ownership of property, as distinct from the uses to which these ideas had been put, were not held to be objectionable. In their own right, ideas of propertied independence and a secure livelihood, although not intended as sanctioning an open-ended pursuit of wealth, had a definite place in Populists" conception of a better life. Their attachment to capitalism was neither an afterthought nor a passion for material advancement. Populists were oriented toward capitalism rather than being solely committed to it. They were capitalists of a subdued kind. They approached the economic system from a wider configuration of values that included, but was not exhausted by, capitalism.

This positive inclination toward capitalism was deeply rooted in the fundamental processes of American institutional and cultural development. Following the decline of Puritanism—and with it the vitality of a pre-liberal, organic conception of the polity—at the close of the seventeenth century, America experienced few internally generated challenges to a capitalistic political framework and value system. Constitutional and legal doctrine was focused on property as the foundation for individualism and basic liberties; seeming departures to the right and the left within the American political universe did not sacrifice in principle the continuous growth of capitalism.

Mercantilism and plantation slavery, though neither corresponded to the political tenets and economic organization of liberal capitalism, could receive legitimation, in their ascendant phases, as part of the reigning national formula of property rights. Prior to the final third of the nineteenth century, the social order could absorb currents of social and economic dissatisfaction from the left with even greater ease because capitalism could pose as the defender of the unfulfilled dreams of farmers and working people. Despite the existence of utopian and communal experiments in the nineteenth century, the dominant pattern on the American land in the two hundred years before the rise of Populism was the commercialization of agriculture. Notwithstanding the realities of subsistence farming and, in many instances, the ideal of self-sufficiency, production for a market was the condition that both established farming as an economic institution and integrated it into the wider economic structure. Populists could only have escaped the influence of capitalism if they had lived in another age, another society, and another political culture, featuring different social and economic development.

They did not escape its influence; except for a specific range of problems, they did not even try. Yet this range of problems, centered on the structure and power of emergent monopolism, was of such importance that Populism could be taken as a major alternative to the contemporary stage of capitalism and its future course. This alternative would remain capitalistic according to any strict definition because Populists had not rejected the property right or a market economy, but in their confrontation with monopolism they were forced to reexamine and modify the very institutional features that led to their original acceptance of capitalism.

Populists found themselves in an ambiguous position. Their selective attitude toward capitalism was a result of their discrimination between the stages of capitalist development. They strongly opposed the existing corporate structure, a framework of business organization that they viewed as operating outside the law and government. The economic mode of emergent monopolism had become socially and politically dominant. It controlled the fate of working people, the security of less-propertied and even middle-propertied groups, and the constitutional functions of the state. All this power was in addition to the specific economic power of a closed system of production and distribution. Populists did not ignore this contemporary mode of capitalism, because it contained basic elements from the previous stages of capitalist development. Instead, they attempted to build from it and at the same time propose a structural alternative to it. This process of conserving, and yet transforming, the system of capitalism suggests the intellectual ambiguity of Populist economic thought.

This ambiguity might be visualized as the attraction and aversion to the same general context, a political economy of capitalism that was founded on principles praiseworthy in themselves but distorted in their current application. For Populists, if not for the detached observer, there was no ambiguity in such a situation; there was merely a need to be selective in shaping an economic system in accordance with democratic values. Their straightforward solution to the problems of contemporary capitalism was to assert fundamental principles as the basis for removing their current application. They would restructure capitalism from within. They would fight monopoly by reaffirming the right of property. They considered monopolism an expropriating force that was destroying the property right for all members of society except those at the topmost levels of wealth and power. Monopolism was gathering property itself into gigantic, impersonally administered holdings, and monopolists acknowledged no responsibility for the general welfare. Monopolism was not accountable to society for its economic power, political corruption, and amoral standards.

Populists believed that they could counter this new structure of wealth through the acceptance of what they took to be the more permanent elements of capitalism, which had been carried by monopolism to unacceptable extremes. This solution, although straightforward, disguised the degree to which Populists were attached to the overall system they sought to transform. They did not achieve a break from capitalism: They did not escape from its influence, and their consciousness was shaped in large part by fundamental capitalistic categories, such as the property right itself. Later I discuss the epistemological consequences of the national political culture for restraining Populist thought. Here it should be noted that the property right informed their understanding of political democracy; it provided a medium through which their ideas of freedom, self-worth, and social progress would be expressed as they strove to develop an independent conception of political goals.

Although the term "ambiguity" often connotes a state of doubt or uncertainty, its application to Populists has a more precise meaning. Their own judgments were sharply rendered; not their state of mind, but the nature of their solution, was ambiguous. They worked toward sometimes contradictory, but not mutually exclusive, objectives: conservation and transformation. They also affirmed in one context what they denied in another: capitalism itself, in its competitive and monopolistic formations. But these two areas of their solution were possible sources of intellectual confusion as much as they were ambiguities properly considered. The ambiguity lies in their combination, which for Populists resulted in consciously opposing one aspect of capitalism to another and neglecting the integrated character of capitalist structure. Solutions addressing only parts of the total formation would necessarily be fragmented.

The conflict in their analysis of capitalism produced a corresponding conflict in their thinking about the remedies for contemporary abuses. Populists sanctioned the private ownership of property; but a central purpose of their analysis was to destroy the powers of economic and political domination connected with private ownership in its consolidated form. Similarly, they valued the natural and harmonious processes they ascribed to a competitive form of capitalism; a distinguishing mark of their position was to advocate the public ownership of business enterprise in the sectors of the economy invested with a public interest in order to enhance competition where it proved workable. The Populists' reliance on public ownership, as a measure both of conservation and transformation, revealed a further ambiguity. This significant enlargement of state power, specifically through direct intervention into the economy to curb monopolism and create an autonomous public area of authority, meant that their allegiance to capitalism would be subject to constant pressure. In the name of property, they would be scrutinizing its uses, its relationship to the community, and its potential limitations on human freedom and economic activity.

Capitalism and Modernization

The tension in Populist thought about the specific aspects of capitalism that would be affirmed or denied had a constructive, if unplanned, consequence. It riveted the attention of Populists on the contemporary setting. It provided their criticism of the monopolistic stage of capitalism with a greater acuity of vision because of the way in which this stage had been made to stand out in relation to previous stages and alternative conceptions of capitalist development. But moreover, it suggested that, because Populists had focused on monopolism, they had accepted the historical growth of industrial production as a necessary fact of the contemporary setting and therefore that they were neither hostile to nor outside the framework of modernization. Notable about their position, however, is their insistence that capitalism and modernization could be distinguished as two separate processes related to the material activity of society. This was important because, among other reasons, it enabled Populists to further isolate monopolism for the purposes of critical analysis.

Populists accepted both capitalism and modernity; they were very much a part of the existing society. Yet they could envision circumstances in which these distinct social configurations worked at cross-purposes, if they were not in actual conflict. For Populists, capitalism was itself divisible into its nonmonopolistic and monopolistic formations, each of which possessed a general disposition toward modernization. The context of modernity, however, was not so divided; in fact, it became a broadly construed democratic standard that they applied to economic operations and the organization of the business system.

Modernity was both an economic and an ethical criterion of societal welfare. It defined what was realistically possible in light of the existing state of technology and the capabilities of the productive system. It served as the basis for uncovering the discrepancies in the social order between the potential for material abundance and the actual conditions of social impoverishment. In their view modernity also provided a standard of rational production: There should be no waste, inferior goods, plundering of nature, manipulation of the labor market or inhumane treatment of workers. Thus when the Topeka *Advocate* called for "a proper use of the instrumentalities of modern production and distribution," it was turning modernity into a critical tool for the analysis of the prevailing structure of capitalism.[1] Monopolism, when judged by the technological and human possibilities of modernity, had fallen considerably short, economically and ethically, of serving the needs of society.

When Populists separated capitalism and modernity, the effect was to introduce an inclusive notion of democracy—political, economic, and social—into their discussion of the productive system. The separation of the two meant that Populists could make distinctions between the forms of capitalism and define the conditions under which economic activity would be compatible with a democratic government and social structure. Their clear preference was for nonmonopolistic capitalism, which had a closer association with democracy. In this formation, property was decentralized. It had noninvidious social implications, and, they believed, originated in productive labor. Monopolism offered a striking contrast, in which property had taken a politicized form. Property had become organized in massive aggregations of wealth. This aggregated wealth conferred power over the work force and in the marketplace. But when aggregated wealth had been extended from the individual firm to monopolism as a whole, it not merely conferred power, but defined a system of power. This system of power was, according to Populists, private sovereignty. It rivaled the power of government, the legal system, and the moral influence of democratic values. It was the antithesis of democracy because it placed the corporate order above the law. The politicization of property involved the broader question of power, and, as can be inferred from Populist arguments, the private domination of society. But its more concrete meaning was also important: control of the state, and the use of the state to secure exclusive privileges necessary to establishing monopolism. The distinction between the nonpoliticized and politicized dimensions of property was crucial to the distinction between the two main formations of capitalism. It was implicit in other concerns of Populists, such as the need for an independent state to exercise authority over the business system.

Monopolism had prevented the free operation of the property right, a system of wage labor, and a market framework of exchange—those basic features of capitalism that Populists had taken as their starting point. Populists believed that the property right should have an extensive application to society's lower and middle strata as the right to an independent holding; the wages system should be based on equitable contractual relations; and the market framework should provide access on equal terms to all participants. What they found was quite different. Property had been concentrated to the extent, as William A. Peffer wrote, that it gave "to the employer a practical ownership of his work-people."[2] Labor had been repressed, the *Farmers' Alliance* observed, as part of a "pauper-manufacturing system."[3] It had been concomitantly cheapened, W. Scott Morgan added, to the "peril to the estate of those who are fortunate enough to accumulate anything."[4] And finally, the market structure had been rendered inoperative as a determinant of exchanges, to be replaced, according to James H. Davis, by corporate directors who were "under no oath of office, obligation or bond to the people."[5] Henry D. Lloyd expressed the salient distinction between these contrasting phases of capitalism when he stated: "The naked issue of our time is with property becoming master instead of servant, property in many necessaries of life becoming monopoly of the necessaries of life."[6]

Populists viewed nonmonopolistic capitalism as compatible with modernity as well as with democracy, for the critical factor was the liberation of productive energies and the consequent stimulation of a mass social base of consumption. They believed that technology was itself the product of civilization, a development of the accumulated knowledge and experience of mankind that should not be appropriated by private interests for restrictive ends. Technology had been conceptualized in public terms. Populists did not oppose private ownership of the machine, but they envisioned societal welfare where all machines were used for human ends. Monopolism flagrantly contradicted the meaning of civilization, which for Populists represented the summary of human achievement based on the contributions and sacrifice of all. Its exclusive appropriation of technology, when this could be realized, had the consequence of enabling monopolism to shape the goals of modernity. Technology, rather than liberating humanity, as a repressive force would destroy the ideal of human progress and replace it with still more intensive means of domination. Not only did monopolism subject technology to the criterion of profit making, but the control of technology became an essential part of its strategy for attaining power in the economy and society. Technology contributed to monopolism's size, market strength, and capacity for inflicting damage to nature and humanity.

Monopolism was more directly antagonistic to modernity in stifling productive energies through its restraint of commerce. Such restraints defied the law, and the power of business over the state was a problem affecting the whole course of capitalist development. Populists contended that monopolism could not have arisen if it were not for the special charters, grants, franchises, subsidies, and exemptions given by the state. This array of subventions comprised an important source of capital accumulation, provided selected firms and investment groups a competitive advantage, and, of course, bestowed the exclusive privileges that confirmed a monopoly status. This favoritism was detrimental to widespread economic participation and technological innovation. The reason was the same in both cases: Control over the processes of production had made possible the more immediate strategy of business growth through scarcity profits. When James B. Weaver observed that "the corporation plunders by the permission or through the agency of the State," he succinctly described the structural and political collaboration between business and government in the monopolistic phase of capitalism. Furthermore, he recognized that capitalist upper groups, in using government to enforce their control of the market, were retarding the process of modernization: "Their Juggernaut must move and the car of progress stand still."[7]

Populists saw modernization as ideally including puristic factors necessary to economic development, such as mechanical power, technological advances, and the forces that integrated the industrial order, such as railroads and communications (both of which they sought to nationalize). A principal criticism of monopolism was that it exclusively appropriated these puristic factors to the harm of the general community. When Frank Doster attacked "the rebellious individuals who thus menace the peace and safety of the state," he was referring to the private control of the forces of nature and technology, primal sources of wealth whose benefits should accrue to the whole people.[8]

Populists endowed what they saw as the imperatives of modernization with a social character. They held that the liberation of productive energies could not be entrusted to private hands, particularly because this liberation contradicted monopolistic practices. The activation of economic forces would require the assistance of a sovereign government, which alone had the power to smash the structural bottlenecks created by concentrated wealth. Weaver's formulation—"government was created to meet and master emergencies with which individual powers and capacities are inadequate to cope"—was a broad assertion of sovereignty in the economic realm that was intended to overcome the constraints on growth imposed by a banker-dominated financial structure.[9]

Populists believed that monopolism appreciably widened the gap between capitalism and modernity. It was prone to stagnation, it denied opportunity to the middle and lower strata of society, and it discouraged both consumption and a strong internal market. It provided a less than healthy climate for enterprise and innovation. Yet they also distinguished the nonmonopolistic phase of capitalism from a modernizing course. It could not be otherwise, given the state of current dissatisfaction. But more important, the legal, moral, and constitutional foundation of the Populist framework had qualified their devotion to capitalism.

Populists did not conceive of capitalism as a thing in itself; their tributes to property were scattered throughout their writings, but seldom, if ever, did they eulogize the system as such. Capitalism was a conditional, not an absolute, good. It was an economic context within political society, not an ideologically defined, all-encompassing way of life. In principle, capitalism was subject to modification, particularly by public ownership. A dynamic reading of state power featured this possibility. But capitalism also, in any of its phases, required continuous supervision to prevent even a nonmonopolistic structure from self-aggrandizement. The polity had to subsume its system of enterprise, rather than the reverse.

An editorial in the *Farmers' Alliance* stated that "individualism incorporated has gone wild." The original value system of individualism had helped to bring about an unstable formation. And, significantly, the *Alliance* added: "Society must enlarge itself to the breadth of humanity."[10] Populists expressed the necessity for supervising the operations of capitalism in their call for the social control of industry. In more implicit terms, their affirmation of the state could be seen as a structural counterweight, if not also a rival, of capitalism per se. In this matter, Lorenzo D. Lewelling's general proposition about the duties of government was not confined to one phase of the capitalistic system: "Government is a voluntary union for the common good. It guarantees the individual life, liberty, and the pursuit of happiness. The government then must make it possible for the citizen to enjoy liberty and pursue happiness."[11] Finally, Lloyd best disengaged modernity from all constraining forms. When he noted that the "new wealth is too great for the old forms,"[12] he showed a full awareness of the bursting forth of productive forces; he also suggested a prior standard for evaluating capitalism that was not derived solely from the economic realm.

Populists had an enriching conception of law that offered clear possibilities for a democratic restructuring of society. The constitutional foundations of their argument for governmental responsibility to society prevented Populism from being easily accommodated within the contours of late nineteenth-century economic development and social power. Industrial concentration led to adapting both law and public policy to the needs of corporate wealth. Populists were not only capitalists of a subdued kind; but they also frankly acknowledged the collective features of modern industrialism, saw that these features could come within the public's jurisdiction, and contended that equitableness and efficiency need not be inversely related. I have, therefore, characterized them as American capitalists of the wrong sort. They grafted modern industrialism onto a democratic political base. Populists' vision of a nonprivileged system of property did not merely re-create the world of the precorporate small producer and enlarge it to define the pace of economic change. Revisionist historians of Populism a generation ago failed to credit the existence of a Populist political economy, and they mistakenly believed that the fragments of the system they found had an obsolete character. The issue of the separation of capitalism and modernity is important because it reveals two conflicting conceptions of the modernization process. The heart of the difference lay in the supposed inevitability of the monopolistic phase of capitalism.

Contrasting Patterns of Modernization

Populists rejected the idea that monopolism was inevitable. They sought to reverse the trend toward business consolidation, which in the late nineteenth century had not yet been made to appear irreversible. They viewed this trend as artificially created by the anticompetitive practices of major corporations and the legal, political, and economic support of a compliant government. In fact, the ascendance of monopolism in the twentieth century required political solutions through a greatly enlarged, specifically capitalist, state. The trend toward consolidation was the product of a structure in which there was interpenetration of government and business, a collaboration through which economic regulation by administrative commissions discouraged competition and encouraged business self-regulation.

The governmental stimulation of monopolism, a stage of capitalism that Populists had fairly well comprehended at its inception, would establish a stable political environment for the expansion of business. In such an environment, not only would popular challenges to the power of corporations be prevented, but a system of administrative capitalism would also be developed to insure that business regulation was placed outside the reach of the legislative process. Government would pursue a foreign policy in which the expansion of markets would promote large-scale enterprises able to operate effectively in international trade, leading to further strength in the domestic market; a degree of internal structural coordination, unprecedented in previous centuries, would result.

By attributing the pattern of modernization to the imposition of economic and political upper groups, Populists anticipated the nature of twentieth-century capitalism in America. In their own period, the problem was not monopolistic stabilization through administrative capitalism but merely the cohabitation of business and government. These parallel structures of power were seeking some form of integration. Populists believed that it was not too late to counter the trend toward business consolidation with political solutions of their own. The first step was to expose the notion of an inevitable monopolism as no more than an attempt to bring about political and intellectual submission.

Populists had met this challenge from the beginning. Even to argue, as they did, that monopolism had antidemocratic implications for sovereign power and threatened the material well-being of lower and middle social groups was tacitly to reject the idea of inevitability. People as a rule adjust to, rather than oppose, what they consider foreordained. Populists not only organized and protested in the contemporary setting; but they also gave substance to their denial of monopolism by expressing an alternative to business consolidation.

What they saw as unsavory cohabitation could be ended by forming an autonomous government that followed the principles of public obligation. If the state was presently a class-state, that forcefully argued for transforming the spirit and purposes of government; however, it did not argue for foreclosing all possibilities of political and structural change. Neither monopolism nor a compliant government in the service of the business community was inevitable. Populists would attempt to build a democratic constituency from the ground up to alter the character of government. Their approach insured that such a change would be gradual, but it also held the promise that people could act in full consciousness of their position. This was itself a repudiation of determinism in all its forms. The powers of the state would be harnessed to broadly antimonopolist objectives. In addition to fostering competition by prohibiting monopolist pressures on the market, these powers would be used to create a social context of public autonomy, a vital and expanding area of public jurisdiction that would contribute to a mass awakening to ethical values in political and economic conduct.

The direction of modernization would no longer be determined by the power of the economic and political elites, but it would reflect the purposes and ensure the welfare of the popular social base. The shift from modernization from above to modernization from below was the main paradigmatic contribution of Populists to capitalist development. Its spirit defied the concept of irreversible trends and deterministic structures. From above came constraint, finitude, a hierarchical social structure frozen in time and place; from below would come the liberation of energies, the predication of abundance, a democratization of social life, and ever evolving relations and social goals. Patterns of political economy were also patterns of either aspiration and freedom or structural and political confinement. Yet in their informal reconceptualization of modernity, Populists clearly flew in the face of the conventional wisdom of their own period and the modern era.

In their own period, the question of preventing monopolism was still intellectually open, although Populists and other social reformers who argued for a deconcentration of power and wealth were already a minority voice in public policy. Corporate publicists, political leaders, and even professionally trained economists and sociologists pronounced in favor of a deterministic theory of economic development. Much of this public discussion was self-serving, motivated by a desire to confirm a structure of monopolism that had not been fully achieved. But proponents of the doctrine that business consolidation was irreversible also found general support in the broader intellectual climate of the late nineteenth century. Opponents of determinism, such as William James, were the oddities, not the popular heroes, of American cultural life. Americans honored the memory of Emerson and Thoreau but did not follow their teachings. And the intellectual climate itself was not wholly above suspicion as a politicized expression of business dominance: The corporate and political leaders, invoking the themes of the destructiveness of competition and the virtues of consolidation as principles of organization, conveniently stated them in the contexts in which bids for monopolistic power were being made. The wider community of scholars and writers also appeared to sanction this contrived social thought.

The notion of determinism, although presented with conviction as an impartial reading of scientific development, was advanced with a frequency and stridency that implied it was a code or a substitute for a less publicly admissible notion: a fear of the people, a fear of democracy. Determinism itself was obviously associated with accepting and furthering monopolism, for in the practical matters of the late nineteenth century, this was the issue of greatest consequence. But even among those who were not consciously the satellites of business, the connection between monopolism and the avoidance of democracy would remain unbroken. (Monopolism represented the safety of property in its ultimate form, within an ordered political structure of national power and deferential masses.) Business had become the alternative to popular rule. Modernization from above was preferable to modernization from below in a society that did not trust its democratic possibilities. Lloyd summarized the threat posed by the Populist pattern of modernization when he stated that "the only true guidance comes from those who are led, and the only valid titles from those who create."[13]

By the twentieth century, the intellectual world had abandoned all pretense of openness to the question of monopolism: Presumably humanity could fashion its own universe, but monopolism was here to stay. Even free will and determinism were not seen as contradictory. The system of modernization from above could tolerate, and in fact generate, ideas about individual plasticity and assertiveness. Individualism had been channeled into an elitist cult of action or the mundane egoism of Babbittry; and individualism (and the individual) had been absorbed into a framework of corporatism. From the time of Herbert Croly and Walter Lippmann onward, individuals were free to follow the dictates of order; they had freedom within hierarchy. As the century progressed, this limited freedom so faithfully reflected the growth of the structure in which there was interpenetration of business and government that the terms "monopolism" and "determinism" were dropped from the popular vocabulary in favor of the inclusive term "order."

But more specifically, the Populist conception of modernity contradicted the conventional wisdom that had been reinforced by the actual triumph of the monopolistic pattern of modernization. In its own period, Populism was a challenge to prevailing interpretations of the economy and society; in the twentieth century, following the movement's decline, its legacy of intellectual criticism, no longer viewed as a challenge to prevailing attitudes, but as an attack on absolute truth, could be effectively isolated and dismissed. The new age was in no mood to measure modernization by the standard of human freedom, except insofar as freedom meant the material completeness of the individual.

The Populist criticism of modernization as it was developing under monopolism had the obvious advantage of any anticipatory perspective on social change: Populists stood on the periphery; they were not totally integrated with the forces that were the object of criticism. They did not have to accept materialism as an exhaustive criterion of development and, once the framework of modernization had been accepted in principle, merely point out where one or another group remained disadvantaged. Because they could stand outside the framework, they were free to examine it as a whole and through evaluative categories of their own choosing. The closed intellectual universe of twentieth-century modernization, however, was able to convert this obvious advantage of Populists into a still more obvious and devastating disadvantage: No one would be prepared to listen when the source of ideas—the organized social movement of Populism—could no longer give them support or embody them in practice. It is a truism that declining social forces often have had original and valuable contributions to make to the clarification of social ideas. However, the meaning of these intellectual and political contributions is frequently distorted by the recipient generation. The ideas are made to exist on sufferance and have been wrenched from their formative context to insure a more innocuous rendering.

Populism has been the carrion of twentieth-century liberalism. Its ideas of social welfare, divorced from the structure of antimonopolism and independent public authority that alone could give them meaning, have been used to promote welfarism. Modern welfarism accelerated, legitimized, and stabilized monopolism and its political system of government-business partnership. In regard to the concept of social melioration, intellectual scavengers at least paid their respects to the victim; the entire society closed ranks in denying the value of Populism's ideas about modernity. There was nothing to appropriate, even for the purposes of achieving an opposite effect from the one originally intended.

History, like the sociology of knowledge, accords greater respect to the victors than the defeated. And historians, like economic and social theorists, admire success more than failure. As a result of this attitude, strongly underpinned by the larger culture, there has been a functional approach to the analysis of social systems in general and to American capitalism in particular. Historical analysis, like its counterpart in other disciplines, has been confirmatory: It judges as valid what exists in practice. What is, is good—or in more neutral terms, what achieves success demonstrates the fulfillment of its function. Observers are connected to what they observe because it appears self-evident to them; the burden of validation is placed on the dissenting perspective, which has already disappeared from historical consciousness.

Specifically, the confirmatory effect of historical analysis was to make *the* standard of modernity the pattern of development that had actually occurred. Modernity was measured by the tests of monopolism and the interpenetration of government and business. As the ultimately triumphant integration of forces, they proved the irreversibility of trends toward business consolidation. Modernization from above was the rational pattern. Conversely, the opposition to consolidation—the belief that it could be stopped—was solemnly pronounced irrational and dysfunctional in political and economic development. Populists insisted that modernity comprised not only industrialization but also the political context that could promote or hinder the shaping of technological and social forces to human ends. These views supposed the human capacity for rationally changing the society. And this paradigm was in disrepute.

From the standpoint of sanctioning particular traits of capitalist development, Populism was indeed "dysfunctional." Populists called attention to the discrepancy between the industrial potential for overcoming poverty and the social misery actually in existence. Weaver described a structure that resulted in denudation, waste, and repressive labor practices when he observed: "We are attempting to build a prosperous commonwealth among people who are being robbed of their homes—a task as futile and impossible as it would be to attempt to cultivate a thrifty forest without soil to sustain it."[14] Populists also saw the cause of deformed moral and cultural standards in the monopolistic organization of society, as is apparent in this strongly worded indictment by Thomas L. Nugent (who himself took pride in the spirit of enterprise): "Thus it wipes out as with a sponge the distinction between right and wrong, makes merchandise of the noblest ideals, sets gain before the world as the highest end of life, and converts men into predatory human animals."[15]

But the significance that Populists ascribed to the state in making capitalism democratically workable constituted perhaps their most serious challenge to the reigning view of modernization. The *Farmers' Alliance* summarized the Populist attitude toward the state on this issue, especially in the West: "To use the power of government in doing something which it is dangerous to permit a few individuals to do is wise statesmanship. In fact that is the only final protection the people have against the oppressions and extortions of monopoly."[16] Ignatius Donnelly was more optimistic when he stated that government was "simply a human device to secure human happiness," and an "instrumentality of co-operation," but his point was the same: Capitalism unaided would not sustain human values and social well-being.[17] In 1894 Lloyd brought together these material and ethical concerns in a speech at Chicago. He expressed the concept of "a people's government," in which the social realization of "the fullness of the divinity of humanity" would ensure that each individual would inhabit a moral universe on earth.[18]

In the twentieth century, Populists were labeled antimodern because they had questioned the predominant course of modernization. Even the moral tone of Populism was considered evidence of economic and social retrogression (the term "retrogression" is revealing, imputing to modernization an organic life of its own), although Populist usage had a high degree of industrial specificity and relevance. Lloyd was commenting on the socially fragmented relations of trade when he observed: "The true law of business is that all must pursue the interest of all."[19] Not moralism, but its content, was the disquieting force. Lloyd's evaluation of the developmental process introduced a norm that superseded, and was outside the dominant pattern of, industrial growth: "The safety of the people is the supreme law. We are in travail to bring industry up to this."[20]

The moral perspective appeared to conflict with industrialism and its material requirements because it raised the anterior, and presumably extraneous, issue of human dignity. Peffer emphatically raised just that issue: "Is not the workman worthy of his hire?"[21] Morgan's apothegm, perhaps the more compelling because of its tacit connection to the institutions of property, revealed the potential for structural change originating from a moral evaluation of the current system: "Any system that is not for the public good—that is detrimental to the public welfare—is and of right ought to be subject to public control."[22] Similarly, the moral factor informed the Populist conception of the state itself, as when Lewelling declared: "I say now, it is the duty of government to protect the weak, because the strong are able to protect themselves."[23]

When Doster contended that the function of government was "to discover and enforce those laws of harmony which raise man above the barbarous antagonisms of the natural state into relationships of social unity and fraternity,"[24] he underscored the larger issue behind the charge of antimodernism: Populists maintained that the political, economic, and moral aspects of modern life were inseparable. This position was in contrast to twentieth-century thought, which has sought to isolate and preserve modernization as a self-legitimating process. Modernization has been freed from the weight of prior rights that rested on a sovereign public and the equally burdensome obligation and responsibility to be assumed by the political and economic structures. The concept of modernization was sterilized to insure immunity from the virus of democracy. Donnelly's criterion for measuring the institutional and cultural life of society, its ability to "conserve the happiness of mankind," reflected ethical and structural priorities inconsistent with a monopolistic social order.[25]

Populists did not conceive of the problem before them as pastoralism versus industrialism. Rather, they focused on the monopolistic patterns within industrialism. They were particularly concerned about increased class differences and corporate political dominance and believed that these had taken precedence over the democratization of wealth and power in American society. Their constitutionally derived premises of a sovereign authority, holding in trust for the polity the principle of a public welfare, stood in marked contrast to what they perceived as a rising condition of private usurpation. Here I must begin the discussion of the dynamics of political consciousness in order to establish more precisely the boundaries of the Populists' challenge to capitalism. This leads, in the next chapter, to a brief examination of the political dimensions of Populism's ideological ambiguities. I present an informal social theory of Populists' inner restraint and place Populism in a more realistic light by questioning the application of the term "radical" to the movement. I am also concerned with preparing the ground for some macroeconomic comparisons in the final chapter.

Internal Sources of Restraint

The Populists' affirmation of public welfare led to political action to achieve structural change that would make possible a public-centered capitalism. Yet this stage also arrested the movement's momentum; Populists were disposed to halt when they approached the ideological barrier of socialism. The ambiguity of their position was expressed, not by alternations between activation and restraint, but by persisting internal restrictions that were integral to their conception and mounting of protest. Their aggressive course of reform checked, although it was a stimulus to reform itself, the expression of radicalism. As a movement, Populism was self-obstructing. It not only confined the democratization of society within limits that its members all too gladly observed, but it partially re-created these limits to contain a radical potential in its ideology.

Populists created an idealized model of the American polity, a model that, in their view, corrsponded with the actual historical development of the United States. They were profoundly committed to this ideal of America, or what I shall term the "American construct" to indicate both their unintentional reification of the national political culture and, conversely, their own role in creating this image of America's political and philosophical setting. A construct by definition has an artificial quality; but the Populists' devotion to America was very real. The problem was that their devotion extended to the construct as well, and this limited still further the breadth of their ideological perspective and approaches to social protest. Their immersion in the American construct, itself a volitional act, was tantamount to Populists' confinement within the basic institutions and values of society.

The direction of protest was inward; Populists reaffirmed the structural core and constitutional doctrines established in the nation's formative stages of political development, for they believed that all democratic rights historically followed from this setting. The most immediate consequence of immersion in the American construct, once the construct itself had been identified with the heritage of democracy, was that Populists fully accepted the political order as the primary, if not exclusive, realm for achieving social change. In their view, the political order was the institutional expression of a deeper set of values: the belief in constitutional processes of political gradualism; the eschewal of class principles of organization, ideology, and social action; and the desire for political legitimation. This would verify their rights of participation in society, the honorableness of their cause, and, at the profoundest level of consciousness, their entitlement to membership in the political community. Populists wanted to belong in, and to, America. They wanted their programs, values, and their very presence to be structurally relevant to America's historical development, and they hoped to preserve the ideals on which the nation was founded.

The logic of Populists' immersion in the American construct is not at issue. The position is perfectly consistent with a framework of reform, advanced or otherwise. Populists were not radicals; there is no reason to expect that they achieved, or even sought, a complete break from the social system. To stand outside America, ideologically and psychologically, they would have had to question the foundations of their beliefs. But from their perspective, their dedication to America was synonymous with their faith in democracy itself. Their idealization of America included their conviction that the nation was morally right and could have redemptive powers if it returned to political and economic justice. America symbolized freedom, popular authority, and the rule of law. Therefore, affirming America meant liberating the democratic heritage that would make the American Constitution and historical experience equal to the task of solving present and future societal problems. It was neither practical nor rational to go outside the political order when that order embodied the political values that guided their protest. Populists' immersion in the American construct was a return to their spiritual, economic, and ethical home.

Yet such immersion, whether or not it was wise, has clear significance for understanding Populists limiting their protest. Because Populists idealized America, their political action and thought and their ideology tended to accommodate the wider social order. The power of their challenge to the existing form of capitalism is not diminished; their viability as a movement of advanced reform is not questioned. But they could not transcend reform, and their interpretation of the historic and symbolic value of America itself indicated that they accepted this limitation. Immersion was for Populists volitional, liberating—and also rational. To reject the political order would betray a lack of confidence in America. It would place them in conflict with democracy.

Still, one begins to perceive, as Populists did not, that the confinement of their protest to the electoral process, and their political dedication, had subduing effects. Other modes of protest—for example, direct economic action—could not be entertained. Class solidarity had to give way to reconciliation of the classes. The desire to achieve a structural relevance to America subtly reinforced Populists' beliefs in the continuity of institutions and imparted a systemic bonding quality to their programs and conceptions of social change. Even the alteration of capitalism had to be compatible with capitalism itself in its supposedly purer form. And the need for political legitimation crowned the Populists' broader perspective: Their inclusion in the community of decent people, partly expressed as the conservation of a law-based society, was dependent on continued professions of loyalty to the basic social structure and underlying cultural values. These professions were completely genuine but nevertheless encouraged social and political absorption.

What did it mean to be bound by or confined within the American construct? Again, on the political level, the fundamental acceptance of the political order had the *net* effect of conservatizing the Populists' ideological perspective and method of expressing dissent. They were sustained by their idealization of America, but it made them cautious. They not only adopted a position of gradualism, but they also checked any tendencies toward radicalism, derived from the growing knowledge and experience of protest, that might violate the political and economic principles of society. The right of property was one such principle, perhaps the leading one. Populists were Americans before they were reformers, and they were reformers only insofar as they considered themselves good Americans. This brings our analysis to the cultural level.

Through introjection, Populists reproduced some aspects of American culture within themselves. Just as they accepted only some features of capitalism, they were selective about the features of the culture that they defined as acceptable or praiseworthy. They were not uncritical; they were not mere members of a mass society who passively and blindly accepted the existing culture or conformed with the established order. What they selected was often quite exciting. It included the idea of the redemptive powers of the national heritage; and their intellectual activity was in itself exhilarating for them. They were historical actors; they were not merely acted upon by stronger impersonal forces of structure and culture. But they were not entirely free agents. Notwithstanding Karl Mannheim's vision of the detached intellectual, it is doubtful that anyone, however exceptional (or exceptionally placed in the social structure), can fully escape the cultural inheritance of the age and the more direct influences of culture stemming from political economy and nationhood. Although culture is a human creation, it also establishes boundaries, through the values and institutions it serves to enshrine, to further human activity and thought.

Individuals influenced the institutional core, and the institutional core affected individuals. The American construct (and America as a cultural entity) was a force to be reckoned with, for although the construct was their own creation, Populists were subject to the shaping powers of the objective factors in their historical and cultural environment. And this proposition would hold, whether we are speaking of the construct or America itself, because one was only the idealization of the other and the cultural influences were the same for both. Language structure is one such objective factor, to the extent that it affects the organization of thought and the range and richness of concepts. (These functions are vital to formulating a social vision and to identifying the causes of discontent.) But the influence of language structure is generic, and our interest is with factors that helped to shape the specific content of Populist values.

Populists were more easily influenced by American culture than some other groups because they consciously embraced the cultural setting. Their very reification of the national political culture insured their susceptibility to cultural influences, compounded the strength of these influences, and made Populists willing, if largely unconscious, accomplices in the result: an ordering of social values and social thought. To them, the American construct was not a reification, but the basis for creating a democratic ideology relevant to the needs of modern industrial society. They affirmed democracy;

yet they also affirmed the property right in the name of affirming democracy. Here one must note several objective factors, originating from the institutional core of society, that placed limitations on Populist ideology.

Populists reproduced, or were responding to, central features of the American culture, and the property right was a foundation of American society. The first objective factor that limited Populist ideology was the pattern of historical development of America. This historical course, predicated on the absence of feudalism, ensured the supremacy of capitalistic institutions. There were no cultural obstructions to their puristic expression that could have been provided from other competing formations at the nation's origins and in its subsequent growth. This uncontested position led to the inseparability of capitalism and America, a structural, political, and ideological union that compelled Populists to affirm capitalism in the process of affirming America. The second factor was the Lockean framework of political thought that, as a rationale for ascendant capitalism, perfectly complemented and described the pattern of historical development. In addition to giving the property right the status of a natural right and dignifying ownership, Lockean thought fused human rights and property rights into a unified conception of freedom. This concept restricted freedom to its individualistic, as opposed to social and collective, applications; and it contributed to the idea that the individual's identity was bound up with property. But it affected Populists most directly, because they partly opposed this usage of individualism, by sanctioning the systemic connection between democracy and capitalism. The final factor was the property right itself, which in American society had come to be regarded as self-evident and was approaching the status of a moral absolute. It was the philosophical crystallization of both the pattern of historical development and the political value system.

There were no barriers to capitalism in America, but capitalism had made America a barrier to noncapitalistic modes of political consciousness and social organization. Property in its myriad institutional forms and cultural expressions had become the ultimate referent of America, whether conceived as an ideological construct or a legal-political order and social system. Populists were a product of the national political culture, and however much they may have dissented from prevailing capitalist practices—the breadth of their dissent distinguished them from contemporary opinion as well as from large segments of the American reform experience—they nevertheless based their political thought on the traditional protection of the property right in America. In this, they were not exceptional; their differentiating feature is not their immersion in America, but their search for ideological clarity as part of this process and the ambivalent feelings and even pain it occasioned. Yet if Populists were critical despite their attachment to America, their very criticisms, particularly of self-aggrandizing individualism, gave them a false sense of security about their position. They claimed to be exempted from the very pressures that governed their attitudes toward the social order; in brief, they were free to rediscover and interpret the American tradition in its pristine, that is, exclusively human, meaning. And they were therefore still more likely to be absorbed into the political cultural system.

The American construct proved to be an epistemological matrix. Acceptance of the political order was the most obvious source of ideological constraint on the Populist movement. It limited and defined the methodology of dissent; the political process screened out unacceptable substantive themes and channeled the means of registering protest. But the more fundamental, because epistemological, limitation on Populist ideology was created by objective conditions: America's history, political and economic structure, and cultural values—all of which affirmed the property right—established the basic categories of knowledge by which Populists came to understand the world and themselves. As judged by the standard of cultural variegation, America inordinately stressed the importance of a property-mediated consciousness in organizing social thought and valuation, if not indeed the perception of reality. The national political culture did not achieve an absolutely closed system of ideology, nor was that necessarily its primary goal; rather, the culture too derived meaning and content from the propertied social order. For our purposes, the structure of knowledge is more important than any specifics of knowledge.

Property, in a society based on its principles, provided the ideological medium through which the individual's thinking about the self and society would be articulated. Political consciousness, despite Populists' resistance to the dominant ideas and practices of business, was and remained an extension of consciousness in the general culture. This broader consciousness had its origins, neither in capitalism as such, nor even in capitalism as it historically operated in America, but in the prior requirements of both: a systemic organization of social relationships designed to conserve property as the source of political power and the determinant of political development and social values. Property had become a mediating force in both the life of the individual and the collective experience, standing between the society's institutional foundations and the individual's social understanding and itself imparting considerable substance to each of these. Finally, what I have said about the ideological and political constraints of a propertied order on Populism as a whole has a more specific application to the South and southern Populists, who further narrowed the boundaries of social ideas and protest. For southern Populists, distinctive regional features, such as a more pronounced belief in order and a racial system that was contested but not surmounted, made culture even more important in the shaping of political consciousness.

The ambiguity of their position, the persisting internal restrictions that were integral to their conception of protest, did not qualify the Populists' acceptance of a progressive historical orientation; this issue of earlier scholarship is fortunately behind us. Rather, their very acceptance invested the ambiguity with its specific content. If Populism had been a retrogressive social force, the problem of restraint would not have existed. The refusal to acknowledge modernization would have required a retrograde solution of existing problems, an antidemocratic hodgepodge of blood-and-soil values, and the search for scapegoats. This did not happen, but the more important point is that it was only when they recognized industrial realities that Populists had a need to check the movement's own potential radicalism.

Restraint would not be necessary in an anachronistic formation; pastoralism could have elicited neither the tensions over how far the movement should proceed nor the anguish at the heart of the ambiguity. There would have been no necessity to face the hard choices over the precise role of the state. Populists did face these choices; they did not adopt a retrogressive mode of thought, in which radicalism would have had little relevance to economic devolution. Antimodernism would have insured that radicalism failed to excite fear or fascination because the structural remedies and programmatic demands in response to contemporary abuses would not apply. But once industrialism is seen as integral to Populist discourse and understanding, it becomes possible to uncover conflicts, perhaps including a residual antisocialism, within the Populist perspective on democracy.

Populism cannot be judged by how well it mirrored the prevailing form of capitalism, for it departed significantly from that form in arriving at its position on the state and the private economy. Populists opposed the partnership of business and government, affirmed the principle and practice of public ownership, and seriously questioned the place of the corporation in society. Now that scholars of Populism have determined the movement was a rational and progressive, rather than a retrogressive, social force, their next task is to consider its gradations of radicalism. Populism's acceptance of modernity indicates its rational position, but it does not presumptively demonstrate its advanced political and social position. The issue of their position on social change has been resolved; however, their advocacy for a radical alteration of society must be shown, not merely assumed. I am skeptical that the evidence supports such a claim.

Dynamics of Political Consciousness

In the course of investigating the political career of the North Carolina Populist, Marion Butler, I became aware of a pattern in the development of his political consciousness that appeared to correspond to the experience of many other Populists. I verified this in my reading of a wider range of evidence. The intellectual development of Populism was the result of an active struggle for political understanding. Populists' groping for awareness directly affected the substance of their views and demands as well as the degree of class feeling they were able to muster. Mental struggle may have resulted in clarity and continuing political comprehension, but it was also responsible for indecision and reticence when dramatic choices involving ideological considerations were being posed.

On the one hand, the painful willing of consciousness suggests the rational features of Populist protest and perhaps even an inceptive class identity and purpose. In turn, such a process reveals the central element of volition in the act of creating a cohesive social movement: Populism created itself as a political culture of protest. But on the other hand, this volitional factor was also expressed in the Populists' perceived need to make choices as their position developed. This need may be inherent in most or all forms of dissent (I am inclined to think it is not), but at each stage of protest reached by the Populist movement the question of how far the radicalization of its position would be allowed to go was precipitated anew. Populism seemed always striving to catch up with itself, to realize itself as a completed political force. Yet its state of incompleteness, an essential part of the dynamics of political consciousness, calls attention to the converse side of volition: the conscious willing of restraint as well as activation.[26]

If one may speak in such terms, it must have seemed to Populists that they stood forever at the existential crossroads. They faced agonizing, and sometimes even paralyzing, choices. In the South, the question of race was, of course, a prime example. Southern Populists' belief in racial separation was indigenous. They had known, and hitherto uncritically accepted, white supremacy as the only political, economic, and social relationship. Nevertheless, when they commenced their protest, southern Populists were immediately made aware of the capability for violence, intimidation, and political suppression in the one-party South. They were also made aware, if they did not already know it, that the racial issue would be used to destroy all forms of political independence. The first choice they faced was whether to start their protest, and not a few expectant Populists, unable to withstand the pressure from the absolutist cultural formula of white southern identity, which pertained to far more than race, dropped away during the summer of 1892. But for those who remained, nothing had really been settled: They were not magically enlightened about the racial issue simply because they had become Populists.

Their next choice was dictated to them largely by concrete political circumstances, although volition had been clearly present, because they did not have to become Populists (in retrospect, this appears to have been the primal choice for them in the course of their protest). The dominant party and the power groups it represented created a political climate of intense racial hysteria. This charged atmosphere was augmented by press and pulpit and supported by an ironclad control of the electoral process that had as its purpose the shattering of both the consciousness of reform and independent politics. If Populists were to survive this onslaught, psychologically as well as physically and politically, they had to come to terms with the issue of race: the specific questions of black participation in the movement and their own racial convictions.

They could be blatantly racist in an attempt to deny the charges brought against them as enemies of the South, traitors to the white race, and abettors in the scheme to restore black domination. But this escalation of racism, they were fully aware, would mean their diversion from reform, the loss of political identity, and a reabsorption into the Democratic party. It would not work when the opposition party was already the authoritative voice of racism; moreover, few Populists before 1895, when black disfranchisement was openly discussed, could stomach such a solution.

Alternatively, they could call for full racial integration; they could launch a biracial political movement for economic and social justice that specifically focused on the destruction of the southern racial system as the prerequisite for all further social change. But however much we might favor this course, it was only a hypothetical option because it was outside the social vision of practically all southern (and probably a substantial number of western) Populists. It violated their racial principles and failed to comport with their idea of the purpose of Populism in the South. That purpose was conceived at the outset as essentially concerned with political and economic reform.

What they did was not by default, as if they could make a choice between putative extremes in some Aristotelian way, for within the bounds of political realism the search for a middle way was perhaps the hardest choice of all. They determined to neutralize the racial climate in the South. Marion Butler, by penetrating to the heart of the problem in the summer of 1892, may have been in advance of many Populists in the South when he asserted that the Democratic cry of "Negro domination" was a subterfuge for preventing the discussion of economic and political improvement. Explicitly, he advised Populists to ignore all appeals to race in order to prevent the fragmentation of dissent. Implicitly, he was developing a line of reasoning that others were also independently working out: that racism was incompatible with reform. Populists observed the growing racial stridency of their opponents. They came to see that the Democratic party was using racial appeals as part of a campaign of terror to stifle reform and remain in power.

This was a major insight into the workings of the contemporary political system, for Butler and southern Populists in general perceived racism as an artificial device, a scare tactic, that had to be overcome if reform were to receive a hearing.

Still, apparently nothing sensational took place. Populists did not directly oppose racial separation and white supremacy. Yet they actually did something quite remarkable. They initiated a process of clarification in southern life. To reach this position meant that they had to clear away a considerable amount of cultural debris. They did not fully succeed in substituting a politics of class for a politics of race; they neither made race an irrelevant factor, nor—and this was more basic—did they make racial democracy or even the specific improvement of the condition of blacks a principal demand of the People's party in the South. If the purpose of southern Populism was political and economic reform, then the conception of reform was socially restrictive: It purposely omitted the alteration of racial social relationships as such, seeking instead the general improvement of political and material conditions within a segregated order. But the goals they set for themselves were greater realism, freer discussion, and, concerning race relations, a new candor about the course of protest. Neutralizing racial appeals was translated as diminishing the hold of the racial factor on the consciousness of white protesters.

Southern Populists, although coming this far, did not provide a clean historical slate from which to move forward. They emphasized their rejection of social equality. They frequently remembered their disaffection from the Democratic party as a wrenching experience in their lives. Significantly, many of them devoted so much attention to attacking that party, as if to explain and justify to themselves the legitimacy of their political independence, that they failed to construct the positive ideological foundations of Populism. The choice of a middle way may have fallen drastically short of modern standards because the rejection of both intensified racism and racial equality left intact the fundamental racial order in the South. But Populists had to struggle for every inch of their progress—not only against the orthodox South but also against their own instinctive feelings.

Although there were state-by-state variations, and, of course, variations among individuals within each state, the new candor brought forth, as early as 1892, a resolute commitment by Populists to a limited form of black political equality. The boundaries of this commitment were carefully drawn. Within the scope of their protest, Populists interpreted political equality to include full voting rights for blacks, an honest ballot in which each vote would be counted, and the active enlistment of black support for the People's party on the terms of the party platform. It also included the infrequently spelled out but valuable items: a pledge to blacks of protection in the execution of their voting rights; impartial treatment under the law when the specific maintenance of the racial system was not involved; a perceptible improvement of the racial climate insofar as Populists, their party, and their newspapers could affect the outcome; and finally, in some states, nominal representation in party conventions.

Populists did not include in their concept and practice of political equality a meaningful participation in the institutional life of the South or, for that matter, the party. The term "political" was divorced from a broadly construed doctrine of civil rights (for example, it was not applied to jury service and educational opportunities) and from the range of party functions—whether as candidates, electors, or officials of the organization. There were exceptions in the make-up of several state parties, and their symbolic value was important. But, omitting the special circumstances of North Carolina, in which fusion with the state Republican party did lead to a more authentic biracial politics, the general picture was not one of political racial integration, either attempted or achieved. And if the term "political" had a limited construction, the more inclusive term "political equality" was knowingly made restrictive because, despite its undoubted enlargement of black rights, it was viewed by Populists in juxtaposition to, and as a possible barrier against, social equality.

Nevertheless, if political equality specifically excluded social equality and also excluded the comprehensive status of citizenship, it did something that cannot be neglected if one is to understand the full meaning of internal restraint. The issue of political equality, strictly considered, tended to make blacks less anonymous in political life—a condition to which whites had previously relegated them for the purpose of social control. The much-vaunted white folk community based on the solidarity of race was slightly cracking under the pressure of independent politics. And, while blacks were not consciously intended to be beneficiaries of this development, they did benefit from it, at least temporarily: They were no longer nameless and faceless, because they were tacitly becoming admitted into the political community.

Populists were continuing the process of clarification through the common experience of protest. To conceive of blacks as political allies, even when the arrangement was under white sponsorship and supervision, and may on occasion have been manipulative, was itself a form of social education, and it strengthened the whites' conception of black identity. A slow momentum was building. This might be regarded as creating the possiblility of a third choice. In some states, where racial gains had barely satisfied the limited requirements of political equality, the third choice never materialized. But in the period 1893-1894 this momentum was sufficient to raise disturbing questions in the minds of southern Populists and place them once again at the existential crossroads.

The choice was not social equality per se; that could not be taken seriously enough even to be ruled out as a real option. Perhaps no one in southern Populism had completely transcended the region's racial system. The third choice rested on firmer ground and for that reason was more difficult to make. The logic of the Populists' dissenting position was the inner dynamic of constant questioning, not because they were particularly intellectual and wise but because they were hounded, vilified, and attacked at every turn. They were compelled to gain a clearer sense of themselves, their goals, and the structure responsible for their persecution.

The term "logic" here refers to the pressure to enlarge the scope of their criticism. Having combatted one aspect of southern orthodoxy, such as the closed political system, Populists were led to other areas of control and to interconnections between the institutions of power in a tightly integrated framework of social organization. If the party, government, land system, and business community could not be separated as distinct factors in the structure of economic and political dominance, neither could they collectively be separated from the racial order that provided the rationale and chief means of stabilization for that dominance. Populists were struggling in a sea of fresh discoveries. The third choice was whether to let their insights into the nature of southern power, including the racial mechanism, lead them toward an indefinite end, an open-ended future that might ultimately raise a challenge to the South itself.

Populists thrashed about in this sea and then sought the safety of dry land. A minority of them continued the struggle until the end; they enlarged the vision of political equality, became freer from notions of hierarchy and paternalism, but got no further. None in this group had drowned; none had played Ahab to the White South. The quest for meaning, even among the comparatively few who struggled, lacked the element of tragedy. They failed to achieve a political or spiritual breakthrough. A larger minority of southern Populists, who exemplified the direct opposite of struggle, became prematurely embittered and masked their capitulation in words of defiance. As for the remainder, they conscientiously held firm to the political understanding expressed in 1892, became somewhat more enlightened about politics and race, and kept their dignity throughout the course of the movement. In this entire process, affecting most, if not all, southern Populists, the racial factor was important, but perhaps not decisive. It helped to bring Populists to the point at which a third choice would become possible, and it helped to keep them from surpassing this point. But the racial factor did not exclusively shape the choice itself or dictate the need for a decision.

Instead, as one moves from the special case to the general case of internal Populist restraint, it becomes apparent that Populists in the South stood in relation to the region as Populists in both the South and the West stood in relation to the nation: In both situations, limits had been placed on criticism; the limitation of race was the regional equivalent to the limitation of capitalism on the national plane. This equivalence was only approximate, but for the South especially it reveals an important feature of the dynamics of political consciousness. Just as Populism in general neither checked nor had reason to check its radical potential until its position had achieved the requisite level of industrial specificity, so also southern Populism had to achieve a higher degree of political and racial specificity before it felt compelled to check its social and cultural potential.

In the South, the racial factor served as a catalyst, perhaps in the way that the structure of monopolism served as a catalyst nationally. But in the South, the catalyst dramatized a potentiality that, if acted upon, would have gone against a whole history, culture, and way of life. The southern identity won out. (One might quibble about whether there was a single identity for the South, as a prominent historian did when he recently attacked W. J. Cash's *The Mind of the South,* but for the greater part of southern history, at least through World War II, there appears to have been a common mental set and personality structure beneath the differences in politics and economics. This prevalent mentality arose from the region's peculiarities of geography, its racial system, and its historical experience.)

Yet if the southern identity won out, it did so after southern Populists, or a portion of them, had progressed to wider criticism of contemporary institutions in the South. The alternatives seemed to them to be either a break from, or a return to, the common bonds based on region, culture, family, and—it must never be forgotten—race. The very success of the process of clarification, which they had themselves initiated, became a brake on their progress. Southern Populists were southern before they were Populists; they were white also, but that was particularly important because they were southern.

When we turn back to the position of the whole movement, it is clear that the consequence of facing agonizing, and sometimes paralyzing, choices was Populism's inability fully to realize the inner possibilities of its ideology. As I have written elsewhere, there was a striking disproportion within Populism between its radical promise and its reform performance. Still, to consider Populism as following an existential course does not imply the presence of imminent tendencies in the movement that had only to be unblocked. Populism did not pursue a foreordained course of reform that would logically follow from its origins, the situation it faced, or the stock of ideas available in America. The element of volition remains significant historically and analytically, and, in fact, Populism was protean inside the walls it had constructed. It is only when the movement has been seen in a wholly nondeterministic light that one can discover internal sources of restraint, including the idealized American construct.

The ideological and structural boundaries that Populism observed help to account for its specificity as a political force. Populists' very perseverance in consolidating dissent in a hostile economic, cultural, and political environment suggests that they grasped, to a degree unusual for American protest, the complex identity of their movement. Nevertheless, the crosscurrents that Populists left unresolved were also a part of this identity, and they were probably the reason for constructing boundaries. In reality, Populism was the product of its contradictions: Activation and restraint together defined the movement.

FOUR

Boundaries of Ideological Growth

Populism had an anomalous position in America. It was a capitalistic movement on behalf of traditionally sanctioned economic goals and principles of welfare, but it met with opposition by the prevailing capitalist order because contemporaries feared that creating an autonomous government could result in exercising sovereign power over capitalism itself. The hostile response to Populism was more than an overreaction to social disturbances at a time of acute economic dislocation, or a predictable result of the harshness that often attended industrial consolidation and rapid growth. The clear danger from Populism lay in its reactivation of tradition, the literalism of its public philosophy of democracy.

If Populism had arisen in nineteenth-century Europe, without its political and intellectual foundations in the American polity, it probably would have been submerged by a confluence of statist and left ideological currents. In that case, it would have been forced either to meld with, or sharply disengage from, the reigning form of capitalism; but it would not have found, as it did in America, its distinctive place within an enclosed capitalist spectrum. In America, the Populist challenge had been magnified and given an ideological as well as a structural significance because it occurred on a spectrum of political ideas narrower than the political spectrum in Europe. This necessitated in turn the attempt by the movement to shape its economic and political understanding by distinguishing itself from the other formations then available within capitalism. In the European context, where the range of political values was greater, this task of creating a specific identity was less pressing. Thus, the suggestion that Populism was capitalistic, while it is a corrective to interpretations that have not made this point explicit, leaves unstated the discriminations that are possible within the spectrum of capitalism. These discriminations became crucial to Populists in defining their own position. The differences within capitalism were critical for determining Populism's ideological location in American history.

Political and Cultural Identity

Populists based their advocacy for an interventionist state on the proposition that capitalism was modifiable. They conceived of a state invested with protective functions as an alternative to both the self-regulative market mechanism of a laissez-faire system and the converse arrangement, a coordinated monopolistic structure of business and government. Neither the Smithian nor the contemporary mode of capitalism could view such a development with favor. An independent state, acting in trust for a sovereign people, would attack the salient feature of each mode: the Smithian belief in the efficacy of a self-adjusting automatism for realizing the general welfare, and the contemporary capitalists' belief in the inevitability of concentration, on which business power depended for its ideological rationale. Populists had posed an independent standard of welfare to be incorporated into the structure of society. They not only questioned the political foundations of a corporate society and economy (and the ethic, now rendered largely ineffectual, of unbridled individualism) but also conceived a separate pattern of capitalism, difficult to classify in the American, or any other, setting.

Populism was sui generis, steering between automatic mechanisms and collaborative powers; it fused its opposition to monopolist restrictions with its promotion of public ownership and yet validated its capitalist credentials by opposing socialism as well. I term this formation the Populist variant of capitalism—a pattern of modernization from below that sought to liberate the productive energies and secure the political rights of the lower and middle strata of society. Populists argued for the modifiable character of capitalism in explicitly democratic terms. For this reason, contemporaries labeled their formation atypical. This judgment was pronounced in light of the already present social configuration of power; it did not derive from a strict regard for the theoretical possibilities still open to American society under a different ordering of wealth and power. The condition necessary for Populist success was the very democratization it could not achieve. To all appearances, this situation rendered the position historically untenable as well as politically unacceptable.

If Populist "radicalism" could not be separated from the constraints on its expression, the process by which Populists came to know themselves still possessed a clear vitality. Two sets of factors operated to form their political identity: First, they defined their political position in relationship to other positions; they differentiated themselves by what they rejected to their right and left. They were aided in this process of identification by the hostility and ostracism they experienced from both quarters, though mainly from the right. Second, their political consciousness also had an independent element. They affirmed a core of moral, constitutional, and structural principles that, although sharpened by the force of opposition, constituted Populism's peculiar autonomy. In creating this autonomy, they combined a qualified acceptance of Lockean ideology, centered on the property right, with a potential counterforce, centered on public ownership. The dynamic interplay of these two standards set off Populism from the prevailing mode of capitalism, from a hypothetical laissez-faire that had not been realized in practice, and from the subsequent pattern of liberal reform in which government-business cooperation would be a given of the political framework. Populist views on public policy, especially in regard to corporate development, did not prefigure twentieth-century liberalism. There was a basic discontinuity between Populism and the form of state activity that started with Progressivism because the independent status and functions of government, including a comprehensive program of antimonopolism, were not pursued in the later period.

In contradistinction to all three of the foregoing modes, Populism would have used the autonomous powers of the state to effect a new synthesis of capitalism and democracy, retaining both elements but varying their proportions to ensure public sovereignty. In broader terms, although Populists labored under a Lockean burden that limited political change, they sought to rearrange the nation's historical and structural priorities: Capitalism was to be secured on the foundations of political democracy. This was the reverse of what they believed was occurring; formal democratic institutions and rights were merely being superimposed on an explicitly capitalistic political and cultural base to the detriment of America's heritage and future prospects alike. Yet because capitalism and democracy were still the prime factors in the Populist formation, Populism was in tension with, but could not transcend, America. For this reason Populism existed in tension with itself as well. Even the literalism with which Populists had invested democracy could not alter this fact.

Figuratively, the Populist variant, a pattern of democratic-capitalist modernization, had internalized America. However, Populists did not blindly immerse themselves in the past. Their American construct involved the search for an active principle of political reconstruction and for a new perspective on social change. Populists had the necessary will, and the movement had the necessary programmatic content, for developing an advanced ideological position. Although their failure to provide adequate organization for fulfilling the potential of their ideology was important, it does not satisfactorily explain why there were barriers to further ideological progression. It is necessary to view the element of restraint in a wider context; the politics and ideology of Populism interacted and checked the progress of dissent when it threatened to go beyond an acceptable limit in its questioning of capitalism.

Populists attempted to find a common denominator for reform, one that would unify the popular currents of social unrest. This political concept—not confined to a single faction, region, or election—effectively blurred Populists' ideology. But their ideology already lacked clarity because their endeavor to democratize industrialism paradoxically reinforced their acceptance of a society founded on property. As long as the marriage of capitalism and democracy continued, the impulse toward democracy would renew commitments and tighten connections to the integrated historical and social framework of which both elements were a part. The influence of capitalism would be driven to a still deeper level because it was now afforded the protective coating of reform. Because of their commitment to the property right, the more Populists sought the modification and improvement of capitalism, the more they became enmeshed in it.

Populism was subject to ideological penetration from the dominant political culture because it had accepted so much of the social order that was slated to be transformed. Its belief in the conservation of basic institutions and values was perhaps integral to its conception of change. But Populism chose to remain within the confines of capitalism, fully aware of the risks to its political identity when a conscious desire for structural relevance governed its protest. In part, the movement was neutralized by its own positive features. It did not court political absorption. Yet the willingness to activate the processes of change even at the cost of its own survival revealed the fact that its moral and ideological dedication, both to America and reform, had become a source of internal fragmentation. This dedication was the source of moderation in equal measure. Populists' protest, because it did not question the basic institutional configuration, gave practical effect to the equation of America and reform: Populism adopted narrowly political means of expressing dissent. This strict political orientation had the positive purpose of strengthening the legitimating force for change, society's democratic foundations. But it also had the negative purpose of checking Populism's own ideological development, which might result in militancy and undermine these same foundations.

Populism was the hostage of its network of allegiances. This situation lessened its capacity to sustain an autonomous course, although it had in fact pursued its own reform objectives, at that moment in its growth when a radicalization of principles was necessary for preserving its independent identity. By 1896, time had run out on the movement. Populists were subjected to the long-term pressures of a repressive industrial and political environment and the exigent demands for sacrifice in a momentous election. When this happened, the customary grounds of reform no longer provided a basis for internal cohesion or continued differentiation from the surrounding agitation. Thus, in 1896, Populism did not simply decline; it collapsed, without, ironically, experiencing a diminution of energy until far into the campaign.

One could diagram the course of Populism as follows: The movement described an ascending curve of political consciousness, moving steadily toward a more radical perspective; this ascent led to the movement's disintegration at that point in which reform had expressed its fullest possibilities and threatened an irreversible conversion to radicalism. The fear of violating the property right had its political counterpart in the tacit recognition, during the campaign, that a further growth of Populism would entail a national and class orientation, thereby transforming the original sectional and agrarian movement into a new and disturbing formation. These tensions reflected, not a spirit of compromise, but the ideological development that had brought Populism to a position in which meaningful choice was presented. Populists' choice of reform was consistent with the internal limits they placed on this development.

Populism's total moral-political stance, in which the sense of mission figured prominently from the Alliance phase onward, had an important role in the movement's destruction. The mission was initially conceived in procedural more than ideological terms; it referred to the manner of marshaling social energies. But the process and content of reform were quickly fused through an insistence that Populist principles were inseparable from the means used to achieve them. In fact, however, the unity of ideology and politics, workable for purposes of insuring an overall moderation, had disguised a more far-reaching, subtle dichotomy.

The political dimension of Populism had consistently derived a measure of prestige from its connection with the movement's advanced ideological position. The means of protesting were not critically examined, because Populists generally assumed that their selected form of protest corresponded in its degree of radicalism to the principles they advocated. But such an assumption allowed politics to be separated from the ideology, leaving the ideology still intact but essentially isolated, while the strategies that promised the greatest effectiveness for a mass awakening and further recruitment were used.

This was particularly important in 1896, when Populists conceived of the election as a watershed in American structural and political development. Because their mission centered on the dedication to principles, the substance of the ideology was perhaps heightened in dignity, but at the same time it was confused with what seemed the more imperative sense of process: to make democratic ideology politically germane. The desire of Populists to be structurally relevant to America was the crux of their endeavor.

For Populists, the idea of mission entailed feelings of responsibility for the outcome of the reform struggle. One motivation for fusing with the Democratic party in 1896 was to prevent the division of the forces of change. Because Populists were doubtful that the Democratic party had thoroughly revised its political and economic thinking, they had additional reason for a still firmer commitment: They wanted to regain the initiative in guiding the reform process and thus prevent the dispersion of the ideological focus by silver Democrats. The Populists' conception of mission, which drew on precepts of conduct antedating their perception of impendent crisis, had made them feel obligated to shape the politically awakened populace into a decisive challenge of the existing order. Yet precisely this conception made them hostage to a pattern of exemplary behavior and converted their moral-political dedication to structural relevance into a strategy of cooperation with the Democratic party that the movement did not survive.

Even the sense of mission and the collective spirit of abnegation and discipline that distinguished Populists from many of their contemporaries worked against them and resulted in absorption by the political system. This occurred because Populists had a false expectation that their asceticism would tide them over the political emergency. The spirit of discipline also misled them into believing that asceticism per se not only gave their cooperation with Democrats moral standing but also made Populism responsible for any activity that might disrupt the coalition. Populists' support for William Jennings Bryan was, especially until the final weeks of the campaign, essentially involuntary; it was a forced support because they had not been free to choose their own battleground. Still, the more important point is not the wisdom of this decision, which in fact they arrived at with varying degrees of reluctance, but the matrix of political values in which it was made. No other choice was thought feasible, and a categorical separation was considered a luxury beyond their reach and unwarranted by the circumstances.

The element of moderation, because it was the result of conflicting tendencies, became remarkably complex. Despite Populism's substantive democratization of the institutions of property, and its more specific demand for public ownership, it reflected the premises of reform in its conservation of property as such, its respect for the political process, and its strong disapproval of violence. The ideology as a whole, including its proto-radical features, also coexisted uneasily with a politically militant temperament that had potential radical significance. Asceticism, while it encouraged adherence to the political process, suggested an inner resolution, a controlled anger, and durable convictions that contrasted markedly with the pragmatic habits of the reformist mind. If radicalism was not entirely out of place in Populism, it existed only in fragments, secondary currents, ideological wedges, or patterns of self-denial that could not form a unified counterstatement. Such a statement was needed to provide the movement with socialist or nonpropertied categories of political understanding. Nor could these fragments redirect the nature and scope of protest to satisfy the requirements of a radical standard: a fundamental transformation of the social order, including its relations of property and class, if necessary, by means of political violence, although violence should not be an end in itself.[1]

To present this minimal test is to see at once the inapplicability of the term "radicalism" to Populism, even when allowance has been made for the movement's ethical premises, structural demands, and political militancy. The imprecision of U.S. terminology that allows us to label all departures from a strict Lockeanism as "radical" has created a series of definitional traps. The usage immediately cheapens radicalism itself by facilely equating it with socialism (whether or not a given social structure possesses liberating qualities) or by minimizing its structural content and the suppression that would follow from its mere presence. Radicalism could be a threat to socialist political contexts that have become bureaucratic; collective ownership in itself has never been an adequate measure of ideological and social vitality.[2] Yet if it is not similarly a threat to capitalist political contexts, one senses its inauthentic character because it would be absorbed, neutralized, or ignored by the social system.

A further consequence of imprecise usage is to preserve historical stereotypes; they not only exaggerate the breadth and depth of social challenges—including Populism, often taken as the embodiment of American protest—but also overestimate the powers of America itself to encourage, rather than stifle, movements of dissent. Crediting the prevalence of radicalism tends to blur the critical relationship between protesting forces and the institutional core of society. When such protest is assumed rather than verified directly, it becomes a testimony to flourishing toleration and structural adaptation. This testimony does not truly reflect the pattern of events, especially of the late nineteenth century. Moreover, it does not sufficiently emphasize the monolithic power of a culture of property over the very formulation of a dissident ideology or the equal power of the total framework over the modes of redressing grievances. The society appears receptive to movements for social reconstruction; but in fact they have had to surmount major obstacles in order to survive.

The important point, then, is not that moderation existed, but that Populism's moderation was earned by honest means. Reform, far from being a term to be derided, represented considerably more than a refurbishing of the old order: It was a courageous stance that defied a part of the value system and institutions in which Populists also located the primal rights of society. If Populists found it unthinkable to cast off America, they still approached the border between reform and radicalism.

The study of Populism's interaction with the United States, in which the property right was an important value that had been internalized—either voluntarily or compulsorily—by society's disadvantaged groups, does not eliminate the possibility of radicalism in the American past. But it cautions one about expecting that such radicalism as may have been present would possess the clarity of ideology and organization exhibited by social formations in which class alignments were openly acknowledged and occurred at formative political stages that were decisive in shaping the outlines of later conflict, as in the French Revolution.[3] Nor could one reasonably expect that radicalism per se would escape the memories of culture that fix a movement's position in society and history.

This placement was particularly devastating in the American context. Unimpeded capitalism brought about the political ascendancy of dominant economic groups, and a rigidly organized system of ideas (Louis Hartz's concept of Lockean absolutism)[4] acted to remove the barriers to capitalism's purist expression. These interrelated factors of structure and ideology led to a narrow perspective and lineal pattern of development quite inimical to political and social diversity. By contrast, for example, England's aristocratic and working-class elements helped to subdue and modify a pure bourgeois impulse; its more variegated historical and cultural setting promoted the vitality of radicalism and conservatism alike. In the United States, which lacked the manifold ideology and experiences of social conflict of both England and France, Populism can be seen as reformist in spite of itself. Populists were unwilling to cease probing to the outer reaches of the dominant political culture, even if they also affirmed and presented in palatable form Lockean notions of property.[5]

The Populist Spectrum of Ideas

Implicitly, I am approaching Populism from the perspective of what I shall term an epistemology of protest: Populism's introjection of the American construct limited the movement to a capitalistic frame of reference. Its basic comprehension of political and economic life was partly mediated by the institutions and values of property; the propertied context was offset only by ethical principles and a constitutional literalism that were found in, yet tended to abrade, the culture of capitalism. This slight margin in which

Populists' independent consciousness had not been wholly overwhelmed by (because it was not exclusively derived from) the dominant categories of the national political culture established the basis for a protest that exceeded the limits of conventional reform.

There were still interior boundaries to political change: In the attempt to identify themselves by the relationship of their political position to others, Populists rejected socialism, total racial equality, and direct action. This rejection was as significant as the reformist-plus position, including advocacy of public ownership, that they had affirmed. Populists appeared to be fighting back, but without knowing specifically against what forces. It was as if they were forming a class movement that could not fully realize itself on class lines; or perhaps the movement was sufficiently close to transcending the American setting that this prompted an arrest of its momentum.

Being on the verge of a historical breakthrough apparently pitted Populists against both their own conception of the democratic heritage and the nation. In general, reform, under the circumstances of facing a challenge to its own basic premises, reveals its nonradical and even antiradical character. This phenomenon is particularly evident when reform has been institutionalized as the dominant feature of an era, as it was in the period of the New Deal; but it is also to be found, even among presumably advanced groups, as the express commitment to stability. This is illustrated by the failure of Radical Republicans to press for the confiscation of land, of trade unionists to endorse a doctrine of class struggle, and of socialists to develop a nonelectoral strategy or a revolutionary posture. When ideology is absolutist, reform and radicalism are thought to lie on the same continuum. They are not seen as mutually incompatible and contesting forces, with reform seeking to obviate the need for, and destroy the principles of, radicalism.

Populism challenged its own premises, producing within itself the protoradicalism missing from the external setting, and in the process it experienced the same stress that characterized the framework of reform in the United States. Yet it demonstrated, for the most part, an inner resilience that checked the progression from nonradicalism to more overtly hostile forms of activity. That Populism never abandoned reform for radicalism should alert the historian to the possibility of the movement's reformist antiradicalism; but I think it will be found that this antiradicalism existed as an exceptional fragment in the same way that radicalism itself did, though perhaps to a lesser degree.

Populism's "inner resilience" was demonstrated by its flexibility toward further radicalization and the willingness to foster alterations of its original, and gradually evolving, conception of social change. In this respect, reformist antiradicalism was present in Populism only as a latent fear, or it functioned as a source of final restraint; it did not impair the vitality of reform so much as it precluded a new direction and set of principles. Reform was not gained at the expense of radicalism; the seemingly elusive distinction between nonradicalism and antiradicalism formed the basis for differentiating Populism from the larger reform experience. Yet because Populists were not of one mind in their response to radicalism, inner resilience becomes a critical factor in the construction of a political typology of the movement.

Despite the conventional wisdom, one cannot assume that the early acceptance of Populism is correlated with advanced radicalism, for such Populists frequently had fixed ideas about the movement's character and ideology, and they evinced little capacity for subsequent growth. In contrast, those who became active later and had less well-developed positions, but who demonstrated a receptivity to widening the bounds of political consciousness, may have held greater promise for advancing Populist ideology than the former group with its putatively radical demands. Orthodoxy can be a snare under changing conditions, and resilience the mark of ideological possibilities and open-ended growth.[6]

Although I do not propose a formal political typology, I would suggest that an important element in shaping discernible positions within Populism was not simply the response, but the quality of the response, to radicalism, specifically a political and ideological rigidity that affected substantive issues and the vision of what the movement ultimately represented. The problem with the midroaders, for example, was that they labored under a regional psychology. Populist orthodoxy in the 1896 campaign had more to do with a regression to the original agrarian-sectional identity, in the face of pressures to create a national (and potentially class) dimension, than it did with a supposed ideological purity, except insofar as this purity was still at the level of the movement's inception. Paradoxically, the ideology that reflected an initial advancement had reached a dead end, and it cracked when Populism gained enough momentum to push against its predefined limits. Even before 1896, a finite vision of Populism discouraged further changes. The Dallas *Southern Mercury,* reputedly the most radical organ in the entire movement, gave disproportionate attention to the financial question, seldom discussing industrial capitalism as a system. Tom Watson, who symbolized this faction, was not the racial progressive that one may have thought,[7] nor was he above a doctrinaire, and perhaps obsessive, antiradicalism.[8]

In the cases of both the *Mercury* staff and Watson, a sense of certitude, despite their original support for a comprehensive program, worked against maintaining a more organic connection with Populism's possibilities of development. Instead, it produced a siege mentality that brought about feelings of isolation and betrayal. These inflexible attitudes had substantive importance. An undiluted agrarianism predominated, because of which the comprehensive program still led to an emphasis on the issues of money and land at the expense of those involving public ownership and the corporate abuse of power. This prevented industrial specificity in the Populist critique of the existing structure.

Moreover, in 1896, the midroad forces in effect faded into nothingness. Watson refused to campaign, and the Texas group openly considered supporting McKinley. Because they favored greenbacks and kept up a running battle with the Democrats, the midroaders have been seen as radical without exploring their motivation for either their political independence in 1896 or their long-term economic and ideological position. Like the midroad faction itself, the recent historian who based his interpretation of Populism on this group dispatched whole portions of the movement into oblivion for not satisfying a particular standard of orthodoxy. This is unfair in light of the myriad forms of repression that Populists encountered.[9]

In a diverse movement such as Populism, any standard of orthodoxy proves mischievous. But particularly in this case, defining a political typology requires distinguishing between a broadly conceived, broadly populated, center position and the offshoots (emerging from many of the same principal assumptions) that were often no more than dispositions to the right or the left. One practical criterion is the scope and character of the power that an individual or specific group assigned to government with respect to the control of capitalism. But even here it was possible for Populists to affirm both state intervention and property, sometimes canceling and at other times reinforcing actions leading to structural change. To complicate matters, the question of Populism's relative advancement was not fully answered by ideological concerns as such, for in the movement there were clear instances in which the advanced elements of ideology had been combined with a political moderation that diminished the power of the overall challenge. This also occurred in the converse situation, in which there was political militancy and a more attenuated statement of the ideology.

In seeking to assess the internal forces that promoted radicalization, the movement's total position—its ideology, its politics, and in the South, of course, its attitude toward race—has to be taken into account. Each of these factors at times was decisive for the resilience with which the movement responded. Even when a favorable position on race—usually the strict observance of limited political equality—was combined with a comparatively uncritical view of politics and ideology, its significance for social change in general cannot be neglected. Beyond the issues of property and political independence, the human element of social decency itself has to count for something in a full analysis of democratic possibilities. Narrow compartmentalizing, which ignores complexity, has little basis in reality and fails to recognize the undoubted vitality of Populism.

The campaign of 1896 was not an ideal benchmark for measuring internal currents because the issue of political cooperation, on which there were honest differences, tended to simplify more complex ideological positions that had emerged over the life span of the movement. Just as the midroad position, which rejected cooperation, did not coincide with radicalism, the fusionist position, which supported Bryan, did not coincide with conservatism; if anything, the fusionists frequently constituted a vanguard, including such figures as Davis Waite of Colorado and Ignatius Donnelly, long-standing critics of capitalist structure and practice. One must bear in mind the limitations of our historical knowledge of Populists below the level of the leaders and agrarian editors, as well as the fact that much pertinent information may never be recovered.

Still, in moving outside the events of 1896, one can reconstruct the following picture: First, the center of Populism maintained basic doctrines that most Populists shared; nuances of difference did not alter the underlying principles. Populists accepted an anticorporate framework in which the constitutional foundations of the polity would become the basis for realizing elemental political rights. They also supported an ethical standard of social welfare and guarantees of the dignity and security of the individual through relations of mutual obligation. The corresponding economic structure, existing under the rule of law, would both balance the claims of capital with the needs of the community and promote opportunity in the middle and bottom strata of society. I would term this position "centrist reformism" because it represented a nonsocialist, but still publicly based, political economy. The belief in a public dimension of society meant that Populism was not centrist within the whole American ideological spectrum, particularly because Populist doctrine made the state fully sovereign over the business system. Weaver, Peffer, Donnelly, Morgan, and Nugent superbly illustrate the diverse strands within the movement's center, which was formed in part through the incorporation of radical and conservative elements from Populism's own ideological universe. While Nugent's Swedenborgian vision made his critique less specific, the broader area of agreement—though even here there were many differences in degree—was the sanctioning of a positive government.

Some individuals adopted a consistent stand that was demonstrably to the left within Populism. Still, it is my impression that radicals, like radicalism, were exceptional and constituted only a fragment of the movement. They left only traces of their existence in the letters columns of the agrarian press, in preambles and isolated demands in county or district platforms, and in communications of outrage in manuscript collections. This embarrassment of ideological riches from anonymous participants—for one wonders why such individuals did not advance in party councils or have their views attended to—contrasted with the ideological hesitance of those who were the advanced leaders. Lloyd was preeminent as a figure of the left because of his acute comprehension and severe indictment of the monopolistic structure and its system of acquisitive values. He combined this indictment with his redefinition of individualism and his social vision of a commonwealth; nevertheless, his vision included the evolution of welfare, which may have obviated the need for a direct engagement of contesting forces. Moreover, he did not abandon his restorative conception of American rights as the source of political and industrial progress.

What endowed the Populist left, including not only Lloyd but also the editors in Topeka and Lincoln, and perhaps also Doster and Lewelling, with a distinctive character was a concern with the specifically industrial workings of society. This concern, because it was focused on issues of structure, led to a penetrating diagnosis of systemic problems related to capitalism. In addition, it tended both to give more emphasis to labor conditions and strife and to credit the significance of class as a principle of social organization. This led to questioning the basic assumptions of society and reform as well. In the *Advocate*, for example, the queries about society's functioning implied the necessity for a fundamental social transformation.

Although these features were less well-developed within the Populist center and comparatively rare in southern discussion, the intensity of the speculation—rather than merely the quasi-socialist pronouncements that resulted—carried the analysis beyond the recognition of the need for independent government to a coherent view of rational production and the circumscribed role of property. Yet the Populist left remained an extension from the center rather than a separate ideological camp. Populists representing the left showed less reticence than the more moderate group about attacking specific features of capitalism, but, with the possible exception of Lloyd, they did not propose a qualitative change of the social order.

However, the Populist right may have preserved a more distinct identity. It was not as forthright as the other groups in its endorsement of basic demands, and it narrowed the construction of antimonopolism because of its mistrust of the powers of government. In addition, it more explicitly credited the property right, a market framework, and the ideal of class harmony because it fused traditional rights and classical liberalism. Here public ownership was a necessary concession more than a declared intention.

The goal, which reflected a cursory treatment of industrialism and the problems of labor, was a structural equilibrium based on the political and economic power of the smaller capitalist. Government would be deprived of its collective impetus. It would not disavow its antimonopolist mandate, but its primary purpose would be to expand the field of opportunity. This was a subtle difference of content and tone. It served to define the structural equilibrium as a balance of forces drawn entirely from acceptable elements within the existing order, and thus made no provision for explicitly new arrangements that might be created by increasing the powers of the state.

Respect for the past as well as the concept of authority had a firm hold on the imagination of the Populist right. Constitutional literalism became more a reversion to a premonopolistic (not a nonmonopolistic) stage than a standard having contemporary application. And the valuing of authority encouraged deference, not only to law and order, but also to the class system in which the bottom groups of society would not take power in their own name or at the expense of stable institutions. In combination, these factors worked to promote a spirit of accommodation; reordering the temporarily deranged economic order was seen as the means of resuming the normal course of development. The purification of structure, synonymous with a model of equitableness, was in contrast to the more incisive aim of democratization, because it was based on the assumption that the cultural and institutional configuration to be repaired was fundamentally sound.

The center, and to a large extent the left, were not prepared to move against the societal framework based on property. This is a clear reminder that on the highest level of abstraction the right still had more in common with these other positions than with political forces outside the movement, particularly because it did not sanction the prevailing form of capitalism. Nevertheless, there was a margin of difference over the areas to be conserved. Trenchant criticism derived its power from the specificity of an industrial perspective; the right embraced a wider range of capitalist premises on the institutional life of society, and at times it was blinded by undifferentiated agrarianism. This was related to its tendency to view laissez-faire as a natural formation if external pressures on economic activity were removed.

This description of ideological traits distinctly fits the South, and Watson's and Davis's positions were consistent with it. However, southern Populism was not coterminous with the right. There were notable exceptions in practically every state, and the issue of race produced differential results for economic analysis and perceptions of class. Yet if the center, and in great measure the left, were bounded by the American construct as an ideological frame of reference, southern Populism was by and large similarly bounded by merely a fragment of the whole: a Jeffersonian system of political and cultural values that, because of its narrow application, was resistant in principle to state intervention in the economy and a more public conception of welfare. This further refraction of Populist assumptions through the medium of southern culture, a constraint within the wider universe of constraints of the political culture and sometimes even at odds with them, produced an ideological inflexibility, often taking an antisocialist form, that gave to the South a special affinity to the right on the Populist spectrum of beliefs. The upper limits to political and social change were reached more quickly, with less tentativeness, and with more hostile feeling toward radicalism than was evidenced on the center and the left. Still, even the absence of hostility meant, in practice, the ultimate rejection of radicalism. This was consequential, but it was only one aspect of the process by which Populists came to define themselves.

In its relational sense of identity, Populism excluded formations both to the right and the left of itself: not only radicalism, but also the unmodified structure of prevailing capitalism. If the purpose of Populism were solely exclusion of radicalism, there would have been little basis or reason for a political challenge to the established order, and its social vision, such as it might have been, would have merged without friction into the existing schema of values and institutions. Populists did not need to place limits on radicalism until their disaffection from the established order had already gained momentum. Beginning as antiradical would have insured a stillborn movement. A preoccupation with antiradicalism would have made Populists incapable of forming autonomous judgments; they would perhaps have emulated dominant-group standards while they veered off into destructive episodes in the classic rightist expression of frustration.

In contrast, Populism's extended period of gestation, in which growth of ideas was sound, if protracted, had led to a basic comprehension and articulation of grievances by the late 1880s. This development was not only aided by the example of previous agrarian mobilization, but it also directly responded to deprivations on the land and the recognition of more general political and economic abuse.[10] This stage had the potential for an independent determination of programs and issues because the adequacy and performance of the major political parties in regard to government policy and farmers' discontents were now implicitly questioned. It also had the potential for organizational solidarity and purpose as the unresponsive character of the political system became more evident. By clarifying inchoate yearnings, the Farmers' Alliance provided, especially in the South, both an educational underpinning and the social framework for a separate community of interest; hence the crucial transition to a fully organized third party was established.[11] There was a comparable ferment in both regions of Populist strength, although the western branch, because it did not fear the political divisions actuated by the race issue, was not as dependent as was the South on this intermediate step. It could go directly to independent politics on the state and local levels by 1890–1891.

In either case, however, Populists' identity did not spring forth whole; they had to discover for themselves what it meant to create a dissenting world view that could exist within, or perhaps even supplant, the established order before they could question their own impetus toward democratization. Their problem at the outset was not that reform normally entailed restrictions on ideology and political consciousness. These restrictions would only follow as a result of active engagement, when the general ties to the prevailing system had been loosened. Populism's limits to change should not be emphasized at the expense of the whole political and ideological construction that brought the movement into conflict with the established order. This unnecessarily concentrates attention on the movement's nonradical dimensions without crediting its challenge to American society.

The Lockean Obstacle to Protest

Here I make an apparent digression to describe the constraints that all movements of social change encountered in the American setting. Populism's experience was a more extreme example of the general problem. My analysis continues with social epistemology: A principal difficulty in expressing protest was that the meaning of democracy had been elaborated through, and made dependent on, the values and institutions of property; this betrayed a static historical pattern that facilitated the capitalist appropriation of social and political ideology. The unique role of liberalism as the philosophic focus of American development compounded the difficulty of protesting, for in addition to its tendency to create an absolutist mental framework in Hartz's sense, it also invested the fully drawn configuration of property with the sanctity of a natural right. The institutions of property were subserved by government through the compact defining its powers. Construing practically all of capitalism as a natural right supported the Lockean equation of freedom and ownership and legitimated unlimited accumulation as being necessary to the fulfillment of the individual and the well-being of the public.

The concept of opportunity was the American emendation of Locke. In the United States, equalitarianism did not apply to the human condition, for in that case, inalienable rights would have resided in the individual, who would be the primal moral and political unit of society. Rather, it applied to the putative opportunity to gather wealth; fundamental rights were still further joined to property, and in the process, property was anthropomorphized. Property was not only endowed with, but also shaped, the attributes of the person, suggesting the precedent integration of human and property rights that C. B. Macpherson demonstrates in the classic texts of liberalism.[12] Moreover, the importance given to opportunity affected the idea of equality itself, transferring it to the narrow legal ground of equal protection for unequal holdings. This fiction of impartial law sanctioned the disparate results of capital accumulation.[13]

Liberalism contributed to the circumscription of the boundaries of protest. If the doctrine of natural rights has been associated with other, and at times contrary, goals, its function in America since the eighteenth century has been popularly conceived as providing a prerequisite for, and then the substance of, a democratic order. As a result, this philosophic connection gave a democratic coloration to whatever internal arrangements were found in practice, including business coalescence, the capitalist appropriation of technology, and continental and commercial expansion. Locke had become Candide. All was for the best; basic features of political and industrial development were seen manifesting the self-evident and inevitable rightness of things. Indeed, to extrapolate from Leo Marx's *Machine in the Garden,* natural rights had, particularly in America, borrowed from the dignity of Nature itself. Nature was an emotionally laden symbol that, whether in the hands of Emerson or William Graham Sumner, heightened the sense of a providential economic and political development.[14]

Capitalism was a formation that had been made to seem natural; it had been set outside both history and the historical dimensions of social conflict. It was a structure for the operation of timeless institutions, for growth that did not alter the fundamental conceptions of property.[15] Social change was limited by an unchanging pattern, which historians have sometimes seen as tokening a condition of innocence: By custom, America had attained a puristic liberalism through its escape from Old World political turmoil and status restrictions. This theme, implicitly deriving its power from a natural rights groundwork, further insulated American capitalist development; the separation from Europe formed an antiseptic context. The escape motif, often elaborated by medically inspired metaphors intended to explain systemic traits,[16] indicated America's movement from political contamination to societal rejuvenation or newness. The dynamism of material forces had come to represent the wider purification of society, establishing opportunity in the guise of pure social motion, which was specifically contrasted to the formal privileges, social barriers, and class antagonisms of the traditional order. A negative quality pervaded the affirmation of liberalism. Democracy was confirmed by default: America became the absence of Europe. Where estates were not found, men were by definition free.

Liberalism sought to reconcile the differences between democratic theory and its application, using the concept of opportunity to provide a functional equivalent to the standard of humaneness rooted in the person. The act of materialistic striving became a moral endeavor—a proper, if not also an exclusive, mode of expressing freedom, that preceded questions of inequality as well as the fate of individual members of society and a collective notion of the public good. The Old World categories of oppression had been shattered. The pursuit of wealth, because it was neither aristocratic nor plebeian in spirit, conveyed the appearance of classless fluidity; meanwhile, the putatively equal starting place encouraged all to struggle and rise and certified that the differential results had been impartially determined.

The concept of opportunity confirmed the materialistic character of striving because it failed to generate an alternative goal. But liberalism's basic political and ideological role was to narrow the range of historical alternatives offered to American society. Not only capitalism but also its social and cultural stabilization became increasingly vital in determining the national welfare.

The period from 1865 to 1877 marked the critical transition to modernity in America. It became apparent that an integrated political economy had emerged from the Civil War and that the humanitarian energies attendant on the conflict had been almost entirely spent. In 1877 an unprecedented rise in industrial violence served notice on upper groups; they countered massive discontent through a combination of widespread repression and the cooptative use of democratic ideology. The systemic conservation that accompanied the industrial spurt in the final third of the nineteenth century was not achieved solely by means of a coercive policy; for the restoration of order, as is clear from the more perceptive analyses of the Gilded Age, also included a transvaluation of the American political value system: There was a conservative implementation of liberal symbols. A frontal assault on values appeared unnecessary; because of its sanctioning of property, liberalism proved readily adaptable to the stabilization desired by business and political leaders.

On the ideological plane, a materialization of democracy had occurred. The polity, inclusively capitalistic in its practices, unified human and property rights. This awakened the latent tendencies toward a private sovereignty, which, by denying all but the formalistic traits of a democratic structure, would undermine the role of government as the center of political integration. The retention of nominal democratic observances was compatible with a restricted course of development that activated the economy on lines fostering the prerogatives of ownership and enlisting popular support of principles of order.

There was a nexus of capitalism and democracy that, although chiefly ideological, reflected a modernizing process in which capitalism had an unobstructed path. This clear field was partly due to the absence of premodern class divisions that in Europe had developed in feudalism and had shaped the structure of capitalism when these divisions were carried over in the transition to a new phase; the historical pattern of America permitted an emphasis on modes of conformity as well as overt compulsion in attaining integration. This nexus was made possible, then, by the absence of structural complexity and cultural variety in American development.

Yet not the mere severance of historical ties to feudalism or the independent force of ideology proved decisive, for if liberalism was the linchpin of American political thought, it was, in addition, a central notation for the system of power. The ideological dominance of Lockeanism depended less on its having created a system of ideas, a blueprint of capitalism, than on its having confirmed economic and social practices already existing in the American setting. This was a feat of legitimation that Locke could not match in England, as Hartz points out. I would add that this was true of England because the puristic values of capitalism made up only one of several competing forces in a course of development that was not devoted wholly to the needs and interests of a bourgeoisie. This class in America was not the entire middle class, but only its upper levels of power and wealth, thoroughly capitalist in orientation. Its triumph rendered democracy, under the auspices of liberalism, primarily a strategy of capitalist development rather than the precedent aim of social organization.

Separation from Europe actually was important because it marked the historical setting for a major political exemption: America, because it did not have a history of feudalism, did not experience the interplay of social forces, or class friction, that in England and France had made the rising bourgeoisie a progressive exponent of democratic rights. This interplay was minimal in Germany, where a weak and late-arriving bourgeois stratum was subordinated to traditional elite groups, and, in the United States, where the bourgeoisie was strong if not omnipotent, present from the beginning, and generally autonomous. In this crucial respect, the United States was opposite to Germany on the world spectrum of capitalism, but both countries lacked the vitality of England, in which the bourgeoisie, pushing against premodern barriers, was compelled to assert its own class position by promoting rights for the remainder of society. Their historical struggle against the old order endowed rising capitalistic forces with the qualities necessary to sustaining a vital conception of rights.

Yet this struggle was conspicuously absent from the American context, in which the bourgeoisie, fully realized at its creation, needed only to conserve privileges that it had already claimed for itself in a society where capitalism was complete from its inception. For this reason, I am dubious about one aspect of Barrington Moore's superb comparative analysis, which demonstrates the connection between an independent bourgeoisie and the creation and preservation of democratic institutions. I question the historical suitability of including the United States in a paradigm of capitalist democracy, especially because the progressive role Moore ascribes to a rising bourgeois class is based on the presence of political conflict and not on an independent status for the bourgeoisie. Whether Moore, in moving from England and France to the United States, has sufficiently allowed for the factor of struggle in the American setting or has bypassed the issue by ignoring the historical and social roots of independence in the other national contexts, it is true that the United States did not exhibit the inner political and ideological vitality of societies where a bourgeoisie had to contest actively against other social forces for a secure place.[17]

Nevertheless, if Hartz's framework were superimposed on Moore's, the conclusion would be that where there was no feudalism, there was no contest between rival upper groups. To this I would add that where there was no contest, there could be no progressive conception of rights derived from such a struggle, and therefore no subsequent cultural manifestation of those rights in the historical course of society. Instead of being catapulted into history as an agent of democratic social change, the American bourgeoisie conceived its direction and purposes defensively. It failed from an early period—early enough to be noted by Tocqueville—to reveal the Schumpeterian confidence in the bourgeois phase of capitalism. A putative vanguard had in reality commenced a holding action against history; like the status of the bourgeoisie, liberalism was fully realized and reproduced completely in each successive stage of development. Therefore, the amalgamation of human rights and property rights originating from Lockean premises continued.

Finally, ideology had become a class weapon. Liberalism did not restructure the foundations of society; it remained cool to the actuation of democratic ideas and tended to immobilize lower groups while offering, as in the case of the suffrage, *pro forma* inclusion in the political community. All of this suggests that a continuing thread in American modernization was a concern for order, and this concern accounted for its static and lineal (that is, nondialectical) qualities. These qualities were still more evident in the constancy of capitalist reproduction.

This system was kept intact, and as it was brought forward historically, it expressed more than the continuity of political and economic development. Retaining the basic internal features of capitalism in each successive phase required that the democratizing potential of economic and technological growth be checked through maintaining a reasonably fixed, if informally sanctioned, class structure and hierarchical principles of social organization. This ensured stable arrangements of property and preserved disparities in power in the course of modernization.

The ideological features of democracy also reinforced patterns of deference—to business as well as to political leaders—in a nominally classless society, in turn encouraging an habituation to social discipline. This discipline affected not only the work routine but also attitudes toward established priorities, particularly the precedence of private over public requirements in defining the general welfare. In addition to diminishing the range of historical alternatives through ideology, there was a formalization of democratic rights. This was a product less of ideas than of class power; an ascendant bourgeoisie, not having experienced the bracing effects of struggle, practically assured a narrow construction in society's espousal of rights. The hardening of democracy into an expression of the property right (or, concretely, into the political implementation of capitalism) reflected a consolidation of the perspective of politically dominant groups. It resulted in a system of government that did not adequately express the human rights component of its ideology or even fully transmit the albeit limited substance of these rights to the whole populace. This was a twofold failure to govern responsively.

Although Robert G. McCloskey's seminal book on the mergence of human rights and property rights has advanced our understanding of a nexus of capitalism and democracy in American ideology and contributed to Hartz's concept of a pervasive Lockean political culture, it is necessary to clarify a point that is relevant to the preceding discussion. McCloskey found the source for the transvaluation of such basic concepts as freedom, equality, and justice in the ideological awakening of late nineteenth-century American conservatism. There was a general conquest of the nation's value system by upper groups. This portended a formalization of democracy, which was made easier because property rights had a more defined form (self-justifying material norms) than the presumably intangible human rights. Conservatives, recognizing the advantages of placing liberalism at their service, had captured democracy. They had materialistically redefined basic democratic concepts; emptied of their previous moral import and substance, they could be narrowly construed as economic.

McCloskey believed that there had been a major departure from earlier American and liberal doctrine. Human rights and property rights merged in the Gilded Age, but this did not reflect adversely on the formative democratic experience, when a clear distinction between those rights prevailed and human rights were given precedence. He rejected the cultural theme of timelessness, investing post-Civil War society and ideology with a specificity that denied the natural rights basis of existing arrangements. But he also accepted on faith a pristine source of human rights at the heart of American institutions, a position that called implicitly for retrieving lost rights and posited the fundamental soundness of political development.

C. B. Macpherson, in his investigation of Leveller suffrage restrictions and in his textual analysis of Locke, provided a corrective to the view that liberal doctrine expressed puristic human rights. He argued that the initial formulations of liberalism already contained a moral-material integration that denied to human rights a separable identity in practice. This perception brings into doubt—particularly in the United States, where the fusion of rights was most complete—the notion of a discontinuity in the statement and meaning of essential values. Even before Macpherson, there were grounds for skepticism because the historical connection between liberalism and capitalism had long been established. The Civil War did promote the pervasive spirit of capitalism, but fixing the broader change in a specific historical moment (and of such recent date) ignores the imbrication of human and property rights. It also exonerates liberalism, for attributing this change of values to conservatism and further relying on a theory of the transvaluation of democratic values obscures the fact that support of the property right lay well within liberalism's province. Conservatism had only utilized the prior ideological synthesis, not capturing, but popularizing, its basic content. In light of the susceptive character of liberal values, a transvaluation seems redundant or merely confirmatory.[18]

The Search for Autonomy

A liberal political and ideological context—rather than radicalism on the one hand, or prevailing capitalism on the other—may have been the greatest challenge facing Populism. The propertied universe of thought had to be opposed if Populists were to offer an alternative path to modernization in America. The difficulty that liberalism posed for the expression of protest was that protest was built on the sands of a property-oriented and culturally absorptive national history; nevertheless, this did not result in a total restriction of political will.

Populists had accepted the institutions of property on many levels. The imagery of family and homestead, which recurred throughout their writing, was based on Lockean premises of an independent competency. They also consciously articulated and refined the concept of opportunity. They rejected it in the guises of aspiration, mobility, and aggrandizement because these emphasized class differences; but they embraced it in its broad social form, the dream of realizing the potential abundance of society. Yet there remained, when the movement was matched against the overall framework, clear political and ideological disagreements; its powers of discrimination had not been extinguished.

Populism was a creation of America, but it sought, and for a time retained, its distinctive identity. The blunting of protest was especially pronounced because Jefferson had subsumed Locke and become a bedrock of liberal doctrine for the nineteenth century. The endeavor to democratize property rights worked, conversely, to propertize human rights. Because property was endowed with democratic symbolism, its influence in the nation's social and political foundations was increased. This synthesis of rights was not easily discerned: Not only was ideological and emotional significance attached to Jeffersonian principles but also such an integration of values corresponded with the actual objectives of subsequent liberal—Jacksonian, Bryanist,[19] and other—statements of reform. Paradoxically, the extension of liberalism fostered more restrictions on structure and ideology; it tended to preclude modernization not founded on property and a separable element of human political and social values. Indeed, conservatism had not captured liberalism. The reverse was true: Liberalism attempted to include the political forces to its right and left by drawing them to the ideological center; all would be putatively equal in their support of the property right, and centrism would be the political label for their common identity. Jeffersonianism, particularly in the South, was partially successful in capturing Populism for America.

Still, blunting protest was not tantamount to political and ideological paralysis. In any event, systemic closure was not attained in the Populist period or perhaps at any time in American history, if that means a successful prevention of dissent once it was conceded that the property right formed the basis of society. This margin between acquiescence and radicalism, however, had a crucial importance for practical affairs, affording the possibility for structural criticisms that could be directed, if not to capitalism, then to its consequences. There was the further possibility of outbreaks of protest that could cast doubt on the putative consensus on values. Protest would focus on the issue that mattered most: whether or not assent was to be given to the particular form the social system had taken. Populism challenged a closed system of politics and ideology, particularly when it was based on the formalization of democratic rights; this was true even when Populists did not fully apprehend the liberal content upon which this system depended. Precisely here one finds the crux of Populism's atypical position on reform: a *detachment from within* the historical and social context of America.

The movement was a twofold political reserve. Populism was a store of energy because its reformist position clearly had radical potential, and it was an island of beliefs, distant from the contemporary rationale for systemic problems. This distance insured a degree of autonomy in the face of the danger of immersion in the dominant culture, so that Populism would be able to continue focusing on challenging the substance, if not the foundations, of capitalist power. Yet the very breadth of this field of engagement could induce a complacent disregard for the political and structural boundaries of change that had long existed but receded from view. Populists were not hampered in their attack on practices that abridged fundamental democratic rights because they had identified these rights with the United States, constitutionalism, and a Jeffersonian synthesis of human rights and property rights.

Detachment from within was a definable part of Populist ideology. It marked the internal affirmation of America, but America freed from what Populists saw as the excrescent features of capitalist economic and political development, notably, monopolism and class favoritism in the implementation of law. As is clear from their treatment of the issue of economic opportunity, Populists believed that the conflict originated in class-based deformations of essentially neutral forms, forms that they considered potentially beneficial if only their neutrality were observed. They did not seek to change the founding institutions or demythologize America's past. They opposed the historical layers of social and structural preferential treatment that had been added to them. These additions resulted in injustice but continued to derive legitimacy from America's formative setting.

The assault on the value system could not be direct; therefore Populism took as its basic political task, distinct from its substantive position on issues, the construction of its own mythology of democracy. This activity did not prevent—in fact it encouraged—a concentration on programmatic remedies; it strengthened the movement's resolve and invested its challenge with moral significance. But this process of construction also meant that Lockeanism disappeared beneath the surface, and Populists were not aware of its influence. There was an unconscious narrowing of choices, as when Populists on occasion somberly invoked Jefferson against capitalism itself. It did not occur to Populists to search for the possible consanguinity between the existing structure of society and the prior stage they idealized. But they did not overlook the element of preferential treatment, the overlay of economic consolidation and its ostensive source in the inequitable policies of government; indeed, this element was at the heart of their antimonopolist contention because class favoritism falsified equal rights.

Not only ideology but also general political development had to be liberated from prevailing class functions, and the resulting benefits from the productive system would extend to the whole of society. Populists sought to undo the class stratification of America, in behalf of a nondiscriminatory rendering of the rights of property. In their view, formalizing democracy meant that privilege was superimposed on a potentially equalitarian political and economic base; in contrast, democratizing property meant that the system of capitalism was subject to popular restraint. Their purpose was to deny existing privilege its sanction in the nation's past, and, through implementing structural changes, to prevent its continuance in the future. Although Populism's vision of a nonprivileged capitalism complemented the movement's nonradicalism, its deep rejection of contemporary political and business arrangements made up for this apparent narrowing of its ideological range and increased its vitality.

While they remained within the spectrum of capitalism, Populists felt free to criticize class dominance and economic privilege. They also endeavored to free themselves from a structure and ideology in which social thought sanctioned prevailing modes of ownership that had been identified with supposedly eternal principles of economic organization. Populists were mindful of the fine line separating the basic framework of property from the institutional modifications that affected its distribution of power and current operation. The attempt to establish autonomous goals despite the immediate political and cultural surroundings, including their attempt to find an alternative form of capitalism, distinguished Populism from other third-party movements in the United States.

In this attempt, Populists simultaneously attacked existing capitalism and retained the broader construct of America, which had been extended to its ideological and temporal limits. The principle of literalism became crucial here, providing a vision of democratic property in the past and enhancing governmental powers to reestablish it in the future. By calling attention to the discrepancies between its creed and practices, their literalistic perspective endangered formal democracy; Populists viewed contemporary democracy as formal. This perspective took the consensual formula of political tenets at its face value and permitted acting directly on principles that historically had served to fend off, rather than guide, social change. This approach provided a basis for political mobilization because it compounded the sense of wholly unnecessary, economically caused hardship, supported through the irresponsible uses of political power.

But literalism was more than a tool for exposing abuses; in applying the literalist principle, Populists could turn the society's own standards against itself. They distinguished between a generalized capitalism, which expressed antecedent democratic values, and the specific abuses of an emergent monopolistic formation that destroyed political and economic rights. Populists were able to present corrective ideas and measures, however basic, because they offered them in the name of restoring fundamental doctrines of American political thought.

To further allay their fears that the property right was being denied, Populists used a literalist standard to construct a defense of protest. The dimension of time had to be freed from its imprisonment in a present-oriented context. Populism's concern for historical specificity in identifying contemporary abuses challenged both the ideological theme of a timeless pattern of development and the presumption against societal alterations that it buttressed. By attacking the prevalent conception of the historical process, Populists could introduce the forbidden topic of its concrete political substance.

Because their perspective embraced the past and future, Populists extended the meaning of America to include the public welfare as a continuously governing norm in political development. They intended to determine if a given situation had violated basic safeguards of political and economic freedom or had comprised a stage that reversed democratic processes altogether. They consciously waged a battle over ideological constants in contemporary thought. The dominant forces of the late nineteenth century had rendered universal their own stabilization of political and social relations, claiming that it was identical with the breadth and substance of the American heritage. Populists, inverting the prevalent view, particularized this formation, exposing the objectionable features that prevented it from being invested with a universal status. Furthermore, in denying the legitimacy of the prevailing order, Populists redefined the universal so that it would incorporate the future; the public welfare criterion became a means of affirming the need for social change. Populists extended the first principles of governance—for example, by finding constitutional sanction for public ownership—because they intended to implement those principles in the light of changing circumstances. The final step was to make their own programmatic remedies, now universalized, the basis for returning the United States to political democracy. Only principles, not the existing organization of society, could be treated as timeless. The challenge before them was the democratization of modernity. Capitalism had an important role, but it was no longer the predominating influence in the social system.

FIVE

The Framework of Democratic Power

The ideological conflict between Populism and the contemporary system of capitalism raised the question of alternative principles of government in a democratic society and, implicitly, the practical meaning of democracy itself. This conflict was dignified by being ideological rather than merely political. It did not merely accentuate temporary political differences over specific policies, despite its occurrence within the limits of a capitalist framework and spectrum of beliefs. The two sides presented incompatible forms of social organization on which to base the rights and well-being of the individual. Each side actively sought (and, in the case of contemporary capitalism, had successfully established) moral supremacy in defining the economic and political foundations of the polity. The roots of this ideological conflict lay in the respective interpretations to be placed on the ideal construct of America; but clearly the fundamental cause of difference lay in the workings of the existing political economy and the attempts to maintain or alter the basic arrangements of capitalism.

The idea of ideological conflict requires closer attention. Populism was essentially a political, rather than an ideological, movement, an admittedly difficult distinction to draw in any organized expression of protest when a conscious emphasis on principles has become the source of action. But Populism's principles were primarily designed to have political application; they were broadly construed as having relevance to relations of power, the responsibilities of government, and individual liberties. Moreover, this very focus tended to minimize matters traditionally taken up by ideology: replacing the political economy as such; questioning the legitimacy of the whole existing social order, not only its supposedly aberrant manifestations; using class organization as the agency of social change or, in the context of conservatism, social restoration; and advocating the direct seizure of power, frequently through extralegal means. In each area, Populism also strongly resisted the conclusions generally thought to follow from ideology. Populists did not think in ideological terms; they thought in ethical terms, with added pragmatism. Yet if Populism was not an ideological movement, it still embodied ideological differences from the established mode of capitalism. The issues raised by Populists had a specific bearing on how the political economy, legitimacy, class, and power would operate in American society.

Ideology had its material counterpart in the way that opposing formulations about America took on a structural importance when they were applied to the current setting. The question was this: What latitude would be afforded to a capitalist society as it attempted to consolidate the foundations of business power? From the perspective of Populists, the question was loaded. It assumed that capitalism, rather than political democracy, would be the ascendant force in shaping the internal character and goals of the polity. Yet in practical terms, the question was allowed to stand; Populists had not transcended capitalism in their understanding of political democracy. They would, therefore, have to fight for circumscribing the boundaries of capitalist influence, the latitude of its power, instead of opposing a capitalist society in principle.

They gave a firm answer, however, to the latter part of the question: Capitalism would not be permitted its final expression as monopolism. They did not reject a capitalist society; they did reject the consolidation of business power. Their response to the situation was sufficiently ambiguous as to place them at a serious disadvantage: They were simply perpetuating the dichotomy between capitalism and monopolism. They had left intact a capitalist economic and social base, hoping to arrest the momentum of capitalism through external political correctives: specifically, the creation of an independent, democratic state.

Populists further weakened their case against contemporary capitalism because they tended to endow property with the status of a natural right, and this had the effect of tacitly assuming the interdependence of capitalism and democracy. But because the property right was not at issue and, according to their reasoning, could be used as a main defense against the corporate organization of property, its status as a natural right actually strengthened their conviction that an independent state was justified. Monopolism did not similarly possess a basis in natural rights; it was the deprivation of the natural rights of others and of property itself.

Apparently Populists had accepted the Lockean vision of the state as the fundamental protector of the property right, but in fact they did not accord the property right antecedent claims on government when it conflicted with what they construed as a still broader and more basic configuration of human rights, including the principle that the people were the ultimate source of political authority. Nor, more subtly, did Populists accord the property right intrinsic value when it was simply limited to property. Unlike Locke, who gave prior emphasis to property, as distinct from the holders of property, they viewed the individual standing behind the property as the recipient of protection. Again in contrast to Locke, they discriminated between magnitudes of property: If property was a natural right, neither was monopolism nor the process of capital accumulation leading to the concentration of property. The state was both independent and democratic, on this underlying philosophical level, because it was exempt from Lockean requirements to treat all capitalism as a single, colossal, inclusive natural right.

Monopolism and Government

The Populist concessions to the existing mode of capitalism, then, did not preclude the class-oriented and reasonably coherent proposal of an alternative pattern of capitalist modernization. There was a dichotomy between capitalism and monopolism; the belief in the natural right of property disposed Populists to give capitalism the benefit of the doubt in determining whether it was democratic; and not least in importance, the positions of both contesting formations were inside the limits of capitalism. Yet Populism and contemporary capitalism actively predicated dissimilar political systems with different concepts of the scope and purposes of governmental power and the determination of public policy. Moral and social priorities were produced by contrasting value systems. These substantive concerns, which affected the operation of the economy as well, indicated the degree of democratization that each mode would accept and be willing to realize structurally.

Indeed, Populism's atypical position was derived from its insistence on the literalness of democratic practice throughout the social order, for this view directly related to the way that capitalism would be articulated with the state and the remainder of society. Populist policies called for prohibiting concentrated private power because this power brought about the capitalist control of the state, prevented the exercise of government's regulative functions, and, therefore, encouraged monopolistic trends. After the Populist era, business and government became partners; Populists anticipated the future by opposing the structural collaboration that had already been set in motion.

There were two distinct areas of analysis in Populism's endeavor to dismount the framework of private controls: (1) the Populists' comprehension of state power, and (2) their understanding of the internal composition of capitalism as a system with its own principles of structure and imperative requirements of development. They appreciated the state's pivotal role in the capitalistic process, but the very confidence that Populists placed in government as a necessary and sufficient force created major difficulties for them when they approached capitalism. Their emphasis on the ability of the state to construct and maintain a democratic matrix, without at the same time abandoning or seriously modifying the capitalist structure per se, resulted in a failure to examine capitalism with discernment.

The outcome was a precarious balance of conflicting elements. Because they confidently expected that the state could achieve a political and social regeneration of the society, Populists regarded capitalism as a malleable formation within which monopolism and its structural containment could be isolated. They did not perceive that the systemic attributes of a capitalistic economy, including the strategies and mechanisms necessary to insure a favorable rate of profit and the sustained renewal of investment, had an effect of their own.

Populists were not blind to the internal features of capitalism. The Populist literature contained a penetrating discussion of surplus value, labor-saving machinery, underconsumption, and the inadequate performance of the market mechanism. Even so, their disposition was to treat monopolism as a special case or an excrescence of capitalism. The power of government would suffice to counter monopoly, and capitalism's inner dynamics would not of themselves lead to monopolistic practices.

When Henry Demarest Lloyd stated that "what we call Monopoly is Business at the end of its journey,"[1] he raised a structural possibility that other Populists usually refused to face, for he implied that corrective action had to go beyond the creation of a powerful and democratized state. There had to be an equal interest in examining the institutions of property. Perhaps it was only the Topeka *Advocate* that explicitly provided for the internal dynamism of capitalistic organization when it observed that "public ownership of railroads, telegraphs, telephones, and all other utilities now monopolized or susceptible of being monopolized for private gain at the expense of the people, would inure to the benefit of the people."[2] In this case the tendencies toward monopolism were also included as a proper subject of action.

The more common observation among Populists was that aggregated wealth had encroached on the ordinary processes of economic life and endangered stable relationships. (Monopolism did not have the technical meaning of absolute market control; it meant disproportionate and restrictive power, usually secured by means of exclusive grants and privileges, in areas affecting the individual's personal security and livelihood as well as those affecting the general welfare.) In sum, an economic force, by virtue of the power it exercised, would have a political complexion. This was an important contention, but the emphasis on the political dimensions of economic consolidation deflected critical attention from the specifically economic components of a system that could eventuate in monopolism, particularly of the kinds that Populists described or modern capitalism engendered.

W. Scott Morgan was representative of Populism, not only in viewing monopolism as a threat to the people "in every relation of their national life" but also in focusing on external factors as the principal source of monopolistic growth: "The root of the evil lay in the laws. Monopolies exist by law, are chartered by law, and should be controlled by law. A trust is a conspiracy against legitimate trade. It is against the interests of the people and the welfare of the public."[3] In addition to protesting against monopolistic encroachment on "legitimate trade," Morgan revealed the strength of the Populist position, the assertion that monopolism was amenable to public law and the restraining force of government; at the same time he revealed its underlying weakness, the implication that monopolism would not have arisen if only the law were impartially administered. The very defense of law and government, at the heart of Populism's conception of a democratic state, was predicated on the belief that they—and not capitalism—were the responsible agents of monopolism; hence, government and law became the prime targets for thorough reformation. The state would be antagonistic to monopolism, but not to capitalism.

Thomas L. Nugent also forcefully denounced the encroachment of monopoly on economic and social affairs in his statement against giving to corporations "the right to dispense for a price services of a necessary and public character—services essential to the existence and well-being of organized society" as the basis for levying "tribute upon the whole community." But when he described an economic setting that enlisted the energies of lower and middle groups, one freed from artificial restraints on its development, his sole attention was on monopolism as such: "To produce results of this kind, nothing is needed but to destroy monopoly in those things which productive industry must have for practical use."[4]

Identifying monopolism, however, meant a consequent broadening of state power. This was the essence of the Populist challenge because augmenting the role of government had the potential for effecting more sweeping internal structural changes than would have been necessary if attacking monopolistic abuses had been the exclusive concern. In the Populist conception of democratic power, if capitalism was a dynamic force, so too was the state. As capitalism progressed toward monopolism, consciously matched by a corresponding enlargement (and a redefinition of purpose, for size alone was secondary) of the state, these levels of economic organization would prove difficult to separate.

Despite their intentions, Populists, because their analysis frequently was based on political principles, made direct inroads into the general context of capitalist behavior and values, implicitly criticizing whatever threatened the public weal, whether or not it was patently monopolistic. Thus, Morgan wrote: "No man has a right to operate against the public welfare and against their expressed will."[5] Capitalism was often questioned through indirection rather than through hard economic analysis, but the result was equally far-reaching; Populists uncovered factors that, although still a part of capitalism proper, contributed to monopolization. When Frank Doster maintained that "it is the business of government to discover and enforce those laws of harmony which raise man above the barbarous antagonisms of the natural state into relationships of social unity and fraternity,"[6] and when Lloyd similarly argued that "the true law of business is that all must pursue the interest of all,"[7] they were providing an ethical standard that contradicted contemporary political and economic life.

The use of political principles to govern the economic realm introduced moral and social priorities into the discussion of capitalism. Property could no longer be taken as an uncontested right; at the very least, it had to share a place with considerations of human welfare as a supreme goal of society. The *Farmers' Alliance* could point to a perversion of the property right in the transformation from individual to corporate holdings, but it affirmed the one element that dignified this right: "The welfare of the individual must be the object and end of all effort."[8]

Ignatius Donnelly, however, best expressed the idea that man anteceded in importance every aspect of society, implicitly establishing human welfare as the objective for which governments and economies had been instituted: "Statutes, ordinances, customs; banks, bonds, money; beliefs, theories, religions; philosophies, dogmas, and doctrines, are only valuable as they conserve the happiness of mankind. Whenever they conflict with it, they must fall to the ground."[9] A generalizing tendency in Populist thought, even when primary attention was given to the state, had the effect of penetrating cultural and institutional defenses of property, as when Donnelly asserted: "Man is the only thing worth considering in this great world."[10]

Lloyd's declaration that Populism arose "to make our government a people's government,"[11] which recognized at the outset the necessity of reconstituting the state to achieve a democratic society, helps to remind us that Populists did not see governmental power as isolated from the general structure of society. They emphasized the state, but capitalism was not excluded from the analysis. Instead, the state had the responsibility of preventing business gains that were detrimental to the public interest. Such gains resulted from not only direct grants and subsidies but also noncompetitive practices in sectors that had a public character, such as transportation, or that otherwise held the populace in a dependent position.

Private administration of governmental functions, including the monetary and banking structure, was to end. If the *Advocate* established the general principle that government had "the constitutional obligation to provide for the public welfare,"[12] James B. Weaver was specific about ending political and legal favoritism: "The man and the family have been driven to the wall, the weak trampled under foot and the choicest opportunities of the century showered upon chartered combinations. Wealth, already possessing great advantages, is not satisfied, and incorporates in order that it may have still greater power."[13] James H. Davis had a clear notion of the state's role in ending dependence on business power: "Congress allows, yea even charters, licenses a lot of cold, faithless, soulless, heartless corporations, to stand between the government and the people, and usurp the blessings conferred by this power, forcing the people to look to these conscienceless beings for money and transportation to carry on their commerce."[14] And the *Farmers' Alliance* described the private arrogation of public functions, as in the case of railroad freight charges, as a nongovernmental system of taxation: "These accumulations are only made possible by the exercise of quasi public powers—by the application over large areas and to great populations of the principles of taxation and the accumulative power of interest."[15]

Conversely, the state had the responsibility of broadening a narrow course of economic development that had denied the authority of government, circumscribed opportunity, and removed the obstacles to a further consolidation of industry. Weaver's remark about the "choicest opportunities" being given to "chartered combinations" indicated this narrowing of development, as did a comment by Morgan: "The relentless, remorseless and unyielding grasp of monopoly is upon every avenue of trade and commerce."[16] Peffer noted the same pattern of contraction: "The wealth of the country is fast passing into the hands of a few rich persons, while the number of impoverished grows alarmingly larger every year."[17] According to Lewelling, in this setting of deprivation it was imperative for the government to act: "I claim it is the business of the Government to make it possible for me to live and sustain the life of my family."[18] Here the *Farmers' Alliance* perhaps best expressed the sense of overall possibilities in the face of a constricting system of enterprise: "Why is all this necessary? It is not necessary. By the aid of invention, machinery and free motive power the work of the world can be performed in about half the time, with less than half the labor that was formerly necessary."[19] Yet such a change would have its source in the power of the state, for the state was "the only final protection the people have against the oppressions and extortions of monopoly."[20]

Consolidation produced impoverishment; more important, it transformed a closed economic process into a system of political power rivaling that of government. It was left to Lloyd to show the antidemocratic implications of the pattern of development. Contending that "our new wealth takes as it chooses the form of corporation or trust, or corporation again, and with every change grows greater and worse," he went beyond the simple statement that such terminology and forms had become irrelevant and claimed that in this trend toward consolidation public authority had been undermined: "Under these kaleidoscopic masks we begin at last to see progressing to its terminus a steady consolidation, the end of which is one-man power. The conspiracy ends in one, and one cannot conspire with himself. When this solidification of many into one has been reached, we shall be at last face to face with the naked truth that it is not only the form but the fact of arbitrary power, of control without consent, of rule without representation that concerns us."[21]

Populists effectively presented a paradigm of nonmonopolistic economic growth in which the state, through enlarging the public realm, would take charge of matters affecting both the general welfare and the sectors of the economy that did not admit of competition. Activating the economic system would increase the benefits of production for the lower and middle strata of society and provide a clearer structural basis for opportunity. In adopting a literal construction of the Constitution, Peffer boldly announced the principle of an enlarged public realm that included within sovereign prerogatives their means of implementation: "The same power which authorizes the Government to open and maintain highways, post roads, and the like authorizes it to build roads for the people without the intervention of any corporation whatever; to build the roads, to own them, to manage them in the interest of the people; and this right to regulate commerce includes necessarily—not only impliedly, but *necessarily*—every function essential to the work."[22]

This case for the public ownership of railroads, an application of Lloyd's broader contention that "there must be no private use of public power or public property,"[23] revealed the way in which Populists had connected sovereignty and antimonopolism: The state alone could prevent the corporate structure from standing between the people and their lawful powers of regulation and restricting economic activity, particularly by appropriating the industries and services on which all in society depended for a livelihood. Citing "the legalization of land monopoly, and interest" as contributing to the concentration of wealth, the *Farmers' Alliance* described the pyramiding of private control through just such an interposition: "Again capital enslaves otherwise independent labor, that which is in possession of land, by monopolizing the means of transportation, so controlling commerce. Standing between producers and consumers and exacting an unjust price for its labor it makes itself a king, levying tribute upon all classes."[24] The newspaper also observed that "capital is concentrating and drawing to itself all power."[25]

The nonmonopolistic paradigm, if it were historically projected, would challenge twentieth-century liberalism, as it challenged in the contemporary setting the prevailing mode of capitalism and for the same reason. Populism insisted on the autonomous foundations of government, while capitalism in both its prevailing and later forms made practical use of the state in creating a secure political environment for continuing the course of business development. In contrast to a political context favorable to promoting and stabilizing consolidated enterprise, the conception of an independent state directly questioned the inevitability of the process of concentration. As Nugent insisted, government had fostered the trends toward monopolization: "Capital could never have attained such ascendancy, but for the legislation which has given it unjust advantages and enabled it to monopolize both natural resources and public functions and utilities."[26] The other modes held the inevitable nature of business growth as an article of faith. This idea legitimated both laissez-faire and liberal regulation on the ground that, at different stages, non-intervention or intervention in the economy would facilitate the integrated operations of a system obeying its own laws of expansion.

But Populism's paradigm of nonmonopolistic economic growth also differed from the contemporary and liberal forms of capitalism on the specific character of government-business relations. Populists perceived in the structural partnership, still in its formative period, the basis for a qualitative change in the functioning of capitalism; this change was marked by the shift from a reliance on the competitive mechanism to the use of political means for resolving internal capitalistic problems. Populists believed that the alteration in capitalism involved the movement from internally generated economic energies, which were consonant with earlier democratic possibilities, to a growth process that supposed the private control of the state and even the social order.

Lewelling's view of the state as responsive to human needs conflicted with such a partnership: "It is the province of government to protect the weak, but the government to-day is resolved into a struggle of the masses with the classes for supremacy and bread, until business, home and personal integrity are trembling in the face of possible want in the family." The stifling of opportunity had now become a threat to survival: "What is the State to him who toils, if labor is denied him and his children cry for bread?" The point of the discussion was to insist, not only on a socially protective state, but on one that would discontinue its privileged treatment of business: "How is life to be sustained, how is liberty to be enjoyed, how is happiness to be pursued under such adverse conditions as the State permits if it does not sanction?"[27] Lewelling's use of phrases from the Declaration of Independence implied the need for a restoration of first principles, literally administered, that would militate against the contemporary uses of government.

Populists valued economic growth because it symbolized the potential democratization of the social order, provided that the productive energies of society were not subject to a monopolistic appropriation and could instead be liberated and used to fulfill the already present promise of social wealth. Nugent defined the problem succinctly: "There is wealth enough and to spare, but it goes to the pampered few."[28] A persistent theme of the *Advocate* was the misuse of technology in the existing social context, specifically the adoption of labor-saving machinery to displace adult male workers, enlarge the labor supply, and employ women and children: "It is thus that things which should afford the richest blessings to humanity, are converted, by a false and malicious industrial system, into instruments of the greatest evil."[29] And Lloyd pointed out the paradoxes of monopolistic control, which retarded economic growth: "Everything goes to defeat. Highways are used to prevent travel and traffic. Ownership of the means of production is sought in order to 'shut down' production, and the means of plenty make famine."[30] The common thread in these statements was a belief that monopolistic restrictions had led to thwarting structural possibilities in the economy. In the view of the Kansas editor there was a systemic anachronism at the heart of contemporary society: "One of the causes of this 'modern condition' is the monopoly of machinery and other means of production and distribution by which the few are benefited and the many are deprived of fair opportunities in life."[31]

Conversely, Populists used the theme of economic growth to highlight the contrast between endogenous and exogenous factors in activating and maintaining the economy. The absence of realizable growth testified to a capitalist system that depended on the state's partiality toward business; a structure of private controls having public sanction created partiality in bestowing privileges, enforced restraints on competition, and brought about general economic stagnation. Populist concerns were grounded in experience. They had witnessed the social deprivation of a whole generation in their own lifetime. Peffer was not speaking of a new trend when he observed: "It appears that every year the individuality of the working man is growing less and less distinct; he is becoming merged into the business of his employer; practically he is out of view."[32] Weaver summarized the long-term conditions of economic and social dependence: "For a full quarter of a century the individual, as such, has been lost sight of in a mad rush for corporate adventure."[33] Nor was he unmindful of the political dimensions of corporate development: "The corporation and the wealth which it brings have become the chief concern of society and the State."[34] James H. Davis alluded to the general privation and dislocation, which he ascribed to the monopolistic control of basic economic sectors, when he described the home as "so essential to human happiness that the decay of liberty, the downfall of society and the wreck of happiness in every age and every country have been measured by the homeless numbers within her borders."[35] Only a widespread social uprooting could have given rise to such a statement. Referring directly to corporate leaders, one farm paper in Nebraska asserted that "they have the power to impoverish the farms, make millions of good men tramps," while "in defiance of law." The corporation was "fast monopolizing every avenue of industry or employment."[36]

The Autonomous State

Indeed, Populists used the theme of economic growth to express the attitudes they had adopted toward capitalism, democracy, and the state, all of which converged in the vision of a people's government. Here once more the late nineteenth-century mode of capitalism and the twentieth-century framework of liberalism were joined; and they are distinct from the capitalist formation envisioned by Populism in their practical acceptance of the necessity, permanence, and even beneficent outcome of corporate consolidation. In this critical respect, liberalism continued, rather than departed from, the prevailing structure; it was a logical and possibly a "higher" stage in the development of capitalist organization. The movement from a supporting to an interventionist state, although it also introduced the limited use of welfare as a means of achieving political and social stability, continued the main economic trends that regularized the status and power of monopolistic enterprise. Liberalism widened the scope of state activity: In the latter nineteenth century, the state merely emphasized corporate privilege, functioning as a caretaker in providing tariffs, subsidies, and other favors; in the twentieth century, it assumed a more inclusive responsibility for systemic coordination based on the needs of business rationalization, particularly the lessening of competition.

Weaver stated that "the corporation has submerged the whole country and swept everything before it,"[37] and Morgan declared that "monopoly is wielding a greater power in the government than the people,"[38] and finally the *Advocate* contended that "every monopoly, as soon as established, shall be seized by the people and used for the public good, instead of, as now, for private gain."[39] These statements all expressed anticorporate sentiment and questioned the legitimacy of integrating capitalism and the state. Legitimation had a literal meaning for Populists; they feared an actual surrender of government's sovereign powers when the private and public structures were combined.

The *Farmers' Alliance* cited one important example, which was meant to represent a wider framework of relationships: "The right to issue money is an inherent government power. . . . In all cases where governments have delegated this right, the recipients have become government agents, as are today our national banks. . . . They have never long exercised the right without acquiring a power which threatened that of their principal. This is the case today with our national banks and their national associations."[40] Weaver perceived a threat to sovereignty in a different area: "The corporation has been placed above the individual and an armed body of cruel mercenaries permitted, in times of public peril, to discharge police duties which clearly belong to the State."[41] Even Davis, who had moderate economic goals, saw the necessity for the state's theoretical and actual supremacy over the business system, if the foundation of political democracy were to be preserved: "The government is the organized agency through which the people rule themselves, and in all governmental affairs we are a great partnership, every person's rights being equal."[42] Only the people were fit partners of government, or, strictly speaking, the government created a partnership among the people themselves. According to Davis, this partnership would set free the forces of opportunity, which were the ultimate weapon against monopolism.

In all three modes of capitalism—the prevailing nineteenth-century formation, the subsequent liberal mode, and the Populist variant—the state had a prominent role, but Populists proposed that it have a distinctive purpose. It would not only break the existing pattern of favoritism but also, as if in anticipation of later developments, provide the ground for rejecting the conjunction of public and private spheres of authority. Populists based their position on the concept of an autonomous state in order to eliminate the artificial dichotomy between the polity and the economy—a division resulting from formalistic democracy and its emphasis on procedural, rather than substantive, rights. A democratic structure had to be vested with specific governmental powers that were applicable to capitalistic operations.

The clearest expression of comprehensive substantive powers was the Omaha Platform, in which every major demand was predicated on strengthening the state to carry out public ownership or define a public jurisdiction. In asserting that "the powers of government—in other words, of the people —should be expanded (as in the case of the postal service) as rapidly and as far as the good sense of an intelligent people and the teachings of experience shall justify,"[43] Ignatius Donnelly, the author of the preamble, not only proposed widening the scope of governmental power but also affirmed a different conjunction of interests in which the state embodied the people's will. The state would be an active force—a literal construction of the Constitution had already provided a model of public enterprise in the postal service—that was based on the people's capability and right, in opposition both to corporate interposition and the integration of the private and public realms, to stand as the final authority in determining public policy. Not surprisingly, Donnelly proclaimed elsewhere that government "is the key to the future of the human race" and that "a higher development in society requires that this instrumentality of co-operation shall be heightened in its powers."[44]

Although the deformalization of democracy, which depended upon a broadly conceived antimonopolism, required strengthening the state, Populists were not disposed to state worship. In Davis's words, the state was an "organized agency," and in Donnelly's, an "instrumentality of co-operation." It was conceived as being simply a political mechanism; it was "a human device to secure human happiness," as Donnelly further explained, that "in itself has no more sacredness than a wheelbarrow or a cooking-pot."[45] Populists did not confuse their priorities; they recognized the antecedent value of the individual over all forms of structure and singled out the state for special mention precisely because of the vast powers conferred on it. Their instrumental view of the state discounted its presumed metaphysical origins and qualities; and this afforded them a measure of separation from the state because they insisted that its purposes, not its existence, commanded respect. It was an instrument of the people, but it also promoted social cooperation, an end, to use Donnelly's words, that alone justified the extension of its activities.

For Weaver, it was inconceivable that "the primal functions of Government" could "ever be rightfully surrendered," except at the cost of democracy itself. Weaver's belief resulted from not an abstract reverence for the state but his recognition that "primal functions" attested to a sovereign public, one that was coextensive with the principles of the republic and, in the immediate context, a locus of "legitimate powers" for combating monopolism.[46] Nugent was skeptical about institutions in general once their formalized character, their tendency "to perpetuate themselves by means of the veneration in which they are held and the dread which they inspire," became apparent.[47] This skepticism was equally relevant to the underlying Populist attitude toward the state: Its value was contingent on its performance.

This conditional standard enabled Populists to sanction state power while rejecting its contemporary form. Lewelling pressed the conditional acceptance of the state to its logical conclusion. The state would be enlarged at the same time that it was subordinated to human needs, in order to insure its dependence on a precedent source of sovereignty in the people. He then set forth a compact theory in which political obligation entailed a faithful discharge of governmental responsibility in achieving the purposes of the democratic heritage. If the state failed of its mission, it would rupture the body politic. This instrumental view of government ensured that the growth and uses of power would be guided by enduring principles. For Lewelling, political consent had no other legitimate basis:

> The problem of to-day is how to make the State subservient to the individual, rather than to become his master. Government is a voluntary union for the common good. It guarantees to the individual life, liberty, and the pursuit of happiness. The government then must make it possible for the citizen to enjoy liberty and pursue happiness. If the government fails of these things, it fails in its mission, it ceases to be of advantage to the citizen; he is absolved from his allegiance and is no longer held to the civil compact.[48]

Although the use of a compact theory was rare in Populism, its essential premise—that it was necessary to grant extensive power to the state, while guarding against its arbitrary rule—was widely shared in the movement.

Eschewing naive forms of state worship, Populists kept their admiration pointedly specific and, in its inspiration, partially restorative. However, they remained oriented toward the future because the state would implement the policy of democratic control of industry. Frank Doster echoed a common sentiment when he observed that "the industrial system of a nation, like its political system, should be a government of and for and by the people alone."[49] This conscious paraphrasing of Lincoln (like Lloyd's terse, "a people half democratic and half plutocratic cannot permanently endure")[50] alluded to both the past and future and merged political and industrial principles into a unified conception of public sovereignty.

The state's involvement was not to be confined to a single area; governmental activism had as its rationale the state's potential for correcting economic as well as political inequities. Populism came into being, the *Farmers' Alliance* maintained, "not to secure political freedom to a class, but to gain for all *industrial* freedom, without which there can be no political freedom; no lasting people's government."[51] Lloyd grasped the dual nature of a democratic polity: "Liberty recast the old forms of government into the Republic, and it must remould our institutions of wealth into the Commonwealth."[52] Moreover, he insisted, as the Nebraska newspaper did, that the two forms of freedom were mutually dependent; one could not survive without the other: "In making themselves free of arbitrary and corrupt power in government the Americans prepared themselves to be free in all else, and because foremost in political liberty they have the promise of being the first to realize industrial liberty—the trunk of a tree of which political liberty is the seed, and without which political liberty shrinks back into nothingness."[53] The extension of the state's jurisdiction to economic matters, reflecting the interrelation of political and economic areas, indicated the continuance of industrialism along capitalist, but not monopolist, lines of development.

Although the state was to be strong, it was expressly not to be a class state or even one that sought an accommodation to the existing forces of business consolidation. For Populists, the essence of the state was its neutral character; the political structure represented an inclusive polity and was governed by antecedent democratic principles: It was not to be a capitalist state, but an independent state that administered a capitalist system. Paradoxically, its neutrality could be sustained only if it performed an activist role that had class implications, given the maldistribution of power and wealth to be redressed. Populists, however, refused to acknowledge the dimension of class when articulating their political and economic demands because it presumably violated the standard of a general public. Instead, the conception of a neutral state permitted them a wider latitude in speaking on behalf of constitutional literalism. They identified the state component with public ownership in such a way as to render antimonopolism the Populist surrogate for class protest. The state would remove the political base of consolidated enterprise, and at the same time it would clear away the restrictions on competitive capitalism. The distinction that Populists made was between, not capitalism and socialism, but capitalism and its politicization, an unacceptable resort to state power for supporting the dominance and economic arrangements of a single class.

Populists argued that the state was in a pivotal position because it had the ability to enhance or, when it operated under different premises, to destroy, the conditions for competitive capitalism. This meant that it had the ability to shape the internal structure of a capitalist *society*. Because Populists emphasized a political and social conformation, not merely economic processes, in defining the industrial order, they invested competition with a wider meaning. Beyond such considerations as an economic predilection, or even the enlargement of opportunity, competition had an important negative significance: If monopolism represented the private aggregation of power rivaling that of government, the presence of competition would verify that political domination by industry had not occurred; the arrest of monopolism would indicate the separation of capitalism from its political support.

In more positive terms, the vitality of competition would be the salient trait of a capitalist stage in which economic processes were internally activated through capitalism. There would be a normalized pattern of activation, which would be neither the subject of political influence nor a basis for class aggrandizement. This stage would permit a recombination of the polity and the economy so as to depoliticize the operations of capitalism, return the flow of power to the governmental sphere, and afford society a free play of economic forces. These forces would complement a precedently valued, independent political framework. The apparent similarity of these concepts to the ideas of Adam Smith is discussed shortly.

A Human-Centered Polity

Populists did not treat state autonomy as a simple structural fact. Lloyd tirelessly asserted that structures had to be ethically charged if they were to effect a permanent alteration, whether of government, society, or human values. The state was neither an end in itself nor a means of discouraging independence in the individual: "Nothing so narrow as the mere governmentalizing of the means and processes of production. It is only the morally nerveless who ask government to do that which they will not rise to do."[54] The autonomous state would be a prerequisite for social change, but it was not to be confused with the substance of change or the conscious will needed to insure that change would possess a democratic character.

Indeed, ethics was fused with rationality, as in the reference by the *Advocate* to "a proper use of the instrumentalities of modern production and distribution."[55] This was more fully expressed in Lloyd's integrated view: "It is not a verbal accident that science is the substance of the word conscience. We must know the right before we can do the right. When it comes to know the facts the human heart can no more endure monopoly than American slavery or Roman empire."[56] Nugent's biting reminder that "we learn to love what we are accustomed to, and misguided affection makes us cling with death-like tenacity to social and political institutions long after they have ceased to be useful or serviceable to the human race,"[57] put into perspective the Populist suspicion that without moral energy any change in structure would ultimately prove barren.

The idea of state autonomy did more than assert that there should be an independent state, an autonomous public realm. It was a condition for defining and promoting basic rights. For Populists, government was inseparable from the legal groundwork it was charged with administering. Moreover, in this conceptualization of sovereignty government not only rested on popular foundations and elaborated the public's will but also had both extensive and potentially extensible powers. The observance by the state of a system of primal law, which I have termed a jurisprudential domain of liberty, sanctioned this application of power.

Although the affirmation of freedom under law could be interpreted to fit practically any law-and-order schema, for Populists it had a more specific reference that related to the extensibility of governmental power. The moral standing of law inhered not in its formal existence, but in its embodiment of principles of sovereignty that fixed human welfare at the center of the polity. The fundamental law, which Populists associated with constitutional doctrine and related eighteenth-century texts, had been precedently transfused with democratic content. They based their argument on the belief that the formative political context defined the framework of governance and, as if by logical extension, the nation's heritage of freedom. When Peffer announced that "the people of the United States constitute a nation,"[58] he was proclaiming a standard of political legitimation. This standard supposed a conjunction of people and nationhood that invested government ("an agent of the people for the purpose of executing the popular will")[59] with self-directed powers and democratic goals. This conception of the fundamental law, strengthened by its connection with a sovereign people, provided a basis and an ethical continuity for American political development: Freedom resided in, and could only be as vital as, the legal groundwork that the people had laid to fulfill their social purposes.

What Populists clearly proposed was an alternative formulation of the ultimate source of power and legality in society, a human-centered, instead of business-centered, universe of political rights. Donnelly, after reducing government to "a cooking-pot," further observed: "The end of everything earthly is the good of man; and there is nothing sacred on earth but man, because he alone shares the Divine conscience."[60] The human-centered political universe also implied a prior valuing of community because community was the fruition of individual expression. For Lloyd, human beings became individuated through multiplying their social responsibilities, a process of growth informed by a dedication to the rule of law: "We can become individual only by submitting to be bound to others. We extend our freedom only by finding new laws to obey. Life outside the law is slavery on as many sides as there are disregarded laws. . . . The more relations, ties, duties, the more 'individual.'"[61] Law was a supremely integrative force, an ethical microcosm of the structure of community, in the life of a democratic society.

The concept of the human being as the fountainhead of government and society had an apparent mystical quality that was dispelled when Populists characterized the institutional setting and its normative political standards in the concrete terms of human rationality. Even natural rights were derived from people's intelligence and potential for cooperation, at least to the extent that Populists would not fracture sovereignty at its foundation by imputing a separate and eternal existence to the law. Sovereignty was indivisible but so also was its source. The progression from individual to law to state did not devalue the law; it affirmed its human content. Rights were fashioned on earth, not in heaven. The reverence for law still left the faith in humanity's primacy unshaken.

Lewelling succinctly revealed the order of priorities: "The people are greater than the law or the statutes, and when a nation sets its heart on doing a great and good thing it can find a legal way to do it."[62] Populists recognized the need to demystify the state because they conceived of it as an instrument made by humans for achieving the social welfare. But in treating both law and the state in matter-of-fact terms, they raised a more significant issue. The political framework required that antecedent rights be located somewhere. They were not to be placed in property, which Populists generally took for granted, and did not elaborate into a system of governance, but in a sovereign public. Doster indicated that the property right was not the highest priority: "I know that humanity is above property, and that profit making on the bread of poverty is an abomination in the sight of the Lord."[63]

The general Populist position had a critical area of shading in which Lockeanism was broken down to identify human rights, although they still retained associations to property, and to reconcile the essential elements of capitalism and community. Property was not displaced, but community was accorded a firmer status. When the *Farmers' Alliance* declared that "the community must now absorb the corporation," it was making a statement about contrasting political forms: "A stage must be reached in which each will be for all and all for each."[64] Lloyd's aphorism, "generals were, merchants are, brothers will be, humanity's representative men,"[65] supported the idea of cooperative political relationships. If a compact theory were to be inferred from Populist thought, its abrogation would probably concern the violation, not of the property right (which was conveniently assumed in America), but of the right of the community, a broader conception of the people's liberties that included the property right and yet already modified it where monopolism was at issue.

Weaver described the potential conflict between business and society, which necessitated a greatly strengthened state: "It is clear that there is some power in this country which is above the Government and more authoritative than public opinion, and which can exert itself successfully at critical moments in high places. A child can tell what that power is. It is the omnipresent, omnipotent corporation."[66] Indeed, the idea of community became a fixed point of reference for determining antisocial forms of capital, as in this definition offered by Doster: "It is that capital which locates nowhere, and identifies itself with no community but which comes to abide temporarily, while it advantages itself upon the necessities of the people, which is the curse of the industrial world."[67]

In advancing a communal standard, Populists were obviously attacking predation and what they believed to be its structural expression, a parasitical mode of capitalism; but they also saw in community a social context of human relationships that encouraged the growth of the individual. This view was among their distinctive contributions. If Populism's sole impetus had been the assertion of a narrowly construed property right, its entire order of priorities and certainly its concept of sovereignty, would have been turned upside down. Instead, one has to consider the matter of potentially extensible powers.

The individual was the basis of political society, and this valuation sanctioned, by aggregation, the vision of community. It also provided a standard for making concrete all other concepts, including the structure of government. The presumption was that, through the values of community, the United States had once expressed its basic political unit and that government could achieve this same end in the future. Populists granted the law an honored, as well as a stable, place in the political foundation of society, as much because it was a symbol of human freedom as because it was an object of intrinsic respect. But they did not confer the same honor on government, which never lost its specifically instrumental character. It was always a means rather than an end, and, at most, one might speak of government as an expression of the natural rights of the individual-in-community to indicate Populists' philosophic position.

Yet, because Populists thought of government as an instrument and also diminished, without abandoning, the Lockean emphasis on property, they were able to create a framework in which governmental power was not threatening. Power became merely additive; the general boundaries of capitalism established the only articulated, predefined limits. Populist constitutionalism rearranged the Lockean political universe in order to conserve what Populists viewed as its specifically American implementation. They were not concerned over power because it was for them an extension of and *from* the people. This conception of the sources of authority resulted in imposing fewer conditions on state activity; the one important condition was the retention of capitalism.

If property, rather than the people, had been the principal basis of legitimacy, the singular force of Populism would not have appeared: its identification of a broad dimension of welfare, contingent on the refusal to reify government and embodied in semicollectivist principles of antimonopolism and public ownership. The underlying, if incomplete, dichotomy of capitalism and democracy (particularly where monopolism was involved) was more significant than these programmatic remedies; it denied an antecedence to property that had hitherto made the political economy impervious to intervention. Populists' insistence on the neutrality of the state reflected their attitude toward power; they were disposed to confer on government the supervisory role that was integral to its neutrality. They would respect capitalism, but they would also compel it to observe prior claims of welfare. In contrast, when property formed the political and moral epicenter of society, there were habitual restrictions on the uses of power, confining its scope to the one right that was to be conserved, that of property. Instead of dividing capitalism and democracy, the conventional Lockean compact resulted in capitalizing democracy. The property right was anterior to humanity, community, and welfare, except insofar as each bore the imprint of property as its defining trait. For Populists, this was a distorted view of what sovereignty and government were supposed to represent.

SIX

Modifications of Laissez-Faire

Comparisons between Populism and the framework of Adam Smith can be fruitful, enabling one to see more clearly the Populist macroeconomic position in the spectrum of American capitalist development. Although the magnitude and goals of an independent state were the essential Populist corrective of Smith, there was a surface similarity in the emphasis on depoliticized capitalistic functions. This similarity warrants starting with the instructive structural affinities between the Populist and Smithian formations. For Populists, depoliticization meant an absence of monopolist dominance and the presence of freely generated competitive processes. The former was a political statement about power in society, the latter, an economic statement about an internally activated capitalism. Populists viewed depoliticization as compatible with an autonomous government and the social principles of community. The Smithian premise of internal economic activation was a decisive element in Populism, even if its application led to quite dissimilar results.

Populists and Adam Smith

Despite a common focal point, Populists had not accepted Smith's ideas uncritically or completely. They were particularly skeptical about the ability of a structure of automatic self-regulation either to impede the transformation from competition to monopolism or even to provide an adequate basis, given the emphasis on egoistic conduct, for systemic social beneficence. On both counts, Lloyd was openly critical: "Liberty produces wealth, and wealth destroys liberty." He explained that "competition has killed competition, that corporations are grown greater than the State and have bred individuals greater than themselves," and that industry, now "in the quadruped state," was "a fight of every man for himself." For Lloyd, social Darwinian values, in reality a shorthand for unrestrained aggressive behavior, were a more naked expression of an underlying Smithian content of individual self-interest: "The prize we give the fittest is monopoly of the necessaries of life, and we leave these winners of the powers of life and death to wield them over us by the same 'self-interest' with which they took them from us."[1]

Lloyd argued that an egoistic standard was amoral and had destructive consequences for both the human being and the attainment of community: "In all this we see at work a 'principle' which will go into the records as one of the historic mistakes of humanity. Institutions stand or fall by their philosophy, and the main doctrine of industry since Adam Smith has been the fallacy that the self-interest of the individual was a sufficient guide to the welfare of the individual and society." Smithian principles reflected a particular stage of development and did not merit the status of a universal formula for social benefits: "Heralded as a final truth of 'science' this proves to have been nothing higher than a temporary formula for a passing problem. It was a reflection in words of the policy of the day."[2]

In Lloyd's view, the expediential nature of Smith's ideas required a frank exposure for the same reason that the state required demystification by Populists: to insure that the needs of a human-centered polity would be served. Lloyd attacked a main tenet of Smith when he presented a two-tiered political framework. His definition of laissez-faire had both economic and ethical implications: "The true *laissez-faire* is, let the individual do what the individual can do best, and let the community do what the community can do best. The *laissez-faire* of social self-interest, if true, cannot conflict with the individual self-interest, if true, but it must outrank it always." In confronting Smith, he began a process of redefining basic concepts; he proposed not only a social self-interest but also a competition that evolved toward mutuality: "What we have called 'free competition' has not been free, only freer than what went before. The free is still to come. The pressure we feel is notice to prepare for it."[3]

W. Scott Morgan was also skeptical of Smithian economics, although he believed that liberated trade could perhaps be efficacious as part of a broader antimonopolism. He declared that "some will contend that competition will correct all inequalities arising in the various conditions of labor." To suggest how inadequate this principle had been in shaping contemporary reality, he quoted a passage in which Smith claimed that competition was "'the great regulator of industrial action,'" that it was "'beneficent, just and equalizing,'" and that its violation was "'contrary to the law of nature and of sound political economy.'" There was not a "like competition in all things," so that "while it [would] apply to the markets of the world in the sale of the products of labor," it had little effect on factors that directly impinged on labor, such as taxes and rents, and was "decidedly injurious" in determining wages. There was "an unhealthy condition of the industrial interests of the country." Morgan had not been overawed by Smithian logic: "Competition in commerce, trade and transportation fails 'at the moment something is expected of it,' because it leads to combination. In proof of this theory we have only to point to the numerous trusts that have sprung up in our country within the past ten years, and to the consolidation of numerous railroad companies."[4]

Yet he did not quarrel with the desirability of competition, provided its operation was not violated in practice: "In the latter part of Dr. Smith's proposition, however, we most heartily concur." This idealized state of the economy had nevertheless been nullified through the growth of monopolism: "Competition is killed by combination, and the laws of trade are perverted to the end that the few are enabled to enrich themselves at the expense of the many." Morgan was implying that public ownership would correct this structural perversion; it would allow the laws of trade to operate in the remainder of the economy where the conditions of monopolism did not obtain, thus restoring putative relations of equity. The railroads, he later added, "are public highways and of right ought only to be operated for the public good."[5]

Nugent's ideas were still closer to a Smithian framework, primarily because he believed that the economy should be internally activated, but his acceptance of laissez-faire tenets was qualified by the recognition, however grudging, that state power, including public ownership, would have to replace an automatic mechanism to insure the prevalence of competition where it could operate. He also advocated a two-tiered structure of public and private economic activity, although the role of government was more attenuated than in the case of western Populists. The effect diminished the influence of the upper or governmental tier, thus checking the potential for socialism that inhered in such a position and weakening the political and philosophic underpinning of a definable public sphere. The tacit rejection of Smith was on grounds of exigency rather than principle.

Nugent lamented that humanity's present "selfishness demands its law of competition." He believed that an Augustinian City of God, founded on the institutions of Edward Bellamy, had to await the future. In the meantime, it was necessary to attack monopolism ("to give back to the people their ownership of public utilities") and to use the initiative and referendum as springboards to private objectives.[6] It was also essential "to recognize the supremacy of the individual in matters of private concern, to restore to the commercial and social world the lost ideas of equity and justice, thus to untrammel legitimate industries and skill and leave them to pursue in freedom the beneficent work of producing wealth." This amounted to a list of Smithian goals that was expanded by a further demand, taken from the significantly earlier 1856 Democratic platform: "and this reform movement necessarily must, upon humane and economic grounds, include 'free trade throughout the world' within its scheme of remedies."[7] This language, taken from classical liberalism, was not unlike that in a passage in another speech in which Nugent discounted the aid of government in helping the laborer and called instead for "employment freely coming to him from the liberated, enlarged and revivified productive forces." However, he once more supposed "beneficent changes in our laws and public policies" in ending monopolistic restrictions.[8]

In a third speech, he predicated the elimination of poverty on the participation of the community, which included the lower and middle strata, in the benefits of capitalism. This was a subtle democratization of Smithian principles because the stimulus to opportunity originated from the social base: "Such a condition could only be brought about, however, in a community all of whose members were afforded fair opportunity for the exertion of their faculties; for thus only could each be enabled to produce a proportion of the common stock of wealth and participate in the general enrichment derived from the co-operating efforts of all." This passage muted the individualistic emphasis of Smith. Nugent's view of community, because of its religious antecedents, necessarily entailed a collective and structural perspective, even though egoistic premises still remained. Moreover, the animus toward monopolism implied that liberating productive forces would require the state's services for removing structural barriers: "In such a community there could be no material waste, no check on production, no limitation to the aggregate wealth by means of monopoly or the possession of unjust advantages."[9] Nugent's conception of rational production depended more on cooperative efforts and the well-being of the community ("aggregate wealth") than did Smith's.

It is not surprising that Adam Smith exerted influence on Populism, for his thought formed a part of the basic stock of ideas, which also included those of Jefferson and Locke, that characterized the historical and ideological construct of America. Populists shared this universe of ideas by way of the broader political culture and internalized the norms of property. (They appear to have associated these ideas with America more than with liberalism proper because they appealed to constitutional doctrine in positing an antecedent general welfare, which was to be set against the unrestricted right of property.) But there was also a more concrete basis for Populism's affinity with a Smithian framework. In *Wealth of Nations* there was an emphasis on nonpoliticized economic processes. Smith had presented the internal generation of the economy as a defense of competitive capitalism specifically considered as a progressive historical force. Populists and Smith had in common opposition to monopolism and the corresponding political formations that promoted restrictions; in essence, corporate capitalism, supported by the state, was for Populists what mercantilism was for Smith.

On a deeper level, a historical element pervaded their perspective on capitalism and fixed it at a puristic bourgeois stage; they regarded capitalist economy as artificial and adulterated to the degree that market forces were constrained. For both Populists and Smith, this judgment was based on an antipathy toward economic politicization, which was achieved by supervening forces of class and power. Conversely, there was an implied congruence between a well-ordered polity and freely competitive economic relations. The confidence that such a framework, in reality a constant laissez-faire model, could be theoretically retained, in spite of altered circumstances of production, was at the heart of this generally static conception of capitalism.

Yet on the basis of laissez-faire, it is possible to isolate Populism's substantive departures from Adam Smith as well: Populists accepted several essential features of the classical version, but they invariably and consciously measured this acceptance against the prevailing realities of a monopolistic system and its politicized nature. The theoretical conservation of the model resulted in the practical alteration of its central factor. Structural automatism was replaced by a governmentally framed market mechanism to insure the continuation of internal economic activation wherever competition remained feasible. There was an overlapping of the Smithian, Populist, and existing modes of capitalism based on their acceptance of the fundamental premise of private appropriation. But the analysis of these modal intersections reveals the creative uses to which Populists had put a laissez-faire framework and its assumptions.

A Critique of the Market Framework

Smith had not provided for the role and power that Populists ascribed to the state, nor had corporate capitalism, for an opposite set of reasons. Smith did not go far beyond the self-adjusting mechanism; economic activation had its source primarily in the system of exchange itself. There was little notion of an energetic but neutral state, or even a clear delineation of power, for it was axiomatic that the economic mechanism would reconcile the factors of production: wages, profits, rent. The state as such was indistinct, given the ostensible sufficiency of exchange as a governing force.

Smith's focus on commercial freedom in theory could be adapted to industrial reality.[10] (In this respect, this theme, like Jeffersonianism, served as a basis for Populists' creative abstraction of moral and economic statements.) But in practice commercial freedom was unnecessarily limiting. The commercial emphasis proved adequate to an analysis of the division of labor, but it did not encourage a direct treatment of industrialization in its prevailing and anticipated forms; this placed a premium once again on the process of exchange as the main stimulus for generating economic activity. In sharp contrast to the specific industrial analysis of Populists, Smith minimized industrialism as a real or potential source of activation. This lack of industrial specificity led to a self-enclosed framework.[11] As a consequence of his emphasis on the commercial factor, Smith largely confined his attention to the presumed automatism of the market structure, and this rendered the creation of general social welfare (from the totality of individual actions) not only an article of faith, but also a scientific principle, insofar as his Newtonian convictions permitted such a claim.

As a result, the invisible hand obviated the necessity for all the political and structural safeguards that Populists considered so vital if the guiding principles were to be implemented. Smith would not face the conditions that made a free market possible. He was a structuralist who isolated structure from its political frame of reference. His simple projection from egoistic premises to the larger social welfare failed to improve his analysis, particularly because he believed that a conscious intending of the common good was not required.

Although Smith and Populists valued the unimpeded operation of capitalistic processes, fixed at a particular stage of capitalism, they basically disagreed on the fixative element. For Populists, competitive capitalism could be retained only through state action; in contrast, Smith tenaciously held to the principle of nonintervention, proposing only minimal solutions outside the framework of the market to correct imbalances of structure; for example, he grudgingly allowed for public works. In his clear order of priorities, the state was subsumed under the economy and given little standing. I suspect this was less because he feared restrictions than because he valued the market framework itself. It was no longer a means, but an end—the self-contained matrix that in microcosm fulfilled the purposes of, if it did not actually supplant, the political community.

Yet it must be said, parenthetically, that although Smith may have given undue significance to capitalism as a social system, his idealism concerning the very conception of the marketplace should not be overlooked. For Smith, atomistic selfishness was the basic motivational unit, and a salutary egoism was perhaps the best one could expect for the foundations of his polity. But the building process, perhaps for no other reason than to keep selfishness operant, nevertheless depended upon economic incentives as the intentional replacement for political mechanisms of repression in stabilizing capitalist society. This rejection of the coercive state must count for something in the world history of capitalism, as a comparative analysis of the modernizing patterns in England, Germany, and Japan would tend to show. The interpenetration of government and business in Germany and Japan, where the state became the agency of conservative elites in promoting modernization, provided the historical configuration that culminated in twentieth-century fascism. Barrington Moore's discussion of the alternative modes of organizing society on long-term economic or political lines within the context of modernization suggests the structural and cultural disposition to repressive frameworks inhering in politically derived solutions.[12]

Although Smith would have found the concept of a people's government improbable, because of similar reasons for rejecting state activity he also ruled out the structural linkages, the interpenetrating design, that were critical to private domination. Indeed, Smith was at his most innocent and humane when he extended the meaning of the division of labor to embrace international trade. He hardly destroyed colonialism, but his emphasis on the exchange framework was sufficiently great to cast doubt on the importance of the nation-state. It is questionable whether Smith possessed a transcendent vision; he failed either to provide for the implementation of his own professed goals or to address the forces of industrialism. Still, he did grasp the *negative* validating condition for what Populists defined as a capitalist democracy: the prohibition of state intervention that gave an advantage to particular groups at the expense of exchange/free-market operations and broader energies and thus promoted a process of concentration that transferred power to ascendant private forces.

Smith's market framework, however, reveals the sterility in his perspective—a pervasiveness and reification of market behavior—that Populists found abhorrent to their cooperative vision of humanity, its freedom, and wider social conduct. Doster's special charge on government was to achieve the "relationships of social unity and fraternity";[13] Nugent's call, patterned on Christ's teachings, was for "the law of human service";[14] and Weaver attacked corporate behavior because it was "void of the feelings of pity and the compunctions of conscience."[15] In addition, Lloyd's writings contained a cogent critique of Smith's market individual, in contradistinction to the Populist conception of the democratic individual.

When Lloyd asserted that "to get it is, in the world of affairs, the chief end of man" and that "in trade men have not yet risen to the level of the family life of the animals," he was speaking of the fragmentation of social bonds, which had resulted in the increase of arbitrary power based on individual self-interest: "Our century of the caprice of the individual as the lawgiver of the common toil, to employ or disemploy, to start or stop, to open or close, to compete or combine, has been the disorder of the school while the master slept." Yet the people were now awakening to discover the social dimension of human development: "The perfect self-interest of the perfect individual is an admirable conception, but it is still individual, and the world is social. The music of the spheres is not to be played on one string."[16] Because it encouraged a sense of mutual obligation, a collective identity needed to be restored.

Affirming that "there is a people, and it is as different from a mere juxtaposition of persons as a globe of glass from the handful of sand out of which it was melted," Lloyd emphatically rejected the Smithian premise of egoism: "A partial truth universally applied as this of self-interest has been is a universal error." In its place he posited the test of civilization as "the process of making men citizens in their relations to each other," which referred, among other things, to a definition of rights as reciprocal and again explicitly qualified the central tenet of Smith: "If all will sacrifice themselves, none need be sacrificed. But if one may sacrifice another, all are sacrificed. That is the difference between self-interest and other-self interest." Perhaps Lloyd's most biting scorn was reserved for the personality of the market individual: "There is a strong suggestion of moral insanity in the unrelieved sameness of mood and unvarying repetition of one act in the life of the model merchant. Sane minds by an irresistible law alternate one tension with another. Only a lunatic is always smiling or always weeping or always clamoring for dividends." The observation complemented his concepts of the social basis and multiple dimensions of human individuation; as he succinctly noted, "men can continue to associate only by the laws of association."[17]

Finally, a more subtle issue was raised by the self-contained matrix, or market framework: its power to penetrate all aspects of the cultural life of society. Lloyd took equally strong exception to this influence: "Art, literature, culture, religion, in America, are already beginning to feel the restrictive pressure which results from the domination of a selfish, self-indulgent, luxurious, and anti-social power. This power, mastering the markets of a civilization which gives its main energies to markets, passes without difficulty to the mastery of all the other activities." The society's confinement within a market standard of valuation meant an inability to respond to the challenges of a truly humane existence: "There is too much left undone that ought to be done along the whole scale of life, from the lowest physical to the highest spiritual needs, from better roads to sweeter music and nobler worship."[18] For Populists, the problem was that the material standard, intrinsic to the market framework, precluded independent normative values that might question, not only the framework, but also its characteristic exchange mentality. In the final analysis, this was the reason for terming the matrix self-contained.

While Populists maintained that internal economic generation served as a basis for stimulating capitalist development, they did not merely occupy a point midway between the Smithian and contemporary modes; they adopted a position within capitalism that was partly defined through what had been rejected in both other modes. The state remained pivotal. Notwithstanding business publicists of the late nineteenth century, Smith's ideas had not provided an exoneration of prevailing American capitalism. His egoistic construct was not identical with the Sumnerian tooth-and-claw ethic of social development, and his emphasis on competition was precisely the factor that business leaders considered a threat to the security of major enterprise. This threat prompted the first modern attempts, as distinct from eighteenth-century mercantilism, to involve government in protective intervention. If Populists were closer to Smith than to the existing capitalist mode on the issue of competition, they did not feel compelled to support an undiluted laissez-faire; instead they sought to correct the Smithian framework by creating a clearly articulated two-tiered structure of the economy through heightened governmental powers.

The Model of Competitive Capitalism

Populists went beyond abstracting Smithian doctrine for their own creative purposes and departed from it. Armed with the benefit of a century of capitalistic practice unavailable to Smith, they questioned the adequacy of a self-adjusting mechanism unless it was within a state framework. In the face of industrial consolidations, they thought that the state should be capable of implementing structural automatism in those intermediate areas of the economy in which competition was still possible. Otherwise, the state should establish a comprehensive antimonopolist position, involving deconcentration and government ownership, in order to subject noncompetitive areas to public control.

Populists had selected from the Smithian model its potentially volatile element, free competition. By confining its application to a structural range that could be enforced by the state, they challenged on ideological and practical grounds Smith's laissez-faire paradigm that included all economic activity within a competitive frame. Consequently, self-adjustment was redefined, taking into account industrial complexities Smith had not envisaged.

The self-adjusting mechanism made sense to Populists only in the context of government supervision. This qualification rendered structural automatism a mere surface description for underlying conditions that had been satisfied and that were specifically confined to the classic version of the market: decentralized economic power in which the actions of individual producers or firms could not determine the outcome of market decisions. Furthermore, Populists shifted the basis of the mechanism's functioning from the process of exchange per se to an internal economic generation that included increased productivity, more equitable distribution, and a state framework providing the requisite controls over industry. For Smith, exchange was the logical and necessary locus for the system's functioning—the one common mediating factor for the myriad of isolated experiences. Finally, as the notion of a mechanism would suggest, it was the sole means for reconciling egoism and welfare.

Populists were not dependent on such an explanation. In addition to a community orientation that would counter material and spiritual fragmentation, the essence of their view on capitalist economics was that structural abuses in principle were open to correction. They held the correlative belief that welfare was the product of conscious intent; it was to be achieved through constructing a democratically centered public policy. This line of reasoning predicated an independent role for government. More basic, it introduced the practical differentiation of competitive capitalism from laissez-faire.

Populists regarded the state as neither an adventitious element to be tolerated nor the political foundation of corporate stability to be embraced; both were inimical to an independent state formation. In regarding the state as essential—at the heart of the distinction between competitive capitalism and laissez-faire—they departed from the concepts of structural automatism and passively realized general welfare, equated traditionally with laissez-faire. In doing so, they presented a sharpened critique of the interpenetration of business and government. Their critique was honed on the whetstone of public autonomy, which they considered the imperative condition, because laissez-faire automatism and its converse, a totally coordinated business polity, were equally to be avoided. In broader terms, welfare was not a spontaneous occurrence, particularly from the unpromising ground of self-interest; it had to derive from an ever-renewed political effort. At variance with the state's uses in the other modes, Populists invested the state with a guardian function, which gave to competitive capitalism its structural *and* social integrity. They refused to separate these two dimensions of organization.

Populists' modifications of laissez-faire raised more than a question of machinery. Because of his inclusive view of the individual and society, Adam Smith was a political philosopher, hypothesizing an ideal social order founded on market relationships. If this social order contained the semblance of geniality and peace as customary Smithian trademarks, it nevertheless reinforced the Lockean statement of moral and political rankings. As a consequence, it treated freedom as emanating from capitalism, or more precisely, from capitalism's proper adjustment in the well-ordered marketplace. Populists considered this rendering of social values and priorities to be a caricature of the individual's make-up and the social relations that were possible in a cooperative framework. Most important, competition had been divested of specific democratic practice. Populists sought a reversal of Smithian means and ends; democracy would take precedence, and the market, merely society's economic invention, would create activity that was not politically injurious to the public welfare. The concentration of private power within the polity had to be prevented.

Populists thus assigned to competition a political sense that was weak, if not altogether lacking, in Smith. Although the Smithian and Populist modes both attempted to retain a particular stage of capitalism, the approach of Populists to this goal was more dynamic, and it changed the meaning for that stage. Competition, no longer exclusively dependent on its egoistic basis, was to be transferred to the narrower sphere of indeterminate economic transactions; it was to entail neither Smithian dissociated social relations nor the harsher egoism of the prevailing capitalist mode. Instead, there was to be a delimited stratum in which the producers maintained an independent position, received the value of their labor, and enjoyed wider opportunity because powerful collusions within the economic community and between the state and business would be prohibited. In contrast, if the doctrines of Smith had been applied without modification to the United States, in the absence of governmental checks, they would have degenerated under actual conditions into the position of Herbert Spencer and constituted the half step needed for rapid corporate ascendancy.

Populists emphasized the state's corrective role in the functioning of capitalism; and yet they did not show a comparable acuity of analysis or criticism of capitalistic internal processes of development. Their concept of governmental responsibility for the public welfare nevertheless led to a misplaced confidence, for the reliance on state power obviated the necessity for a fundamental restructuring of capitalism per se. Reform would be a matter of containing, more than of dismantling, the basic economic features of the system. Populists consciously limited structural alteration; their exactitude in proposing social change was already evident in their application of laissez-faire to the intermediate economic range. But this exactitude also affected their ideological perspective. The movement experienced and desired to make firmer the moral and structural attachment to America. This sense of being related to, immersed within, and pertinent to the nation's institutional heritage and growth resulted in a selective remedying of abuse in both government and business to conserve the whole of society.

Populists' self-restraint had a positive motivation. Their affirmation of America spoke to their belief that the framework of democratic governance could be retrieved. James B. Weaver expressed this idea, integral to the Populist conception of mission, in its full historical dimensions: "Throughout all history we have had ample evidence that the new world is the theater upon which the great struggle for the rights of man is to be made, and the righteous movement now in progress should again forcibly remind us of our enviable mission, under Providence, among the nations of the earth."[19] Yet this deep fount of inspiration, especially when it had become unavoidably identified with the institutions of property, was restrictive. Populists rejected the normalization of private power in their attack on corporate organization; but they would not abandon the notion of entrepreneurial liberation, at least insofar as it comported with a nonpoliticized economic course and respect for the rule of law. The abridgement of the fundamental law, manifested in the imbalance between the public and private spheres, denied the antecedent standard of community interest and *human* worth. But the moment Populists thought that a nonprivileged form of capitalism was practicable, their criticism reached its outer limits.

In seeking to transform the economy so that it would be compatible with a democratic political order, Populists had, perhaps without knowing, placed an immense burden on the state; they charged it with insuring both equitable social relations and freely generated economic activity. The result was a structural paradox. A steady augmentation of governmental power would be necessary even to keep abreast of internal capitalistic processes and prevent a renewed coalescence of monopolistic forces. Meanwhile the broader systemic contours of capitalism were left intact. Here the moral dimensions of political authority, in which the concept of sovereignty was derived from primal understandings of freedom, assumed greater importance as an exhortation to right conduct: One suspects that in Populism, the final barrier to capitalist dominance in the polity rested more on moral-exhortative than structural grounds. Government would delineate the welfare principle and create a climate for it, but it was to be externally imposed upon ongoing capitalistic operations.

Populists reinforced the structural context they were endeavoring to change; they wanted to maintain a system of capitalism, but not the prevailing mode. The conflict in their thought occurred because of the issue of antimonopolism; there was a tension between a radicalization of awareness and an objective radicalism that few Populists really considered as the ultimate destination of the movement. A practical resolution of this tension was found in competitive capitalism; the provision for public ownership enabled

Populists to adopt a broader pattern of restraint when it appeared that private industrial and financial dominance had been safely checked. If government furnished the structural locus of regenerative political and social relations, stimulating extracorporate economic development, such regeneration nonetheless had for its purpose the security of traditional patterns of organization within an industrial context, including the literal application of constitutional rights. Modernity was not at issue; rather, the inclusion of smaller holdings and the principle of just rewards became the test of its democratic orientation.

To be a viable force, competitive capitalism had to provide the methodical structuring of beneficence; the realization of public welfare could not be left to chance, impersonal laws of the market, or the prevailing organization of industry. Populists required a degree of public intervention to fulfill this goal, to further legitimate the principle of popular determination, and to support nonmarket social ethics. In sum, Populism's differentiation from the Smithian political economy lay in its attitude toward the polity itself.

A capitalist system divorced from welfare was unacceptable; perhaps the very retention of capitalism supposed the democratic control of industry. On ethical and practical grounds, Populists insisted that the social framework could not allow business development to express its fundamental purpose. In their conception, an internally activated economy was inseparable from a deeper configuration of political rights and observances. These would support the state as the mechanism of final resort in implementing a propertied democracy. The independent state, merging individual rights and public sovereignty, was capable of circumventing a monopolistically organized future.

Moral Sources of Intervention

Not the state alone, however, but its direct purpose and its matrix of values proved of decisive importance to Populists. In Smith, these factors were at best materialistically derived or subordinated to the prior claims of the market. It could be said that in a Smithian framework the citizenry was made up of so many calculators of personal advantage, encouraged to pursue the materialistic goals of individual advancement. Populists would rely instead on an independent citizenry, cognizant of its rights and standing and encouraged by that knowledge to establish political and social relations of mutual harmony.

Lloyd best captured the spirit of mutuality, which appeared only when the maximizing of individual advantage was renounced: "We are to become fathers, mothers, for the spirit of the father and mother is not in us while we can say of any child it is not ours, and leave it in the grime. We are to become men, women, for to all about reinforcing us we shall insure full growth and thus insure it to ourselves. We are to become gentlemen, ladies, for we will not accept from another any service we are not willing to return in kind."[20]

The conception of a meaningful political community, as the structural basis of the polity, necessitated precisely this acceptance of social obligation. Human betterment depended upon affirming the nation, not because Populists suffered from sterile patriotism, but because the nation embodied a potential for welfare and selfless conduct that contrasted with the value system of the prevailing economy. Lloyd implicitly distinguished between a fragmented market framework and an interdependent political community, and between the patterns of behavior within each formation, when he envisioned America's social possibilities. He made a tacit distinction, as well, between human and property rights:

> As we walk our parks we already see that by saying "thine" to every neighbor we say "mine" of palaces, gardens, art, science, far beyond any possible to selfishness, even the selfishness of kings. We shall become patriots, for the heart will know why it thrills to the flag. Those folds wave the salute of a greater love than that of the man who will lay down his life for his friend. There floats the banner of the love of millions, who, though they do not know you and have never seen you, will die for you and are living for you, doing in a thousand services unto you as you would be done by. And the little patriotism, which is the love of the humanity fenced within our frontier will widen into the reciprocal service of all men.[21]

The affirmation of government intervention questioned the adequacy of the self-adjusting mechanism and, more subtly, the process of internal economic generation whenever this process was left unhampered in an industrial-capitalistic setting. Populists viewed the state as the necessary complement of capitalism. It would function in the interests of capitalism, but the formation would bear the imprint of political democracy rather than corporate wealth. The critical factor here was the acceptance, not of capitalism, but of industrialism—a distinction Populists were quite able to formulate. Populists did not believe on a priori grounds that capitalism required stricter governance or correctives but that action was necessary when the system attained a more mature organizational and technological character. The state was a response to contemporary realities, and it would be called into being as an autonomous force for that reason. Populism's specificity of industrial concern differed from Smith's commercial emphasis, and this difference opened the way for the critical appraisal of the premise that egoistic behavior was fundamental to human nature.[22] In addition, the focus on industrialism provided the basis for the dissection of modernity, an accomplishment that could be credited to neither Smith nor late nineteenth-century American laissez-faire.

When the *Farmers' Alliance* claimed that the economic and psychological impoverishment of the individual was the prevalent condition of industrial life in a capitalist society, it presented a series of questions implying the need for a fundamental change: "How is he to have more time and more energy to develop his faculties except by lessening his hours of labor and increasing his wages? Can this be done under the present system? Has there been a better system in the world? Does not the problem of humanity demand that there shall be a better system?"[23] The attention devoted to labor's problems was itself a way of applying the criticism to an industrial and modern context: "The number unemployed is made to grow constantly greater and wages less by the pressure of poverty, our employing and distributing system being an autocrat-producing, mass-enslaving, pauper-manufacturing system."[24]

Industrialism, considered as a class relationship, had bred a pervasive condition of underconsumption: "Now what is life and so-called liberty if the means of subsistence are monopolized? Hunger-scourged, the dependent laborers must accept the wages that independent employers choose to offer, and the wages are made so low that the dependent cannot become independent."[25] It was doubtful that the market mechanism operated satisfactorily, or even that it operated at all: "How is it that the products of labor are in the hands of those who do not need them and will not use them, and the money too, while the people who produced all the goods have not money, or were found with insufficient money to buy back their products?"[26] The corollary of cheapening labor was denying laborers the means of self-protection: "In the condition of the labor market today, the laborer without an organization is at the mercy of an organized capital that knows no mercy. And capital's combines have issued the edict that labor organizations must be destroyed."[27]

The *Advocate's* discussion of labor-saving machinery, Peffer's treatment of modern production, Lewelling's concern about a reserve army of labor, Donnelly's description of an industrial underclass, and Lloyd's analysis of business organization all indicated the same general response to industrial conditions. Populists identified the problems of massive consolidations, widespread unemployment, and endemic collective disturbances. In these circumstances, it is not surprising that Populists would be led to discard egoistic premises and, more important, call for a reexamination of structural automatism and the means of achieving the social welfare. They would take little on faith, except the nation's political principles. With the rise of industrialism, the presumptive case was made for government intervention. Yet the principle of intervention had also, perhaps, a moral dimension. Populists not only questioned economic and political factors—automatism and welfare, respectively—but also maintained that the ultimate fate of the polity would rest on properly determining these factors. For this reason, the question of workability and the necessary connection between capitalism and the state had clearly exceeded narrow economic boundaries.

Furthermore, government intervention, especially when it took the form of public ownership, was an operational as well as an ideological repudiation of Smith; the operational repudiation had significance precisely because the conflict occurred within a capitalistic framework. The confrontation with Smithian economics was far more pointed than it would have been if Populists had adopted a noncapitalist mode and thus stepped around basic questions that were pertinent to capitalism's principles of organization.[28] Their intention to keep competition within bounds was opposed to the customary perspective on how capitalism functioned; in the conventional view, whether the frame of reference was structural automatism or government-business cooperation, an equitable distribution and greater productivity were taken as articles of faith. Populists acted to confine the range of competition because they recognized that independent state power was necessary to preserve competitive activity where it could exist; and they acted to stimulate the inner workings of the total economy because the restrictions of monopolism tended to result in depression.

The state would not resolve the problem of distribution directly, but it would counter two general trends that Populists associated with systemic breakdown and social misery: underconsumption, which was promoted by the power of business to set policies of low wages, prevent the formation of unions, and create a labor surplus; and the pattern of economic concentration, fostered by a compliant government, in which a process of selective growth stifled the capitalistic energies of the middle and lower strata of society. The state's effort to nullify monopolistic power would bear also on the issue of increased productivity, for the attempt to widen the scope of opportunity would entail loosening rigid prices and strengthening the social base of a vital domestic market. Unlike contemporary business opinion, Populist theory did not regard productivity as threatening the economy with the potential curses of overproduction or stagnation; Populists welcomed it as a challenge to be met by more equitable distribution and used it as an index of potential social health.

Observing that "labor can only, under its present conditions, have such a portion of that which it creates as suffices to forever keep it dependent and enslaved," Nugent shifted the focus from production to distribution: "Let us not forget that the millions of toilers are in more pressing need of remedy that shall prevent the unjust concentration of wealth, than they are for one which only can insure the increased production of wealth."[29] The fluctuations of the business cycle had little to do with overproduction, which was to be remedied through the aggressive search for foreign markets. Instead, Populists saw the basis for this alleged condition in long-term agricultural price declines, labor repression, high mortgage indebtedness, and the numerous points at which organized capitalism—notably railroads—impinged on productive activity in an exploitative relationship.

Populists distinguished between competitive capitalism and laissez-faire; although rejecting the latter mode, they did not embrace socialism. Rather, they sought its capitalist equivalent in the form of active state power because they wanted to retain competitive economic processes. They elevated the guardian role, making it a primary function of government; this countered both an ethic of social fragmentation and the legitimation of capitalism as the purpose of existence. The market should not define the individual, nor should the individual resolve merely to humanize the market. Populists had altered the meaning of the economic stage they wished to conserve: Indeterminate transactions and relations of power, based on a comprehensive notion of democratic opportunity, and given a political as well as a moral import, would create an openness of structure in which domination could not occur.

In contrast, they believed that unregulated laissez-faire was historically and organically connected to an emergent system of monopolism and threatened the survival of constitutional democracy founded on a sovereign public. Through state activism, Populists would modify the Smithian framework; this was also the prerequisite for addressing the modern form of capitalism. Through the process of clarification, they were able to identify corporate power as the supreme negation of autonomous government and individual liberty. Lloyd, for one, was confident of the future: "Mankind belongs to itself, not to kings or monopolists, and will supersede the one as surely as the other with the institutions of democracy."[30]

SEVEN

Comparative Economic Systems

It is necessary to enlarge the scope of my theoretical analysis to show more clearly the structural intersections of these capitalist modes and the place of Populism within the spectrum of capitalism. There was an affinity between the Populist and Smithian modes of capitalism because they both valued internal economic generation. It is equally significant that Populists qualified this position by ascribing heightened powers to the state in order to assure a competitive framework. The following discussion supposes the evidence and interpretation of the previous chapters; it is intended as a speculative essay in the largely uncharted area of historical macroeconomics as applied to Populism.

Preliminary Lines of Modal Conflict

In rebounding from Adam Smith, Populists appear to have embraced the contemporary capitalist mode, because both formations relied on government intervention. In fact, the role of the state was the differentiating factor in any comparison between the Populist and the contemporary mode. One might suppose that Populism was caught between opposing historical phases—the past economic theory of Smith and the present structural reality of the prevailing mode; but the attempt to apply a theory that no longer seemed operable was scarcely the beginning of their problem. In Smithian and contemporary capitalism, Populism confronted two formations that precluded the idea that the public interest had the principal claim on the authority of the state.

Populists believed that the public interest could not depend on existing capitalist mechanisms or patterns of wealth distribution for the predication of welfare. They did not concede that there was a foundation of welfare in capitalism as such, especially one deriving from either egoistic premises or a partnership of business and government. Populists were skeptical about the capitalist predication of welfare because the putative well-being of society merely confirmed the existing structure of power: The closed system failed to provide for the whole of society in the distribution of the social product. They appear to have realized that a predication of any sort, except one derived from an independent structure, would fail to sufficiently guarantee democratic opportunity and would present a plea for acquiescence in the idea that welfare was a natural product of the system. Populists advocated the autonomy of the state to compensate for the inability of the Smithian mode to implement welfare, but they also intended to counter current state practices because they encouraged the coalescence of privilege. The governmental factor was conceived as the mainspring of a sovereign public.

While in Smith's theory, the self-adjusting mechanism minimized the need for state activity, Populists believed that the mechanism could be preserved only through government intervention. They would counterpoliticize the total framework and create more favorable conditions for democratic growth through an infusion of independent state power. The result would be a modification of the contemporary capitalist mode as well. The rehabilitation of market operations in the intermediate range, imparting vigor to competition, was antithetical to a system of administered prices and private clusters of power; dislodging private monopolies from the remainder of the economy meant that their larger antimonopolist position was also preventative. The Populist and contemporary modes agreed about the need for a strong state, but there were profound differences in the purposes they believed the state should serve. These differences extended to the valuation they placed on capitalism, insofar as the state had the power to define its character and possibilities.

Populists showed less perspicacity in their analysis of the internal structure of capitalism than in their concept of the state, but they did not treat capitalism as an abstraction separable from the political order. Although they accepted the interdependence of capitalism and democracy, they did not regard capitalism as a pristine formation that (as it affected their understanding) had been mediated through the political culture of America. Populists' immersion in the American construct was both conscious and cautious; the burden had been put on capitalism to demonstrate its long-term historical connection with the democratic tradition.

One finds the Populist attitude toward this connection informally worked out in the body of Populist writings through several tacit premises. First, unimpeded capitalist operations were feasible on the condition that systemic energies and the attendant growth of the economy were not nullified by disproportionately powerful economic units. Second, the role of government, acting impartially, was to make the economy more progressive (that is, competitive), or, in the absence of private aggregations of power, to remain comparatively removed from the economic process. Third, this historical setting, or capitalist stage, was in the constitutional period, when government was dedicated to the principles of structural opportunity. It continued into the first half of the nineteenth century, when productive dynamism, supported by Jacksonian democratic activity, performed the roughly equivalent function of promoting competition.

Fourth, capitalism in America could still be endowed with a competitive and democratic capability in spite of the changes that had occurred, provided the state would assume increased powers consistent with the new realities, thus fulfilling the same underlying objectives. Populists accepted the idea of an irretrievable past; it had existed, however much it was politically romanticized, in a preindustrial situation that could no longer be duplicated. Fifth, these objectives centered on a course of nonpoliticized development, economic activity that in fact retained its *economic* complexion and did not become the basis for a system of private domination. The economic growth had to take place in a way that did not violate the broader principles of justice or penetrate the political-social realm of democratic society. Meeting politicization with counterpoliticization was not, in the opinion of Populists, a mere sleight of hand; it was a conscious attempt to penetrate beyond the deceptions of a formalistic democracy, and it was perhaps a precondition for retaining capitalism in any form.

Populists did not concede to capitalism a prima facie legitimation, nor did their immersion in the national political culture fully account for their ultimate willingness to equate capitalism with democracy. Populist economic thought had unusual clarity and subversive implications unusual in America because Populists subjected capitalism to a mental reservation. Not Lockeanism, but the way capitalism functioned in the historical process, was the primary basis of its legitimation and the test of its social efficacy. Populists' critical bent suggests this prior consideration: They found capitalism attractive because, and only to the degree that, it was modifiable.

In their view, factors intrinsic to capitalism shared a place with extrinsic factors; the latter stimulated the former and invested them with merit. Populists believed that the state had the power to restore the harmonious processes of a less complicated age, processes that, since the period of the Civil War, had appeared ill-suited to the features of more modern capitalism. Even though they had an almost reverential view of the early Republic, they accepted the capitalism-democracy equation that was derived from that period because, in their estimation, it deserved to be accepted, not because it was to be accepted on faith. The later period, of course, was treated more critically. For their own age, a forceful, specific, restorative intervention would be required if the presumption in favor of capitalism was to be freely granted. Capitalism was to be tested by not only the Populist version of the American past but also the system's current and future potentialities. Although the property right was not contested, the particularities of capitalist organization did not receive the same approval; they were considered harmful to the national welfare, and they presaged the further integration of monopolism and a compliant state.

The capitalism-democracy equation, however, led to complex results. Because public intervention was essential for uniting these separate elements into complementary parts of society, the Populist affirmation of the equation became an energizing force for political protest. Yet precisely because capitalism was a main constituent of this balanced formation, the equation also encouraged accommodation to society. In light of Populists' acceptance of the property right, this accommodation helped to define the outer limits of permissible reform.

Populists' reservation about capitalism sanctioned their questioning of capitalist foundations. The Populist counterpoliticization, which delegitimated the current framework, depended on the enhancement of state power, so that a public guardianship of political and human rights could be affirmed whenever capitalism exceeded acceptable limits. This was Populism's incipient compact theory. Still, their reservation did not condemn these foundations, nor did it provide a release from political obligation as it was traditionally conceived. The relational basis of Populism's identity must constantly be kept in mind. Competitive capitalism clearly was a form of capitalism; it rejected socialism as well as the Smithian and contemporary capitalist modes.

On the matter of political obligation, the compact represented an injunction to continue striving to achieve necessary alterations of society, but it did not confer a categorical right of social repudiation, through either separation or revolution. The act of striving was itself a sign of confinement within the political process, and while this act became a warrant for antimonopolism and encouraged a sense of mission, it also provided a stimulus to immersion in the Populists' construct of America. For Populists, separation was untenable because it suggested more profound rejections. It would have been necessary to repudiate their own animating spirit, including the search for political relevance, and their deeper attachment to America, specifically the democratic part of the equation.

Smith's framework of ideas had been modernized and rendered workable, but not transcended or abandoned altogether. The programmatic trend of

Populism altered the Smithian concept of the impartial state perhaps beyond recognition. The very call for an autonomous government introduced intervention and a clear standard of control. This stance could nevertheless be considered neutral because it posited a general welfare that conflicted with the narrow prescription of rights and priorities in the other modes of capitalism. A neutral state would affect structural automatism and a government-business partnership alike. Yet Populists also viewed Smithian nonmonopolistic principles as necessary to their case against the prevailing system. There was a degree of compatibility between Populists and Smith, even influencing Populism's structural revision of laissez-faire, that enables one to state the relationship between the three modes with greater precision.

The neutrality of the state entailed state activism. Populists found activism absent from the Smithian mode and politically charged in the contemporary mode. In the latter case, state activism resulted in converging structures of power; private and public elites formed a unified ruling stratum that was divorced from, but still manipulated, political democracy. If Populists had been limited to the choice of resurrecting laissez-faire or supporting the current framework and confining their goals to improvements within the given order, it seems likely, because of their belief in competition and their corresponding hope of more widely distributed power, that they would have favored the first course of action.

There were clear difficulties with laissez-faire. It was already identified with conservative politics and opinion; and although it theoretically recalled a simple economy, laissez-faire had actually been used to sanction the growth of a corporate economy. On the other hand, supporting the current system would have negated Populism's reason for being because Populists primarily opposed the deprivations caused by the established mode. They refused to confine themselves, however, to this binary paradigm, and for that reason Populism deserves study as a variant of capitalism in America. The affinity between the Smithian and Populist modes had a logic of its own that was based on a common historical placement and precarious existence in the face of the political and structural realities of capitalism's development. The question of historical placement also had relevance for Populism's relationship to the third formation.

An Inversion of Historical Dynamics

In the half-century following Smith, laissez-faire prepared the ground for monopolism by preserving intact an explicitly capitalistic value system and institutional context, which was absorbed by corporate capitalism once the industrial phase had begun. The result was not a purposeful direction; it was precisely the outcome that proponents of the laissez-faire stage, whether or not they anticipated industrialism, had sought to avoid. No ineluctable capitalist motion drove the historical process forward, but a possible explanation for what occurred lies in the transitional nature of laissez-faire itself. Even when it was ascendant and did not serve as a rationale by which to obscure privileged charters and monopolistic activities of a lesser scale, laissez-faire represented essentially a progressive interlude. It was the springtime of a nascent bourgeoisie that had rebelled against the political and economic restrictions of mercantilism, only to find that the formation was unstable because the necessary state power to prevent further business consolidation had not been established. Nor was it likely to be established with industrialism. To secure its position, the new upper stratum, acting as the consolidating elite, promoted the breakdown of the system responsible for its rise. The state brought into existence by this process would register the needs and wishes of dominant capital.

The bourgeois were heroic figures who, through their success, betrayed their own vision. Here the realities of capitalism's development were critically important. Smithian principles, except for the short-term purposes of an initial takeover, were unacceptable. They left a political void that had to be filled by a responsive government if the minimal, yet mandatory, setting for a mode of capitalism based on unrestricted accumulation and growth was to be achieved: the protection of property, often against competing entrepreneurs; the stabilization of class power not only to confirm prerogatives of ownership but also to compel public observance of social tranquillity; and the normalization of sources of enrichment, gained in part through an access to government. Implementing order required nothing less than this agenda, and in mature industrialism it required considerably more. In sum, capitalist trends worked through laissez-faire despite, or because of, this formation's unsuitability (except in its early stages) as an inclusive political structure.

But the more consequential main direction of capitalism was the progression from mercantilism to the contemporary stage. Capitalist development had leap-frogged over laissez-faire. Laissez-faire tended to be self-destructive because capitalist energies eventuated in the concentration of wealth and could not be replenished without drying up their original source, individualistic competitive activity. Moreover, it emphasized structural automatism, which was not adequate to the task of economic rationalization and social management under corporate capitalism. Laissez-faire increased its vulnerability by failing to dismount the preceding political and economic stage. Although mercantilism had been in temporary suspension as the demands of a new class were being satisfied, it remained a serviceable framework, the paradigm of the statist encouragement of monopolism. This framework, combined with the difficulties expressed by laissez-faire, provided important continuities of political and economic development. Prevailing capitalism became the reproduction of a mercantilist order that could encompass the requirements of modern large-scale enterprise. The process of leap-frogging was pertinent for Populism as well.

The Smithian and Populist modes had a still deeper affinity than might be suggested by their common opposition to monopolistic restrictions. In addition to rejecting the prevailing form of capitalism in its practical necessities, each mode threatened the historical process through which capitalist development had been embodied in a particular construction of the state. Although Smith emphasized the market and Populism emphasized cooperative conduct and values, both modes opposed a power complex that protected its own reproduction, wherein the enlargement of capitalism took on the proportions of a closed system that virtually corresponded to the nation-state. It was as though corporate capitalism represented the seemingly irresistible conflux of history, structure, and culture. In these circumstances, the challenge posed to the prevailing order could not be considered a mere intrusion or the continuation of an effort to achieve internal reform. The stages did not mesh. Something had to give way, and it clearly did: Both laissez-faire and Populism were destroyed.

Although it is possible to distinguish unintentional consequences from intent in assessing these frameworks, the fact remains that the adherents of laissez-faire and Populism identified with capitalism. Yet the arrest of synchronous institutional growth had been objectively projected by both modes. The self-adjusting mechanism and the neutral state alike would have fractured the contemporary structure because each would have severed the connection between the internal features of capitalism and their political support. In practice, this connection had become tantamount to an unbreakable foundation.

The increasingly systemic character of the political coordination of intraeconomic relations promoted monopolism and served as the vehicle for the continuity of economic development. Essentially, power underpinned what ordinarily appeared as exigent growth. Historical movement became the display of authoritative force; in this case, structural integration required the total organization of society. Even intrusive forces had a catastrophic import, not because they violated an ideological commitment to stabilization, but because they portended what an alternative structure of control would mean for continuing business-defined social contours.

Two distinct political economies, acting in the name of capitalism, endangered the basic capitalist framework as it was constituted then and in subsequent periods. Although the Smithian mode was centered on property, it opened, unlike the Populist mode, a vista of absolute chaos in the contemporary stage of economic development. To dispense with the protective state, in the presence of economic carnivores, might eventually lead to social war. But the more likely result would be a winner-take-all consolidation and deepening poverty. The absence of coordination, which removed the barriers to competition in enterprise, would accelerate the systemic fragmentation that government was designed to check. A structure that produced combativeness, regrouping into monolithic units, and pervasive social tension was hardly conducive to the security or predictability of capitalistic operations. In this configuration of forces, business members would have had to fend for themselves; therefore they had a strong incentive to construct a state that gave maximum attention to order and perhaps sacrificed democratic observances to direct business rule.

However, the Populist mode, less rigidly attached to property than the Smithian mode, represented a more practicable, but equally inconvenient, alteration of the existing stage. It could not be as readily dismissed by contemporaries. Populists' emphasis on political and structural realism made their alternative course viable. Laissez-faire could be used for rhetorical purposes by the governing synthesis of power, but not even the symbolic appropriation of Populism was possible for upper groups while the movement remained vital. The Populist variant appeared as an implosive force. It emerged from the same national matrix as the dominant mode, affirmed many of its key institutional features, and yet attacked the roots of contemporary power. For this reason, Populism was feared more than the earlier capitalist formation and more, perhaps, than it would have been if the movement had experienced a totally independent line of development.

Furthermore, in marking the dimensions of its challenge, Populism clarified the options available to prevailing capitalism in response to menacing systemic changes. The Populist variant did not threaten a structural rupture of society and hence did not furnish a pretext for antidemocratic solutions, on the grounds that it was infeasible or politically incoherent. Therefore coercion by the existing system was less easily disguised, and the elite were reminded that the conservation of the dominant position of business was the product of their conscious action.

Although this was, of course, a reminder and not a surprise to the political and business leadership, the result of stripping away the myth of an inevitable pattern of growth and its imperatives occasioned more than embarrassment. It encouraged the instrumental view of basic democratic principles, in which formal democracy, in contrast to a business takeover, would be continued as a developmental strategy, provided it met the test of total stabilization and proved impervious to the counterpoliticization envisioned by Populism. Business, reacting to the erosion of a class state, now saw more clearly that the basis of conflict with dissident forces was in the control of government and that the state was indispensable for the political coordination of the polity.

Business, like nature, abhorred a vacuum. But it abhorred even more the modern relevance that Populism had given laissez-faire; the apparent vacuum of political economy would be filled by the independent state. This would activate the laissez-faire formation, which had been largely overridden by long-term structural trends. In recurring to the affinity between the Smithian and Populist modes, the process of leap-frogging has increasing significance. A puristic bourgeois nation had hindered the vitality of a bourgeois stage through preventing the rise of competing historical fragments: The bourgeois element in American development was old before its time because it contained the newness of a monopolist disposition toward economic and social organization. This disposition in turn thwarted the development of forces necessary for operating on a separate historical track. The Smithian and Populist modes both had a precarious existence, but there was no social geometry involved here. Two negations of the same configuration did not necessarily make these negations equal, in either their cogency and critical thrust or the frameworks they sought to inaugurate. Instead, the similarity had meaning only when the Populist mode corrected for the deficiency in the laissez-faire mode by subsuming its antimonopolist principles within the structure of a democratic state.

Because Populism and laissez-faire were outside the main contours of American capitalist development and because their shared opposition to monopolism could be integrated into a unified position, the political means existed, as contemporary observers seemed well aware, for an inversion of long-term historical and structural dynamics. Populism embodied the potential for a reverse process of leap-frogging economic stages that would have retrieved the Smithian framework of values and modified it. The purpose was to remove the prevailing industrial forces from the political context in which they were currently administered and subject them to rules that would end the practices of collusion, restriction, and the creation of scarcity profits, thus correcting the existing condition of underconsumption.

Emergent monopolism, not history, was to be arrested. The bond between the two modes pointed up Populism's orientation toward the future. Populists envisioned a conversion from antimonopolist to postmonopolist goals; political democracy would liberate technology from the restraints of a property-centered framework as well as attack class privileges and the ideological supports that justified submissive behavior. Populism incorporated and then transcended laissez-faire.

The synthesis at least partly remedied laissez-faire's incompleteness. Under the aegis of Populism, a structural fracture would rearrange power rather than merely create chaos. Populists believed that it would also furnish the basis for a more stable polity, for only if opportunity were democratized would capitalism achieve an acceptable degree of social harmony. Ideally Populism would appropriate the future by closing all paths to antidemocratic solutions.

Populists focused on the state because they were concerned about the possibility that corporate power, with or without provocation, was already transforming the nature of government. They had observed the evolution from the informal partnership of business and government to a rigidly stabilized arrangement that was dimming the prospects for any but a narrowly conceived entrepreneurial freedom. The urgency that helps to explain the terms on which the People's party entered the 1896 presidential campaign suggests a merger of political and structural objectives in attempting to prevent the next stage of capitalist development. In this light, a reverse process of leap-frogging signified not only that the Populist variant would skip over prevailing capitalism but also that it would intentionally seek its replacement. This was the essential condition of democratization in any meaningful form, even if, as Populists insisted, capitalist premises still remained.

Democracy, Capitalism, and the State

The Populist experience, based on the realities of power, becomes a study in the varieties of capitalism. Descriptively, the Populist variant, as an alternative modernizing pattern, represented a people's movement to restructure government; and politically, the outcome of the experience testified to the disparities of strength between the contesting formations. In the monolithic corporate order varieties of capitalism had no place, legitimation, or basis for advancement after the late nineteenth century. One is forced always to treat Populism in the conditional sense, as an actuality that United States historical development reduced to a hypothetical construct because it was never permitted a proper test. Despite its emphatic and concrete protest in which it delineated positions, maintained an organization, and actually won some campaigns, the movement only projected the dynamics of political and social change. It did not have the opportunity to carry out its plans for restructuring American capitalism. The authoritative retribution that followed under Progressivism and in later periods took the form of a liberal counterrevolution to forces already successfully checked; this was the political significance of the 1896 election. The reaction appeared necessary, not because the state realized an autonomous status and the polity assumed an antibusiness direction, but, on the contrary, because the very existence of Populism presaged a system of structural development and social ethics that could not be allowed even an ideational representation in the twentieth century.

Populism had to be kept permanently submerged beneath the historical surface. One perforce deals with failure, but not with nonexistence: Populism was removed from the historical agenda in spite of every endeavor to become a politically consequential vehicle for dissent because the forces of property believed that a substantive confrontation was undesirable and outside the grounds of legitimate debate. A dream might possess greater reality than the reality that denied the dream. In the case of Populism, an efficacious program for social welfare was a certain ticket to oblivion. Yet the hypothetical construct still has immediacy because so little has been changed in the dominant outlines of the political economy. The pertinence of the Populist variant is in what has failed to happen since its disappearance: a democratization of industry, government, and the foundations of the polity.

Populists saw that their choices were not limited to laissez-faire and contemporary capitalism, and they selected an independent path to the future. They relied on an autonomous state but left the capitalist framework comparatively unscathed once it had been denied its political support, thus creating a precarious balance of conflicting forces. It was natural for Populists to emphasize the state because they viewed it as the guardian and implementing mechanism of political democracy, but they may have reversed the error of Smith, who assigned disproportionate weight to the economy. They reposed such trust in the powers of government that their dissociation of capitalism from its political support obscured their understanding of the power residing within capitalism itself. Under the Populist variant, the internal features of capitalism would exist within, but create pressures antagonistic to, the new political framework. These pressures in turn would require the active countermeasures of a neutral state when capitalist features took on monopolistic proportions.

The cost of failing to dismount capitalism, thereby making government responsible for containing it, would have been a constant tension between the economy and the state. The tension could be resolved only if the state continuously enlarged the public sector to keep pace with the dynamic force of capital accumulation. This magnitude of involvement had not been sanctioned or even contemplated by their ideology in what Populists regarded as normal circumstances; but the problem, of course, was that circumstances could not be normal so long as the economic structure had the potential for recombining its elements and becoming monopolistic whenever public surveillance lessened or the political climate changed. Realistically, the Populist variant, despite Populists' expectation that the pattern of capitalism would be muted under a regime of strict antimonopolism, had not provided the structural safeguards needed to arrest internal systemic motion.

This basic irresolution derived in part from the very affirmation of political democracy because this induced a complacent attitude toward capitalism and a confidence in government as an agency of restraint; but it also resulted from Populism's rejection of what was conceivably the only barrier to renewed capitalist ascendancy—the alternative of socialism. The containment of capitalism would have been a consuming task, but democratic capitalism under Populist guidelines would not have been impracticable, especially if antimonopolism was treated as a principle of public responsibility and a focal point of political mobilization. Rather, the analysis points up the imperfect nature of the transcendent vision of Populism; there was to be a democratization of property, and not a transformation leading to its abolition. In positive terms, Populists questioned the ideology that presented property as an absolute right; they intended to modify capitalism from within through an ethic of humaneness and the creation of social bonds. Their cooperative outlook denied the atavistic premises of existing conceptions of wealth.

Because they saw political attachment rather than internal processes as the more threatening aspect of capitalism's historical make-up, Populists were not fully aware of the need to assess the features of capitalism under the influence of political democracy as well as in the prevailing order. This omission reinforced their dependence on externally derived solutions rather than on the elimination of critical systemic attributes. Yet their approach to capitalism was not tangential, for in identifying the partnership of government and business as the salient trait of the modern capitalist political framework, they grasped the unitary nature of the monopolist paradigm, even when they had not taken the measure of its private component. Populists may have too facilely equated nonmonopolism with freedom, particularly because capitalism would remain in the democratic structure, but it was important that they accepted the converse proposition: They equated monopolism with the absence of freedom.

Capitalism had to be integrated with the Populist variant and not become a bridgehead for private sovereignty. A faint stigma was attached to capitalism even when it was transposed to the Populist context, especially in the treatment of corporate organization, whether or not the requirements for monopolism were present. For Populists, not only the size but also the systemization of operations caused concern because they feared that internally cohesive major enterprises had introduced an economic form that was potentially incompatible with a democratic polity. The corporation had become a self-contained entity. The business firm impersonalized economic development and became a law unto itself: cold, calculating, sealed from public inspection, unwilling to subordinate its needs and welfare to those of society. Populists used the term "bloodless" to describe this process of drawing inward.

While accepting the details of everyday capitalist life, Populists were more critical when their analysis moved up the scale of business; the categories of capitalism were retained, approved in principle but, in varying degrees, qualified in practice. They assumed that the wage relation would govern employment policies, but when they considered labor's rights as a broader social question, thus identifying issues of class and power in which the stakes appeared higher, they frequently criticized the wage system and specifically approved unionization as a means of redressing the imbalance between labor and capital. They similarly credited an entrepreneurial function, but their support of labor led them to oppose customary habits of deference to upper economic groups, build alternative power bases, and, when the principle of a labor theory of value had been stated, question existing patterns of distribution and incentive. The experience of cooperative activity, especially, refuted the single-minded absorption in profits and the primacy of exchange-value over use-value in production. By qualifying these categories of capitalism—the qualifications have relevance for other categories as well—Populists did not prefigure an anticapitalist formation, but they did begin separating the political and economic elements of the tightly integrated structure of contemporary capitalism. Even slight modifications of this structure would have an effect on the whole because the categories themselves were interconnected. According to Populists, the precarious balance of forces created by their own analysis should ideally result in benefits to the public.

Because both capitalism and democracy were essential parts of the variant, Populists considered such a balance healthy if business could be depoliticized and prevented from intervening in the organization of society. This condition required implementing a public sovereignty. Yet an active state would break the bonds between contemporary capitalism and democracy only to re-create them under more satisfactory conditions. Within the Populist variant, the state would function through the ascription of its effective control to assure the inclusion of capitalism. This incorporation was more matter-of-fact than if a capitalist economy had been held to be less governable. Transformed capitalism invited Populists' profound regard and had a preferential status as the logical expression of the Populist variant's structure.

The process of extrication from the Smithian mode suggests Populism's deep-seated commitment to capitalism, for the purpose of a structural revision of laissez-faire was to maintain capitalism as a functional system in a democratic polity. Mechanisms inadequate to the requirements of political democracy were to be eliminated, but the internal features of capitalism as such were to be retained. In the industrial phase of development, structural automatism had ushered in an unregulated capitalism with neither systemic provision for welfare nor acknowledgment of an anterior public interest; this mode loosened all constraints on the progression of economic forces toward monopolism and private aggregations of power.

On the one hand, Populists sought to initiate political change through a closed system that they could not go beyond. They confronted the prevailing mode as if it were definitionally sound but currently misshapen. They did not view it as the advent of a new capitalist stage that required more than modifying laissez-faire to bring it within the framework of political democracy. Populists had not broken the continuum. Using Smith with the intention of replacing contemporary capitalism, they actually traversed a long historical corridor. Notwithstanding their vision of the future, this would have produced a revised version of the old context rather than a new one. The process of extrication from the Smithian mode was less dialectical than sequential because Populists limited their alteration of contemporary capitalism to the changes that competitive capitalism permitted. Their commitment to capitalism was reinforced through their adopting a political orientation, which narrowed the range of dissent and directed transformative energies inward to basic institutions. Protest was confined to channels that society had established to legitimate existing patterns of dominance and neutralize popular impulses toward change.

On the other hand, to maintain capitalism as a functional system would require disarranging the parts of the existing system and changing the historical process. The Populist perspective was accommodating, but it disturbed even as it submitted to the basic flow, for Populists had assigned to competitive capitalism an element—public guardianship—that was not derived from the old context and could not be reconciled with the new one. Their proposed structural course was sequential, but it was not lineal. They added modern features to laissez-faire by advocating a postmercantile independent state that would support antimonopolism and social cooperation. Moreover, they added seemingly obsolescent features to contemporary capitalism, particularly a viable system of competition, that were drawn from their partly mythical version of laissez-faire.

The transpositions were not made indiscriminately. The genius of Populism lay in the way it had recast laissez-faire. This involved more than a structural revision; it had pertinence for modern capitalism as a potentially disruptive force. The creation of another historical choice depended on Populism's almost uncanny insight into the systemic vulnerability of a monopolist formation when its political foundations had been successfully reclaimed for democratic governance. Populists advocated modifications of both the old and the new structure, even though they had few capitalist precedents to guide them.

Populism was innovative in the finest sense of the term; it distilled political and economic principles that might have been retrograde if they had not been integrated with a democratic state. Without the Populist translation, laissez-faire, as a self-contained position, represented an outmoded formation that was incapable of controlling economic forces in the industrial context. It was powerless to regenerate itself because a free market had no support under the prevailing organization of business. Laissez- faire without the Populist modification was an open field for the invasion of monopolism: a reactionary configuration in which the polity was unable to defend itself against economic concentration and therefore had to accept the inevitability of contemporary power arrangements and the modernizing design.

The historical circumstances that originally invested laissez-faire with a progressive meaning had ceased to exist in the new order. Populists supplied the vital spark to laissez-faire through the provision of an active, neutral state; and, in a more subtle process of historical disarrangement, they added a new dimension of class forces that alone gave the formation its progressive direction. In sum, Populists introduced a modified laissez-faire into the setting of corporate capitalism in an attempt to duplicate the operative context that had inspirited the Smithian system. They were not, however, representing an ascending class in conflict with a previous mode, but a submerged populace in desperate straits in need of a variant as a political and structural alternative to the prevailing mode. The fight made by laissez-faire in its initial surge was now placed at a higher stage of capitalism. Populism was perhaps the last authentic bourgeois social and political force; or rather, from the standpoint of comparative history, it was the functional equivalent of such a force.

Conclusion: The Liberal Counterrevolution

Finally, Populism can be distinguished from twentieth-century liberalism because it anticipated and responded to the interrelated challenges of monopolism and government-business partnership, thus helping to clarify the meaning of modern reform. Here one might speak of a contemporary/liberal mode to suggest that American capitalism had a unified political and economic phase of development from at least the period that saw the rise of Populism. Business consolidation was a main indicator of this phase. However, it is necessary to add that liberalism historically signified the form of state intervention, beginning in the administrations of McKinley and Roosevelt, that was designed to achieve a more systematic integration of the business order. It expressed and extended the framework in which business and government were interpenetrated. Since the demise of Populism, the reform process has been serviceable to large-scale enterprise by preserving the fiction of the popular control of industry in the face of a contrary economic reality. Among the major components of reform, regulation became the rationalization of the market structure in consultation with business, planning became the public authorization of private-corporate anticompetitive practices, and welfare became the compensatory spending to make up for deficiencies in consumption while business pursued a strategy of profits through underutilized human and productive resources.

Populism revised the Smithian mode, but it was equally, if not more, resistant to the contemporary/liberal mode. Its resistance to liberalism took on special meaning because Populism differed from liberalism in its conception of the state in relation to capitalism. The purpose of modern reform—the enlargement of a capitalist state to stabilize the power of corporate wealth—was in contradistinction to a politically autonomous state, which would maintain an independent regulative function to superintend the direction of capitalism. Liberalism possessed an affinity with monopolism, so long as the state was left free to expand its welfare activities. The result was a denigration of welfare because its existence supposed the very arrangements of power that made it necessary, suggesting a perhaps inadvertent tolerance of oppression in order to meliorate its consequences.

The discontinuity between Populism and modern liberal reform is apparent in the response of each mode to this question: Does capitalist industrialism entail monopolism? The liberal mode has permitted a lax antitrust policy, reflecting the normalization of the government-business partnership. It has also been coextensive with the unprecedented growth of monopoly and the increased disparity in the distribution of wealth (as measured by income-tenths) in the course of the twentieth century. This historical performance, including the more recent militarization of the industrial economy, was hardly conducive to democratic gains in the two critical areas, business concentration and income shares, that were most germane to the exercise of power in American society.

The pattern of liberal reform did not improve when landmark measures affecting a comprehensive federal labor policy had been added. Instead, the welfare sector was integral to the systemic coordination of the political economy. It fostered predictable operations and reduced social tensions, just as the broader social emphasis was a part of ongoing economic stimulation in response to business fluctuations, stagnation, and declining rates of profit.

Liberal reform was absorbed into capitalism. Reform not only provided social palliatives, but it also became a political force in the shift from emergent monopolism to a monopoly-capital stage: The Wilsonian framework of administrative centralization gave way in the interwar years to monopolistic self-policing under private auspices, and then, in the New Deal, under public auspices. Major enterprise formed a constant around which government programs had to revolve. The response of liberalism to monopolism has been regulation, which invariably failed to match public with business power.

Liberalism did not require the deconcentration of industry, and it was still less likely to require government ownership, which was considered an improper recourse that was not built into the regulatory machinery. From their inception, regulatory commissions in the United States constituted a structural extension of the business system; they provided sympathetic guidance to, and functioned as assemblies of, representatives from the sectors to be regulated. In broader terms, for much of the twentieth century the supervision of business has been removed from the political process to the higher ground of administrative decisions, abstracting corporate power from legislative remedies and control and from any kind of adversary relationship. In practice, liberal reform has answered the question of whether capitalist industrialism was possible without monopolism by inverting the purported objectives of regulation. It sought to demonstrate an antecedent public interest through successfully placing the corporate order at the foundation of the polity. Liberalism was the logical inheritor of structural tendencies toward a closed political and economic system.

In contrast, Populism was predicated on the entire feasibility of antimonopolism; its fundamental premise was the negative relationship between monopolism and industrialism under capitalism. The political character of capitalist development—a reliance on the state to buttress economic concentration—was to be reversed by installing an autonomous government. Populism's distinctive feature—if still falling considerably short of socialism—was the authority of the state, which was given effectual powers and jurisdiction. The comparison was more telling in regard to liberalism, which claimed the same semantic ground on regulation, than in regard to the Smithian and prevailing modes, which did not make this claim.

While in Populist usage the literalistic interpretation of basic principles repudiated all inversions of constitutional power when political democracy was involved, the implied criticism of liberal reform in particular was that the strengthening of the state under the nominal aegis of social welfare principles still meant the abrogation of public sovereignty. Liberalism rejected the state's independence and supported the coalescence of internal capitalist features that made practicable the next capitalist stage. The effectual powers of the state had relevance to not only the contemporary mode but also its subsequent liberal refinement. More was involved than preventing monopolism. Closing antidemocratic paths to the future would open the pattern of development itself; there would be a movement toward structural indeterminateness and political fluidity that could create a favorable setting for social reconstruction and democratic opportunity.

Populists proposed to confine an indeterminate course within the limits of competitive capitalism, without appreciating the contradiction. Yet despite their being capitalists, they were perceived as a menace to the contemporary structure of capitalism. Capitalism had left them behind in their own time, not because the Populist formation was outmoded, but because it was depoliticized, asserting an essential neutrality of the state that was unacceptable to upper groups. It posed clear lines of authority and denied the political framework needed to maintain an emergent monopolist mode.

The Populist variant illustrated the way in which the varieties of capitalism differed in their interpretations of power. For Populists, the relation between industrialism and monopolism was based on the locus of sovereignty in American society; this view was in opposition to modern capitalism's insistence on a state favorably disposed to business. Through a vision that excluded the full political dimensions of capitalism, Populists had initiated a conflict not only between varieties of capitalism but also between a rapidly accelerating dominant mode and a mode that perhaps came closer than any other in America to being a people's formation. It had only an ideologically mobilized lower stratum to resist monopolism.

The bourgeois were heroic figures who, through success, betrayed their vision; the Populists were antiheroes who, confronting failure, expressed an antimonopolist countervision of a people's government. The entrepreneurs, as befitted their position of dominance, merely decreed their "vision" of sterile order and gain; and the liberals, the beneficiaries of a prior stabilization, benignly pronounced what they intended, not as a vision, but as reality: a responsible corporatism in which major enterprise, given a soul, was settled within a framework of countervailing powers that pointed toward the vital center. The elimination of Populism was the historical condition that made possible modern corporate liberalism, itself an emergent monopolism that was then actualized. The prime casualties of this process were not only Populism and its doctrine of a public guardianship but also political and structural fluidity.

There was a drastic narrowing of historical alternatives in response to Populism's countervision of independent governance. Populism disrupted the model of equilibrium that a business polity sought to confirm for itself. It protested against private sovereignty and state-activated monopolization, and because the setting was so rigidly maintained on behalf of the political security of business, this protest was interpreted as a total ideological challenge. That the challenge occurred within capitalism did not make it acceptable; in fact, it was probably more keenly felt because of its indigenous, nonsocialist origins. Populists found themselves in a strange fix because their being capitalists was no defense against the attack of capitalism. This situation would have been unlikely in a society based on more variegated social and political principles.

The ideological rigidity of American capitalist development magnified differences that existed in the same institutional range. It must be said, however, that never before in America's experience had a capitalist (and largely agrarian) movement evinced enough critical penetration to question the structural attributes of capitalism. Populism was reform-oriented, but the issues it addressed fell more properly in the domain of radical political forces. Nonetheless, Populists were unable to adopt a radical identity because of the binding nature of American society's historical pattern and political culture. This identity might conceivably have been realized in a setting in which unrestrained capitalism and the inordinate commitment to stability did not exist.

Populism's location within the American historical framework had ambiguous consequences for shaping its protest. The magnification of differences acted as a catalyst to political awareness. At the outset, it encouraged the voicing of grievances in a hostile climate that offered little hope of conciliation. The stark contrast between the Populist effort and the climate itself promoted a greater sense of radicalism than the position warranted; an innocent, but not harmless, false consciousness sustained Populists in the face of grave difficulties. Yet the exaggeration of differences also retarded protest by engendering their conviction of great ideological breadth. Populists were concerned that their differences with the existing order might carry the movement beyond the spectrum of capitalism, and this paradoxically recommitted them to a dialogue in which it appeared unnecessary to go outside the prescribed range of dissent.

The entire context of history and culture militated against self-discovery, and yet, in spite of their tendency toward immersion in the United States, Populists persisted in their quest for a humanly fulfilling capitalism. They ascribed vitality to the past because it offered an unequivocal declaration of political rights. Moreover, it posed a standard of capitalist performance in contemporary society, acting as a springboard to a democratic future. But despite Populists' emphasis on the past, their innovative theory of autonomous government was derived from experience as much as from the political and ideological guides they believed were present in the American heritage. They exhibited a conscientious devotion to, and yet an instrumental use of, the principles of the Republic, creatively adapting the past while drawing from it both inspiration and precedents, real or contrived, for legitimating current antimonopolism.

Although it is difficult to imagine, if Populists had succeeded in breaking free of American political culture to discover the sources of their ideology within themselves, the process of democratization would have been unhampered by a prior structure of thought. Their consciousness was limited by capitalistic premises and political inhibitions. But because Populists were not outside of history, they must be viewed in terms of the imperfect transcendence they achieved. They fostered an ideological growth that emanated at least in part from the experience of protest, and they questioned capitalist power as it functioned through a compliant government. The achievement was considerable because it took place within a reformist context that was less resistant than radicalism to cultural and structural absorption. In fact, Populism is best revealed by its transvaluation of the meaning of reform.

If Populism was not radical, it also was not liberal; it had set itself against a formula of political development that, in encouraging administrative regulation and the corporate integration of society, would determine the twentieth-century liberal strategy of welfare-supported domestic underconsumption and state-supported commercial expansion. Liberalism strengthened monopolistic enterprise by synchronizing it with government; and Populists regarded this process as the antithesis of democratic modernization. Populism's own formula, which, unlike later reform, emphasized the indeterminateness of political and structural development, was a truism of formal democratic theory: Monopolism *was* preventable.

This truism took on grandeur when matched with subsequent events. The basic features of modern capitalism were developed under a liberal framework precisely when, if Populism's conception of reform possibilities had been followed, the whole edifice might have been dismantled or reconstructed at a critical stage. The narrow ideological spectrum in America, thinly populated outside the middle range in support of property, still revealed here gradations that constituted a qualitative difference.

Although it rejected radicalism, Populism was the incipient revolution within reformism that must be contrasted with the liberal counterrevolution of political and economic stabilization in the twentieth century. Populism envisioned an inadmissible future; it advocated the change from systemic interpenetration to a political democracy as the organizing principle of society. This intent reflected the broader goal of creating a socially concerned and responsive polity.

In summary, Populists sought an alternative path that brought them to the outer limits of capitalism. They approached the border between radicalism and reform: a position of authentic reform, which would establish democratic capitalism. They transcended liberalism, if not America—decrying as enemies of human freedom the privately dominated state and the materialism of contemporary society, which were negating the existence and very meaning of democracy. Populism was more American than America had any right to expect.

Epilogue: Property and Democracy

Populism shaped a distinctive pattern of capitalist development in America. It rejected both the structural automatism of laissez-faire and the political integration of emergent monopolism in favor of an autonomous framework of government. Populists called for an independent state that would guide economic forces, using moral, legal, and constitutional standards derived from the concept of an antecedent general welfare. Possessing the historical vantage point of the late nineteenth century, they perceived the breakdown of a market system founded on the principles of Adam Smith. They believed this structural instability was rooted in a state formation that could not preserve freely competitive activity after the rise of modern industry. Their vantage point also enabled them to appreciate the crucial change that was occurring in the relationship between capitalism and the state in the context of modernization: the interpenetration of business and government, which they believed not only shattered the market mechanism but, in fusing the private and public realms of power, destroyed the foundations of sovereignty in a political democracy.

These criticisms did not originate from anticapitalist premises. Populists began their analysis with an acceptance of the institutions of property; and, particularly in the American setting of pervasive Lockean values, such an orientation placed their capitalist identity and the ultimately nonradical character of their movement beyond question. Yet a basis for serious political and structural disagreement still remained. Through their ideology and concrete protest, Populists demonstrated that historical varieties of capitalism were possible. In turn, the very suppression of Populism as an alternative force of ideas and development testified to the inflexibility of the prevailing mode of capitalism in responding to divergences from the main pattern of growth. America's own lack of historical, ideological, and structural resilience made the Populist challenge appear greater than it was (even for the Populists themselves) in what remained a struggle representing essentially intracapitalist differences on the nature of the polity.

The primary issue was this: Could property and democracy be reconciled in a workable system? Populists valued both property and democracy; they believed that they had once existed in harmony and could be unified in the future through a political economy of democratic capitalism. But they also found that in contemporary society the very form of property was being altered; it was being transformed from a means of livelihood, personal security, and social-political independence to a massive, impersonally administered unit of power that had the potential for expropriating individually based holdings, exercising domination over others, and controlling the state itself.

Property was taking on a politicized character. Through a process of consolidation, it was exerting influence through the entire range of society's activities. Populists believed that this organized appropriation through corporate mechanisms made necessary the assertion of the rule of law, if capitalism were to be subsumed under the control of legitimate authority. In ways that the rising middle classes in England earlier in the century would have understood, Populists conceived their mission as a property-oriented defense of human freedom. They performed the functional equivalent of the bourgeoisie in its ascendant phase, representing a progressive social force in the historical creation of democratic institutions.

The terms "reform" and "radicalism" are not helpful in analyzing Populism. The general spirit of Populism was clearly moderate. It rejected class principles of social organization and political change. Populists offered in their place a doctrine of constitutionalism that would establish the polity, including its economic structure, within the framework of law and historically interpreted principles of justice. They thereby accepted the fundamental social order in which this framework of law and justice was conserved. And they willingly confined their protest to societal boundaries consistent with their understanding of the American past.

Yet Populism demonstrated political and ideological vitality. The movement's primary allegiance to an exceptional America, which became identified with the democratic heritage itself, inspired a wide-ranging critique of the existing capitalist system. An acceptance of property did not preclude (indeed, it encouraged) the modification of the prevailing system. Populists would alter contemporary capitalism's systemic features, ideological values, and social relationships, all for the purpose of asserting the standard of the sovereign public and the achievement of welfare and individual human dignity.

Public ownership, as derived from constitutionalism and the sovereignty of a people's government, was particularly important for demonstrating autonomous state power. This power, given its legitimating sources, enabled Populists to range freely across the political spectrum with the confidence that extensive structural change would not endanger the property right or a capitalist economy as such. Yet the effect of public ownership would be far-reaching: It would correct concentrated private power in decisive sectors of the economy; it would weaken the universal application of the property right; and it would liberalize economic processes by opposing monopolistic pressures that restricted the growth of enterprise in the middle and lower strata of society. In essence, it would change the configuration of social rights and participation that defined the structure of the political economy. Public ownership would broaden the social base of capitalism. At the same time, it would also attack the idea, if not completely the practice, of class dominance.

However, the force that was potentially more damaging to the contemporary mode of capitalism was the rule of law, which had deep symbolic meaning for Populists. The law represented constitutional democracy. It alone perhaps could serve as the counterweight to prevailing capitalism as a total system. The law and capitalism derived from the same fundamental social order, but this only heightened the applicability of the law to the needs of, and the direction taken by, the polity. The law and monopolism were diametrically opposed as formulas of social legitimacy for establishing the permanent basis of authority. They were also opposed as frameworks of political obligation for defining the responsibilities as well as rights of the diverse social elements. The law would primarily become the voice of the individual and the community and then secondarily of the business system. Law connected capitalism and democracy; their interdependence would hold true only if capitalism accepted the prior restraints propounded in the legal foundations of society.

Law is conspicuously associated with reform; yet it endowed Populism with radical possibilities because it supported the proposition that capitalism was governable. This idea contradicted the axioms of Sumner, who believed that the social system was governed by its own material norms, so that independent ethical valuations of its principles and performance were not valid. Populists feared that the absence of ethical and social criteria in judging capitalism had led to the materialization of democracy. This form of the polity was inhumane and lifeless, and it rejected basic principles of liberty. Furthermore, the idea that capitalism was governable enhanced the political argument for government power. The state would serve as the guardian of liberty. Populists sought an autonomous position in addressing capitalism: They inhabited a capitalistic universe, but were bound by antecedent moral, political, and legal values. The state, because it was responsible for the public welfare, should create a jurisprudential framework of political rights that would advance broader social and moral claims and affect the status of corporate capitalism as well.

Populists, in their view of freedom, revealed unmistakable signs of classical liberalism. In Populist ideology, the ideal of individualism and the recurrent imagery of the home suggested multiple economic and philosophical connections between freedom, independence, and personal identity that were rooted in a system of property. Populists did not fully transcend the tenets of a Lockean political culture. Still, they expressed the liberal impulse in a more vital setting of ideas, which included the ideal of commonwealth and the belief in individual fulfillment through social cooperation. Both of these also helped to define the meaning of freedom. In Populism, this social vision did not necessarily have a socialist content; it did, however, provide a basis for reapportioning the political and legal claims that were assigned to the polity and its system of enterprise. Within American ideology, a notion of community struggled for recognition; capitalism was not the exclusive purpose for social existence.

Finally, the law served to legitimate state action with respect to capitalism. For Populists, law was inseparable from human powers of reason and self-governance. Moreover, because it also dealt with substantive rights, the law tended to demystify a national-cultural past that had been too narrowly identified with the institutional goals of property. Populists had enlarged the contextual meaning of political democracy. Their reasoning on law and the state led directly to a second basic proposition: The public welfare had precedence over contemporary sanctions of private wealth. Not only was capitalism governable, but the impartial role of the state would take on structural significance.

Three specific contentions are evident: The preferential treatment of government toward business had to be stopped; the moral and social claims of the free person had to be extended to the economic realm in order to insure a meaningful participation in the productive community by those who were currently dispossessed of opportunity; and the state itself had to be endowed with independent powers, to give vigor to the public jurisdiction. For Populists, government was the people's sovereign exercise of political authority. This view of government not only legitimated, but also *mandated,* active intervention in economic affairs.

Populists argued that a pattern of unimpeded capitalist development had been established; there had been a progression from laissez-faire through corporate capitalism to a fully realized monopolistic order. The traditional notions of liberty that were founded on the spirit of individualism had spawned a monster in the form of consolidated holdings that destroyed the marketplace. The independent state could stop this concourse that began with classical liberalism. (Populists recognized a qualitative change with the corporate growth that occurred in the post-Civil War society; they treated monetary contraction as one symptom of the fundamental collaboration of business and government.) But equally important, the state had also to address the more immediate political consequences of a monopolistic abrogation of the marketplace.

Populists granted that industrialism was an irreversible process and that it could entail a significant degree of economic concentration. Yet with utter realism they took these factors as grounds for their advocacy of public ownership. In addition to public functions that were already the responsibility of the government, natural monopolies had arisen that could not be entrusted to private hands. However, if the necessary condition for government intervention was the growth of monopolism, the sufficient condition for government intervention was the inherent inability of laissez-faire to maintain its own existence.

Populists did not approve of a self-adjusting mechanism as such. They were little interested in seemingly objective laws of allocation as a guide to the overall regulation of the economy. Rather, they associated laissez-faire with historical circumstances and structural conditions that might encourage the freer play of economic forces: Specifically, the market would be based on the decentralization and dispersal of power. Units capable of exercising control of production and exchange would be eliminated. Conversely, the consolidation of property created an undue influence in, and a retardation of, the economic process; the formation of private aggregates held the political components of a broader system of dominance. Economic dispersion worked against private and public collaboration; monopolistic coalescence virtually insured it.

Populists therefore feared that the breakdown of the older political economy would lead to a class state, the organization of property into a new system of power. Augmenting the powers of the state would correct the inability of laissez-faire to preserve competition in the face of cumulative business growth. It would also challenge a rival center of power in the contemporary mode of capitalism that had resulted from the combined patterns of the classical and later prevailing stages. Laissez-faire was structurally anachronistic; emergent monopolism was politically undesirable. Through an autonomous government, Populists sought to liberate the progressive forces they believed were still latent in capitalism—including its potential for overcoming conditions of poverty—as the first step in achieving a greater equity in productive and social relations.

An autonomous government, founded on the principle of public sovereignty, would modify laissez-faire. The state would bolster the market mechanism by circumscribing it, an apparent paradox that expressed for Populists the realistic assessment of existing relationships of power.

A mixed economy was necessary if any form of nonmonopolistic capitalism were to exist under the conditions of modern industry. Competition would be enhanced where it was practicable; the affected economic arena would represent a multitude of transactions and common possessory rights that would not create the prospect of private domination in society and government.

Populists considered capitalism as it operated in the lower and intermediate economic and structural reaches of society to be largely unobjectionable, except in social values. To conserve this range of activities, they sought to make collective the topmost level because it both restricted the levels below it and exerted maximum pressure on the market mechanism. They asserted that the economic stranglehold of corporate wealth would be broken through government ownership of monopolies and more particularly through government power over public functions, as in banking and transportation. Therefore, the state was enlisted to modify the contemporary stage of capitalism as well, to break the structural connection between the classical and prevailing modes. Populists favored a form of capitalism based on the democratization of modernity.

Populists believed that monopolism flourished because of government favoritism. Political assistance accounted for the privileges that placed the corporation above the law and defined its method of achieving continued stimulation. The resort to political solutions, business control of the state, had replaced the internal generation of economic forces in laissez-faire. They had no quarrel with the latter process. They questioned, not the legitimacy, but the workability, of laissez-faire; but on the politicization of capitalism there could be no compromise. An autonomous government would establish more than public ownership. It would lay the foundation for an alternative pattern of control over the system of enterprise; the paramount status of the state would mean restoring legal processes and sundering the more immediate and decisive connection between government and business.

In a political democracy, internal economic generation would symbolically represent the subordination of the system of enterprise, so that business would no longer exhaustively define the polity and its purposes. Populists took the *absence* of a strong, autonomous government as a significant factor in the process of capitalist development. They reasoned that if special economic privileges were prohibited, or prevented, capitalism would no longer be propelled toward monopoly, and it could resume a presumably normal (that is, market-oriented) course. Antimonopolism implied both an important public realm and the legitimation of capitalistic institutions that had been excluded from this realm. This suggested the creation of a two-tiered economic structure in which the integrity of each sphere of activity would be preserved. This specific example of a structural balance of forces was a part of the larger Populist conception of just governance. It meant in this case a variant of capitalism that was equally opposed to unmodified laissez-faire and politicized emergent monopolism. In practice, the latter formation raised the more explicit challenge to Populism.

Yet, despite their dedication to property, Populists were curiously indifferent to structure in one respect: They did not delimit modernity as either capitalist or socialist because they thought that the nation, not capitalism as a system, was in a state of fundamental disrepair. Monopolism was the central problem, for it corrupted the state, obstructed the economic process, falsified basic values, and exploited the broader populace, the small holders of property as well as the laboring poor. But monopolism was not essential to capitalism; it was an excrescence produced by historical conditions rather than by structure. The very progression of the criticisms enforced this sense of the separation of monopolism and capitalism. Although Populists investigated the activities of a compliant state, they did not conduct as bold an inquiry into the specifically capitalistic basis of monopolism. For this, as they perhaps knew, would have shaken their confidence in the redemptive powers of an America that they had identified with the democratic heritage.

The result, as if by default, was to preserve a consciousness shaped by the institutional foundations of property. Staying within propertied boundaries, however, had unexpected positive consequences for the expression of protest. The Populists' emphasis on an unresponsive government had the advantage of forcing attention on the issues of public sovereignty and the role of an independent state. The deflection of critical analysis from the systemic character of monopolism also strengthened their belief that capitalism was in principle modifiable. This confidence helped to account for Populism's programmatic focus. They believed that structural problems, even when derived from a monopolistic framework, could be solved through technical means and were not an integral part of capitalism. The support of the public realm was not, for the most part, anticapitalistic; the support of the private realm neither compromised the attack on monopolism nor denied the responsibility of the government for advancing the general welfare.

When the issue of the property right did not arise, Populists were free to act in consequential ways. They could view the problems of production and exchange as matters facing any political economy, so that their departures from contemporary capitalism appeared unself-conscious, and it became unnecessary for them to parade ideological banners. Their primary allegiance was to elemental conceptions of political democracy, which had intrinsic value and tended to discourage ideological classifications: Freedom was more than capitalist freedom; law transcended the function of preserving property; the polity was based on strong social bonds. Populists used a strict political language that was supported by a system of ethics applicable to all properly regulated societies. Humaneness cut across the lines of social structure. Its haven would be a society that respected the individual.

Notes

ONE
Foundations of Social Degradation

1. William A. Peffer, *The Farmer's Side* (New York, 1891), 8–9.
2. *Ibid.*, 29.
3. *Ibid.*, 9.
4. *Ibid.*, 42.
5. *Ibid.*, 47.
6. *Ibid.*, 51–52, 53–54.
7. James B. Weaver, *A Call to Action* (Des Moines, 1892), 5.
8. *Ibid.*, 5–6.
9. *Ibid.*, 27–28.
10. *Ibid.*, 86.
11. *Ibid.*, 88.
12. *Ibid.*, 445.
13. W. Scott Morgan, *History of the Wheel and Alliance, and the Impending Revolution* (Fort Scott, Kan., 1889), 16–17.
14. *Ibid.*, 15–16.
15. *Ibid.*, 16.
16. *Ibid.*, 21–22, 24.
17. *Ibid.*, 24–25.
18. *Ibid.*, 25.
19. *Ibid.*, 26–27, 29–30.
20. *Ibid.*, 608.
21. James H. Davis, *A Political Revelation* (Dallas, 1894), 14, 15.
22. *Ibid.*, 70–71.
23. *Ibid.*, 73.
24. *Ibid.*, 82.
25. *Ibid.*, 96–97.
26. *Ibid.*, 92–93.

27. Lorenzo D. Lewelling, manuscript of speech of July 28, 1894, Kansas State Historical Society.
28. Lorenzo D. Lewelling, Inaugural Address, Jan. 9, 1893, in *People's Party Paper* (Atlanta), Jan. 20, 1893, Library of Congress.
29. Quoted in Michael J. Brodhead, *Persevering Populist* (Reno, 1969), 87, 74, 88.
30. *Ibid.*, 55.
31. *Advocate* (Topeka), Sept. 19, 1894, Kansas State Historical Society.
32. *Ibid.*, Apr. 11, 1894.
33. *Ibid.*
34. *Ibid.*, Aug. 15, 1894.
35. *Ibid.*, Nov. 22, 1893.
36. *Ibid.*, Nov. 22, 1893; Feb. 14, 1894.
37. *Alliance-Independent* (Lincoln), Aug. 24, 1893, Nebraska Historical Society.
38. *Farmers' Alliance* (Lincoln), Aug. 30, 1890, Nebraska Historical Society.
39. *Ibid.*, Aug. 23, 1890.
40. *Alliance-Independent,* July 28, 1892.
41. *Farmers' Alliance,* Oct. 22, 1891.
42. *Ibid.*
43. *Ibid.*, Mar. 3, 1892.
44. *Alliance-Independent,* Aug. 11, 1892.
45. *Farmers' Alliance,* Feb. 28, 1891.

TWO
The Vision of a Sovereign People

1. *People's Party Paper* (Atlanta), Nov. 26, 1891.
2. Thomas E. Watson, *The People's Party Campaign Book* (Thomson, Ga., 1892), 213.
3. *Ibid.*, 187, 188.
4. *Ibid.*, 218, 219.
5. *Ibid.*, 216, 219.
6. *Ibid.*, 216.
7. *Ibid.*
8. *Ibid.*, 219–220, 220–221.
9. *Ibid.*, 221.
10. *Ibid.*
11. Ignatius Donnelly [Edmund Boisgilbert, *pseud.*], *Caesar's Column* (Chicago, 1890), 4–5.

12. *Ibid.*, 22.
13. *Ibid.*, 40, 44–45.
14. *Ibid.*, *46*.
15. *Ibid.*, 122.
16. *Ibid.*, 129.
17. Ignatius Donnelly, *Doctor Huguet* (Chicago, 1891), 63.
18. *Ibid.*, 309.
19. Ignatius Donnelly, *The Golden Bottle* (New York, 1892), 291.
20. *Ibid.*, 125.
21. *Ibid.*, 168–169.
22. *Ibid.*, 167–168.
23. *Ibid.*, 171.
24. *Ibid.*, 270–271.
25. William A. Peffer, *The Farmer's Side* (New York, 1891), 190.
26. *Ibid.*, 122–123.
27. *Ibid.*, 190–191.
28. *Ibid.*, 193.
29. *Ibid.*, 190.
30. *Ibid.*, 193–194.
31. *Ibid.*, 195.
32. James B. Weaver, *A Call to Action* (Des Moines, 1892), 333.
33. *Ibid.*, 267.
34. *Ibid.*, 333–334.
35. *Ibid.*, 334–335.
36. Catherine Nugent, ed., *Life Work of Thomas L. Nugent* (Stephenville, Tex., 1896), 195–196.
37. *Ibid.*, 176.
38. *Ibid.*, 160–161.
39. *Ibid.*, 185.
40. *Ibid.*, 222–223.
41. *Ibid.*, 185.
42. *Ibid.*, 196.
43. *Ibid.*, 176.
44. *Ibid.*, 168.
45. *Ibid.*, 161–162.
46. *Ibid.*, 165–166.
47. *Ibid.*, 177.
48. *Ibid.*, 182–183.
49. *Ibid.*, 183–184.
50. *Ibid.*, 195.

THREE

Tensions: Conservation and Transformation

1. *Advocate* (Topeka), Apr. 11, 1894, Kansas State Historical Society.
2. William A. Peffer, *The Farmer's Side* (New York, 1891), 52.
3. *Farmers' Alliance* (Lincoln), Oct. 22, 1891, Nebraska Historical Society.
4. W. Scott Morgan, *History of the Wheel and Alliance, and the Impending Revolution* (Fort Scott, Kan., 1889), 25.
5. James H. Davis, *A Political Revelation* (Dallas, 1894), 96–97.
6. Henry D. Lloyd, *Wealth Against Commonwealth* (New York, 1894), 494.
7. James B. Weaver, *A Call to Action* (Des Moines, 1892), 88, 27–28.
8. *Advocate,* Sept. 19, 1894.
9. Weaver, *Call to Action,* 333.
10. *Farmers' Alliance,* Feb. 28, 1891.
11. *People's Party Paper* (Atlanta), Jan. 20, 1893, Library of Congress.
12. Lloyd, *Wealth Against Commonwealth, 521.*
13. *Ibid.,* 535.
14. Weaver, *Call to Action,* 5–6.
15. Catherine Nugent, ed., *Life Work of Thomas L. Nugent* (Stephenville, Tex., 1896), 183.
16. *Alliance-Independent* (Lincoln), Aug. 24, 1893.
17. Ignatius Donnelly [Edmund Boisgilbert, *pseud.*], *Caesar's Column* (Chicago, 1890), 122, 129.
18. *Times* (Chicago), Nov. 4, 1894.
19. Lloyd, *Wealth Against Commonwealth,* 495–496.
20. *Ibid.,* 496.
21. Peffer, *Farmer's Side,* 9.
22. Morgan, *History of the Wheel,* 608.
23. Lorenzo D. Lewelling, manuscript of speech of July 28, 1894, Kansas State Historical Society.
24. Quoted in Michael J. Brodhead, *Persevering Populist* (Reno, 1969), 87.
25. Ignatius Donnelly, *The Golden Bottle (*New York, 1892), 125.
26. Popular disturbances of themselves do not necessarily create a democratic vision or embody class behavior. But they cannot merely be assumed to represent a historical and political vehicle of social reaction, as if the ideology of the lower classes were by definition opposed to human freedom. Scholars of working-class culture have generally shown the presence of a high order of political comprehension in

movements of social protest. The response to deprivations frequently revealed a striking rationality; grievances were fitted into a coherent view of social oppression. In many cases, the experience of social misery led protesters to frame generalizations about the nature of political and economic power. Specifically, the recurrent cry for bread (probably the most political of all terms in calling attention to relationships of power) in demonstrations both in Europe and America implicitly raised these questions: Why have we been denied bread? What in the social system has caused widespread impoverishment?

In the face of cold war pressures toward structural acquiescence and cultural conformity, social historians, beginning in the late 1950s, gradually opened paths to the discussion of class, power, repression, and protest. The latter appeared as the yearnings of lower groups expressed through self-defense organizations of their own making. From E. P. Thompson's *The Making of the English Working Class* (London, 1963), one finds that the process of collective realization was slow, painful, and without guarantees; yet it was all that the common people had at hand, all that was theirs, not to be denied them. Although the historical contexts differed markedly, a lesson from the English situation could be applied to Populism: Protest movements did not simply spring up spontaneously. Political consciousness helped to convert objective circumstances—working people in the aggregate, laboring under the same regime of hardship—into subjective understanding of common bonds and a mutual destiny.

FOUR
Boundaries of Ideological Growth

1. Political violence has to be candidly discussed in an evaluation of radicalism. As an agent of social change in revolutionary epochs, it historically appeared as a necessary element in countering the intransigence of upper social groups bent on conserving the structure of the old order. In each situation, including the French Revolution, one might wish to develop a moral calculus in measuring violence against the long-term suffering, malnutrition, and illiteracy created by the existing society, but the larger point remains: How can a fundamental social transformation be effected in the face of absolute resistance on the part of those who generally hold the levers of power?

The historical role of violence, of course, can be a mere pretext or apology for the mindless, vicious, inhumane terrorism that slaughters innocent people, as present-day events painfully demonstrate. Yet I do not see any intrinsic connection, philosophical or historical, between this form of nihilism and radicalism as such. I include violence as an element of radicalism, neither to discredit radicalism nor to glorify force and bloodshed, but to call attention to the logic of a position that presumably seeks the *implementation* of far-reaching structural changes, and not only their passionate advocacy.

Perhaps radicals have to be distinguished from revolutionaries, but unless they are willing to adopt a revolutionary position, one suspects that their radicalism is specious and that they are incapable of acting on their professions of faith. To demand a major transformation of the social order is a serious enterprise; "radicals" always have the option of returning to the more comfortable world of reform. In the case of Populism, the rejection of violence illumines its presuppositions of reform: an acceptance of the canons of political legitimacy and individual well-being in a property-based society.

2. The attempt to treat radicalism as invariably synonymous with socialism reduces the dynamics of political consciousness to narrow structural terms. For humane writers in the Marxian tradition, the abolition of private property does not exhaustively define liberation; it is only the prerequisite for this liberation, and the burden still rests on the people to create and continually renew humanly fulfilling institutions and values. In practice, socialism has often forfeited its claims to being considered radical. See Herbert Marcuse, *Reason and Revolution* (New York, 1941), 315–322, for a classic Marxian statement (although many Marxists have opposed its essential spirit) on the role of conscious will in shaping a historical context of social emancipation. Marcuse wrote: "Once mankind has become the conscious subject of its development, its history can no longer be outlined in forms that apply to the pre-historical phase. . . . Not the slightest natural necessity or automatic inevitability generated the transition from capitalism to socialism. . . . The realization of freedom and reason requires the free rationality of those who achieve it" (316, 318, 319).

3. Barrington Moore, in *Social Origins of Dictatorship and Democracy* (Boston, 1966), has treated revolutionary moments in the capitalist West as formative political contexts for defining a society's institutional growth. The alignment of social forces, in the cases of the English Civil War and the French Revolution, prefigured the degree and vitality of class traditions and class differences; these were unlike the case of the American Civil War, in which significant class feeling had not been engendered.

Moore demonstrated the importance of unified ruling strata for preventing the rise of a separate political consciousness from below—a point that has specific relevance to reactionary formations but that he also applied to America: "The war reflected the fact that the dominant classes in American society had split cleanly in two, much more cleanly than did the ruling strata in England at the time of the Puritan Revolution or those in France at the time of the French Revolution. In those two great convulsions, divisions within the dominant classes enabled radical tendencies to boil up from the lower strata, much more so in the case of the French Revolution than in England. In the American Civil War there was no really comparable radical upsurge" (141). The absence of a formative revolutionary experience still better testifies to the political foundations of subjective classlessness, except among upper groups that could themselves appropriate national symbols to their own advantage. For a fuller statement of Moore's relevance to my ideas on American historical development, see *The Just Polity* (Urbana, 1987), 347–348.

4. In Hartz's analysis, the historical development of America is presented as primarily ideological, taking on the dimensions of a closed system of thought because of the way key political definitions were successively elaborated and refined within an exclusively Lockean framework of ideas. Because of the central importance of Hartz to my thesis of the epistemological dimensions of Populism's interaction with America, I herewith reproduce in abbreviated form a relevant footnote from *The Just Polity*, 348–349:

Although Louis Hartz's *The Liberal Tradition in America* (New York, 1955) is widely regarded as the apogee of the consensus framework in American historical writing, with the attendant conservatism thus implied, this judgment misconceives the level of analysis that the book attained and the potentialities for a serious criticism of America that its perspective could support. Hartz's ideological portrait, even when it tended to dissociate liberalism from its specifically capitalist foundations, was not flattering: a pervasive Lockeanism that reached absolutist proportions, and that required a like rigidness of response for its conservation. The context of thought was one of unrelieved drabness, reflecting an equally static pattern of history and conception of time. Hartz described liberalism as follows: "Here is a doctrine which everywhere in the West has been a glorious symbol of individual liberty, yet in America its compulsive power has been so great that it has posed a threat to liberty itself" (11). A comparative perspective, as in Moore's case, sharpens one's focus on the nature of America.

Further quotations substantiate the critical possibilities of the analysis. Hartz found a political complacency rooted in uncontested dominance: "Frustration produces the social passion, ease does not. A triumphant middle class, unassailed by the agonies that Beaumarchais described, can take itself for granted" (52). He also found a narrow range of ideology, in which liberal premises had been gained without the experience of struggle: "This then is the mood of America's absolutism: the somber faith that its norms are self-evident. It is one of the most powerful absolutisms in the world, more powerful even than the messianic spirit of the continental liberals which . . . the Americans were able to reject. That spirit arose out of contact with an opposing way of life, and its very intensity betrayed an inescapable element of doubt. But the American absolutism, flowing from an honest experience with universality, lacked even the passion that doubt might give" (58). Throughout his analysis, he emphasized the absence of a politically and historically variegated pattern of growth, which makes it difficult to consider the American bourgeoisie as a progressive social force. There was not an adequate basis for the release of positive energies leading to a social transformation: "It is this business of destruction and creation which goes to the heart of the problem. For the point of departure of great revolutionary thought everywhere else in the world has been the effort to build a new society on the ruins of an old one, and this is an experience America has never had" (66).

5. A superb place to begin an exploration of what Populists did and did not borrow from the Lockean political universe is the discussion of John Locke in C. B. Macpherson, *The Political Theory of Possessive Individualism* (Oxford, 1962), 194–262. Although I will, at another time, take issue with Macpherson on his treatment of Hobbes, particularly on the relation between sovereignty and property, his textual analysis of Locke reveals implicit and explicit assumptions that carry beyond the meaning of the property right as such and point toward differential rights in the political community and differential powers of rationality inhering in the possession of property.

Populists would fall within the outlines of a proprietary conception of the individual; they would not, however, accept the rationale for the unlimited accumulation of capital, nor the political, moral, and intellectual inferiority of laboring people. When I say, in the text, "palatable form," I mean more than a softening of Lockean philosophy. Populists adopted the property right without the additional invidious distinctions intended by Locke to convey a system of economic and political class dominance. Capitalism as a total social order was not a natural right, nor was there any place for Locke's doctrine of "just dependence" in a democratic political system.

6. I derived the concept of inner resilience, as the test of an ideological flexibility that gave promise of further widening a given framework, from my investigations of Thomas Hobbes's commitment to stability, once his scientifically constructed political order had been set in place. One notes a built-in limitation in Hobbes's perspective on government. Although he made a transcendent leap in rendering sovereign power antecedent to property and in connecting political security with human potentiality, this initially advanced position was abruptly halted when he realized that the finite character of his political framework would be threatened by the continued unfolding of human reason. The combination of a forward motion and carefully stipulated boundaries could be termed a stabilization of perfection—a phrase that would suit many Populists as well.

7. For the first critical article to deal incisively with Watson's pre-1900 racial perspective, see Charles Crowe, "Tom Watson, Populists, and Blacks Reconsidered," *Journal of Negro History* 55 (April 1970): 99–116. I am presently writing at length on Watson, seeking to relate his position on race to his wider political and structural conservatism. A first installment, analyzing his economic views, can be found in *The Just Polity,* 189–217.

8. Stanley L. Jones, *The Presidential Election of 1896* (Madison, 1964), and Robert F. Durden, *The Climax of Populism* (Lexington, 1965), refer to Watson's antisocialism. A more complete account, showing its peculiar virulence, is Robert Saunders, "The Transformation of Tom Watson, 1894–1895," *Georgia Historical Quarterly* 54 (Fall 1970): 339–356. Saunders, like Crowe (see note 7), tends to underestimate the retrograde features of Watson's thought by failing to treat race and economics as parts of a unified view derived from a strong paternalism. Watson did not sour in the aftermath of Populism; a sophisticated fermentation was taking place throughout his Populist career.

9. Lawrence Goodwyn's *Democratic Promise* (New York, 1976) is a defensively written, narrowly proscriptive treatment of Populism. The entire life of the movement appears to have turned on disputes over the monetary question, a focus affording little incentive to examine the Populist position on railroads, the process of monopolization, and indeed the whole corporate structure. His petty attack on John D. Hicks, who wrote the first (and still the only) comprehensive political account of Populism, suggested that the pre-1888 Alliance experience in Texas was the essence, and even final crystallization, of acceptable Populism:

"Unfortunately, while John Hicks believed he had interpreted the central meaning of the agrarian revolt, he had not. He had produced instead a detailed chronicle of what was in fact a superficial derivative of the farmers' crusade—the shadow movement" (xv). And Goodwyn wrote of William V. Allen: "For his part, Senator Allen joined the reform movement belatedly—in 1891, five years after its fundamental political principles had been initially fashioned and three years after these doctrines had reached their final basic form" (xvii). My concern is not to defend Hicks and Allen, but to point out the absurdity in these seemingly minor matters: Populism had been prefixed before its political birth; it had been further localized to certain hallowed ground; its subsequent political consciousness and protean nature as a movement had counted for nothing. The "incubating germ of greenback insurgency" (24) became an exhaustive description (as if the national-structural dimensions of antimonopolism had never existed) that served to make agricultural cooperatives the infrastructure, greenbackism the ideological touchstone, and C. W. Macune the prophet-hero, of Populism (see page 653 for one of many recurrent summaries). Goodwyn failed to show that cooperatives were a seminal experience, that they were extensive and instrumental in generating a culture of protest, or that they bore an ideological connection to greenbackism; nor did he demonstrate that the two together were an integrated structure, formed a unit with the subtreasury program, reached the more destitute farmers, or posed an alternative to the American financial structure. Was finance capitalism per se in fact the center of American business power? Did Populists so narrow their own field of economic and ideological vision? The "shadow movement" is for me frequently central, and, in any case, is not to be disparaged.

10. The traditional accounts of Populist grievances, although they require a more detailed analysis drawn from Populists' own writings on the broader issues of political degradation and economic deprivation, can be found in John D. Hicks, *The Populist Revolt* (Minneapolis, 1931), esp. chapter 3, and C. Vann Woodward, *Origins of the New South* (Baton Rouge, 1951), esp. chapters 5, 7, 8. Woodward succeeded better than did Hicks in capturing the realities of their respective regional political economies, particularly given Hicks's ambivalent discussion of the railroads and, more important, Woodward's major interpretation of the southern framework of internal colonialism.

11. See Robert C. McMath, *Populist Vanguard* (Chapel Hill, 1975), chapter 5 ("Brothers and Sisters"), for a penetrating and thorough discussion of the communal structure, spirit, and purposes of the Farmers' Alliance. This chapter is a model of scholarship dealing with the cultural and social foundations of popular movements. The North Carolina State Farmers' Alliance charter and related materials can be found in the Southern Historical Collection, University of North Carolina Library, Chapel Hill.

12. While Macpherson, *Political Theory of Possessive Individualism,* only broadly hinted at the anthropomorphic conception of property, his analysis of the possessive characteristics of individualism—that one was "essentially the proprietor of his own person or capacities, owing nothing to society for them"—suggested the moral and political antecedence of property both as a defining trait of human freedom and as a fulfillment, sanctioned by natural rights, of individual appropriation (see esp. 3, 220–221). Not only in Locke, but also in the Levellers, human and property rights were intermixed to such an extent that a separable human rights component, owing nothing to property, failed to emerge from the formative context of English liberal philosophy. The idea of proprietorship did not humanize, but reified, property. It was based on the premise that property in oneself was the archetypal right of ownership that legitimated its expansion to other areas and on an unlimited scale. That property invested the individual with differential political *and* natural rights further testified to its inviolable status (221–238).

13. The vast majority of Populists uncritically accepted the political slogan, "equal rights to all, special privileges to none," which was particularly misleading as an unrestricted view of economic or any other form of strict equality. In fact, it explicitly derived from a Jeffersonian and Jacksonian affirmation of entrepreneurial freedom that, by synthesizing human and property rights, was intended at best to realize the democratization of opportunity, but emphatically not equality of condition. Populists, of course, did not thereby sanction monopolism, but to the degree that they construed this formula as a comprehensive symbolization of the democratic heritage, they provided unwitting testimony both to their own immersion in an American ideological and political construct and their generally reformist convictions.

14. Leo Marx, in *The Machine in the Garden* (New York, 1964), provides an excellent cultural perspective on the meaning of nascent industrialism in the earlier nineteenth century. I am extending his analysis to suggest that the very conception of Nature in America, worked up from its raw state into "the middle landscape," incorporated a seemingly neutral expression of the ideals of property. A distaste for unmodified nature already made clear the strength of possessive values in American society.

But the more serious consequence of using natural imagery in the period was that capitalism and the machine alike had been rendered sanitary. They were not only denied explicit political and economic referents, but, ultimately, they were celebrated as puristic forces: This naturalization of the productive order could be carried over to the post–Civil War generation as the further incasement of capitalism within Nature and the exemplification of a providential national development. Without intending it, Leo Marx made Emerson the father of William Graham Sumner; in an elliptical way, perhaps he was. There was a transcendent flight into *existing* social reality, which was perceived as inspiring truth. In Emerson's words: "Machinery and Transcendentalism agree well" (232).

15. Hartz, *Liberal Tradition,* superbly delineated the factor of timelessness in American political thought and its role in encouraging a linear historical process and the social values of conformity. First, he emphasized the nonprojective, antiutopian component of the American Revolution itself: "For if the messianic spirit does not arise in the course of a country's national revolution, when is it ever going to arise?" (43) For Hartz, America started sober-minded and remained so, aided by a particular view of traditionalism: "The result was that the traditionalism of the Americans, like a pure freak of logic, often bore amazing marks of antihistorical rationalism" (48). Yet this was not surprising, because rationalism justified the self-evidence of capitalism—an article of faith that, both in historical and structural terms, was frozen into place. In the process, "the past became a continuous future" (50), a formulation that enabled Hartz to reconcile tradition with rationality. Still, although he saw this pattern as a part of Lockean absolutism, and by definition the sign of a rigid ideological context, he refrained from mentioning the specifically social and structural consequences of this: namely, an unwavering political development that maintained the consistency of class and power relationships.

16. The use of social-medical metaphors was based on the premise that society existed in a framework of equilibrium. Society was fundamentally sound but readily susceptible to, and threatened by, external perturbations. The idea that the structure itself might possess integral defects capable of producing hardship could not be admitted; instead, the need was to eliminate presumably extraneous factors and thus restore the good order (health) of society. This attitude clearly militated against a social transformation. Although Populists revealed a partial acceptance of the model of equilibrium in their conception of a political and economic balance of forces, and even more in their treatment of monopolism as an excrescent form of capitalism, they rejected such a theory in its modern guise—when it was applied in order to confer legitimacy on existing political and structural arrangements and to maintain a restorative perspective.

I had Parsonian sociology in mind when I raised the issue, but this orientation was actually widespread in the late nineteenth century and in Progressivism. It was part of the political vocabulary of repression and social discipline. In retrospect, I believe that Parsons's own usage of an equilibrium model was a good bit more decent, although I sympathize with C. Wright Mills's critique of his theory and its social implications in *The Sociological Imagination* (New York, 1959), chapter 2.

17. The character of the historical pattern of bourgeois ascendancy was critical to determining subsequent democratic institutions. Did the bourgeoisie struggle to achieve its rights, which were primarily concerned with political, religious, and civil liberties, or did it merely declare, confirm, and perpetuate them in the absence of a decisive internal contest? The specific mode of the historical acquisition of rights affected not only their continued inner vitality but also their potential extension to other areas of human freedom. Basically, rights gained without struggle were in danger of remaining inert, ossified, formalistic—in fine, privileged and limited in application. They would lack the social dynamism necessary for being incorporated into the structure of power and principles of governance. They would not create the grounds for a historical or ethical progression from formal to substantive democracy.

Barrington Moore identified several crucial factors in the modernizing experience of England (and to a lesser extent France) that enabled capitalist societies to retain democratic features and avoid the twentieth-century fate of Germany and Japan, where capitalism culminated in fascism. These features revealed a variegated political culture and society that also promoted the existence and consciousness of nonbourgeois elements. In America, liberalism had a stabilizing quality that corresponding social forces in Europe historically opposed; it was a liberalism of the old order, if this contradiction is possible. See Moore, *Social Origins,* chapters 7–9 for the broader issues involved in this discussion and the need to think constantly in comparative terms.

18. Robert G. McCloskey's *American Conservatism in the Age of Enterprise 1865–1910* (Cambridge, 1951), is a passionate and quite rigorous defense of the human rights component of liberalism. McCloskey, later an outstanding scholar of the Supreme Court, argued that an "inversion in liberal principles" (vii) had violated the original statement of priorities in the hierarchy of liberal values. The "morally free individual" possessed a right to "moral self-development" that could be traced back to the Levellers' emphasis on "spiritual or humane values," in contradistinction to the "instrumental or secondary character" that had been assigned to the property right (3–4). McCloskey was not alone in returning to the Levellers as the fount of democracy; many, from George Sabine to E. P. Thompson, used this source. This underscores the significance of Macpherson's analysis for the discussion of liberal philosophical foundations (see above, note 12, chapter 4). Yet in proceeding in this way McCloskey was under no illusion about the meaning and importance of Locke: "In his hands, at least in the *Second Treatise,* the right of private property became in effect an end in itself, became indeed the typical right, the analogy on which the argument for all other rights was based" (5); and again, "the practical effect of his thought was undoubtedly to justify not only the Glorious Revolution but Western capitalism" (6).

This is important because it suggests that McCloskey recognized in principle the amalgam of human rights and property rights occurring under Locke's auspices: "So, whether intentionally or not, Locke fastened on democracy the idea that the right of private property is fundamental; he set in train a materialization of democratic ideals that led ultimately to their perversion" (6). However, since materialization was at the crux of democracy's perversion in the first place, either his statement does not follow or it suggests the earlier onset of this perversion. For McCloskey, America's formative context of political philosophy nevertheless remained sacrosanct, in the same way that it did for Populists. Concerning jurist, Stephen J. Field, he noted: "The democratic ideals to which Field paid his respects were radically different and logically incompatible with the humane philosophy of the Declaration whose terminology he borrowed. But by taking advantage of an initial ambiguity, by exploiting the vast prestige which the businessman had acquired, Field, William Graham Sumner, Andrew Carnegie, Bishop Lawrence, and other lay and clerical apostles of the gospel of wealth were able to weld capitalism to the democratic creed. They were able thereby to capture democracy and make it hostage to conservatism, so that the aims of democracy and those of business became indistinguishable in the popular view" (14–15).

Given the pervasive influence of business thought in the late nineteenth century, it is noteworthy that Populists could return to the founding philosophy for ideological sustenance and still proceed exactly to the foregoing distinction. Although they did not question the property right, they insisted that contemporary business development was separable from, and prejudicial to, democratic government. On the process of transvaluing democratic values, McCloskey wrote that "the traditional terms were drained of their old significance; a new content was injected; and it was generally supposed that nothing had happened, because the labels remained unchanged. The conservative exponent of a basically antidemocratic ethos could now bolster up his argument with the language of democracy itself" (16). To the degree that a qualitative shift in the meaning of fundamental doctrine did occur, one comes to appreciate the significance of the Populists' emphasis on the principle of a literalistic construction of the Constitution and canons of political democracy. This element represented a necessary cutting away; it was a tentative first step in the direction of an epistemological break. They recognized (this was also the spirit of McCloskey's book) that the restoration of original meanings at the foundation of American political thought was a prerequisite for any kind of political consciousness and democratic progress.

19. Despite the comprehensive biography of Paolo E. Coletta and the general interest shown by historians, William Jennings Bryan remains a puzzle in the critical areas of his political, legal, and economic thought. Bryan is often dismissed as having little theoretical value. It is fashionable to consider him in the light of Bible Belt stereotypes, one who blended a reincarnated Jacksonianism with a silver-only entrepreneurial radicalism and who was capable merely of sporadic political gestures based on this retrogressive standard. This view has little to do with the reality of his undoubted capabilities and powers of reasoning. Bryan had mental discipline as well as stamina. He was politically astute and intellectually multifaceted; his performance at the Scopes trial in 1925 cannot, with fairness or accuracy, be read back into the events of the 1890s.

In the portion of my work on Marion Butler dealing with the campaign of 1896, I discuss Bryan's sophistication, sympathy toward labor, and grasp of capitalist development. He expressed subtle yet basic differences with Populism, beginning nonetheless from a common appreciation of the democratic possibilities inhering in fundamental law. If one were to construct a Bryanist model of capitalism, it would reveal a distinct political economy that stood between the Populist and the contemporary modes of capitalism and leaned decidedly more toward the former. Although Bryan rejected the concept and practice of public ownership—this advocacy of public ownership differentiated Populists from the major parties as well as from the majority of their contemporaries—he strongly endorsed the idea of strict government regulation as necessary to a framework of impartial law. In regard to the issues of regulation and impartial law, he was a completely unorthodox member of his own party. Bryan's devotion to the property right was more constant (that is, unreservedly Lockean) than was the Populists'; but his resilience concerning popular rights and public-spirited government was exceptional when measured by the record of the Democratic party.

FIVE
The Framework of Democratic Power

1. Henry D. Lloyd, *Wealth Against Commonwealth* (New York, 1894), 6.
2. *Advocate* (Topeka), Feb. 14, 1894, Kansas State Historical Society.
3. W. Scott Morgan, *History of the Wheel and Alliance, and the Impending Revolution* (Fort Scott, Kan., 1889), 29–30, 16–17.
4. Catherine Nugent, ed., *Life Work of Thomas L. Nugent* (Stephenville, Tex., 1896), 183–184, 185.
5. Morgan, *History of the Wheel,* 608.
6. Quoted in Michael J. Brodhead, *Persevering Populist* (Reno, 1969), 87.
7. Lloyd, *Wealth Against Commonwealth,* 495–496.
8. *Farmers' Alliance* (Lincoln), Feb. 28, 1891, Nebraska Historical Society.
9. Ignatius Donnelly, *The Golden Bottle* (New York, 1892), 125.
10. Ibid.
11. *Times* (Chicago), Nov. 4, 1894.
12. *Advocate,* Feb. 14, 1894.
13. James B. Weaver, *A Call to Action* (Des Moines, 1892), 247–248.
14. James H. Davis, *A Political Revelation* (Dallas, 1894), 73.
15. *Alliance* (Lincoln), June 26, 1889, Nebraska Historical Society.
16. Morgan, *History of the Wheel,* 15–16.
17. William A. Peffer, *The Farmer's Side* (New York, 1891), 29.
18. Lorenzo D. Lewelling, manuscript of speech of July 28, 1894, Kansas State Historical Society.
19. *Farmers' Alliance* Oct. 22, 1891.
20. *Alliance-Independent* (Lincoln), Aug. 24, 1893, Nebraska Historical Society.
21. Lloyd, *Wealth Against Commonwealth,* 511.
22. Peffer, *The Farmer's Side,* 193.
23. Lloyd, *Wealth Against Commonwealth,* 523.

24. *Farmers' Alliance,* Mar. 10, 1892.
25. *Ibid.,* Mar. 3, 1892.
26. Nugent, *Life Work of Thomas L. Nugent,* 183.
27. *People's Party Paper* (Atlanta), Jan. 20, 1893, Library of Congress.
28. Nugent, *Life Work of Thomas L. Nugent,* 236.
29. *Advocate,* Nov. 14, 1894.
30. Lloyd, *Wealth Against Commonwealth,* 499.
31. *Advocate,* Apr. 11, 1894.
32. Peffer, *The Farmer's Side,* 53–54.
33. Weaver, *Call to Action,* 247–248.
34. *Ibid.*
35. Davis, *Political Revelation,* 99–100.
36. *Platte County Argus* (Columbus, Neb.), Oct. 15, 1896, Nebraska Historical Society.
37. Weaver, *Call to Action,* 86.
38. Morgan, *History of the Wheel,* 17–18.
39. *Advocate,* Aug. 15, 1894.
40. *Alliance,* June 26, 1889.
41. Weaver, *Call to Action,* 5–6.
42. Davis, *Political Revelation,* 97.
43. *National Economist* (Washington, D.C.), July 9, 1892.
44. Ignatius Donnelly [Edmund Boisgilbert, *pseud.*], *Caesar's Column* (Chicago, 1890), 129.
45. *Ibid.,* 122.
46. Weaver, *Call to Action,* 333–334.
47. Nugent, *Life Work of Thomas L. Nugent,* 161–162.
48. *People's Party Paper* Jan. 20, 1893.
49. *Advocate,* Sept. 19, 1894.
50. Lloyd, *Wealth Against Commonwealth,* 521.
51. *Farmers' Alliance* Oct. 22, 1891.
52. Lloyd, *Wealth Against Commonwealth,* 517.
53. *Ibid.,* 530.
54. *Ibid.,* 533.
55. *Advocate,* Apr. 11, 1894.
56. Lloyd, *Wealth Against Commonwealth,* 535.
57. Nugent, *Life Work of Thomas L. Nugent,* 161.
58. Peffer, *The Farmer's Side,* 190.
59. *Ibid.,* 190–191.
60. Donnelly, *Caesar's Column,* 122.
61. Lloyd, *Wealth Against Commonwealth,* 527.
62. *People's Party Paper,* Jan. 20, 1893.
63. Quoted in Brodhead, *Persevering Populist,* 88.

64. *Farmers' Alliance,* Feb. 28, 1891.
65. Lloyd, *Wealth Against Commonwealth,* 535.
66. Weaver, *Call to Action,* 88.
67. Quoted in Brodhead, *Persevering Populist,* 55.

SIX
Modifications of Laissez-Faire

1. Henry D. Lloyd, *Wealth Against Commonwealth* (New York, 1894), 2, 494.
2. *Ibid.,* 494.
3. *Ibid.,* 497.
4. W. Scott Morgan, *History of the Wheel and Alliance, and the Impending Revolution* (Fort Scott, Kan., 1889), 23–24.
5. *Ibid.,* 24, 608.
6. Catherine Nugent, ed., *Life Work of Thomas L. Nugent* (Stephenville, Tex., 1896), 176–177.
7. *Ibid.,* 176.
8. *Ibid.,* 222–223.
9. *Ibid.,* 185.
10. For an analysis of Adam Smith's emphasis upon the commercial factor and its implications for structural automatism, egoistic premises of conduct, and the comparative weakness of the state as an administrative force, see the admirably lucid discussion of Elie Halevy, *The Growth of Philosophic Radicalism* (Boston, 1955), esp. 88–120. This is a reprint of the three-volume study published in the 1920s. It still ranks as among the finest commentaries on Smith's ideas and their intellectual setting.
11. I cannot emphasize enough the significance for Populism of basing its political and economic analysis on the specifics of contemporary industrial development. Populists' critique of the prevailing mode of capitalism was thereby freed from a dependence on the framework of exchange and the process of automatic self-regulation as guiding principles in organizing the political economy. By focusing on existing relations of production and contemporary trends toward monopolism, they were enabled to identify and confront the problems of underconsumption, economic misery, and the growing loss of political rights.

Industrial organization raised the crucial question of power and its private uses in a democratic society. There were simply no assurances that the totality of individual actions would lead to the general welfare.

I shall argue below in the text that industrial realities, even more than capitalism per se, determined the Populists' case for enlarging the powers of the state. They could not credit the exchange mechanism as an avenue to a just polity. For a handy summary of evidence suggesting the role of industrial specificity in deepening their political and economic perspective, see Norman Pollack, *The Populist Mind* (Indianapolis, 1967), esp. 3–15, 16–20, 82–87, 348–349, 403–466, 478–480, 505–513, 527–533.

12. Barrington Moore, *Social Origins of Dictatorship and Democracy* (Boston, 1966), esp. chapter 8. Moore showed that antidemocratic patterns of capitalist development had their origins in labor-repressive systems of agriculture, which, in the transition from feudalism to capitalism, supported a dominant role for the state in consolidating economic institutions and the power of established elites. The old order, generally unmodified, has been carried over into the modern setting. Industrialism essentially has been placed on a premodern cultural, political, and social base, in which modernization was divorced from the potentially liberalizing trends of economic growth. Such a society did not experience a revolution in its historical advance to modernity. In contrast, when a modernizing process was founded on the commercialization of agriculture and the rise of an independent bourgeoisie, two historical factors that were closely associated with a revolutionary break from the old order, the conditions were not present for a repressive state formation in promoting capitalism and industrialism. The stabilization of society could be achieved primarily through economic controls.

In part, the contrasting situations reflected the degree to which a unified ruling stratum had retained command of the political order and encouraged the maintenance of premodern social foundations and reactionary cultural values. But in addition to a unified ruling stratum as such, the original economic context, as in the cases of Germany and Japan, had acted as a brake on modernization, thereby disposing elite groups to look to the state to accelerate industrial development. In these circumstances, the state willingly provided the force to insure labor discipline and an attitude of docility on the part of the masses. But it also provided more technical requirements for industrial success, including a good part of the capital formation that established basic industry. This forcible process of modernization from above had nothing in common with Smith's emphasis on the internal generation of economic forces.

13. Quoted in Michael J. Brodhead, *Persevering Populist* (Reno, 1969), 87.

14. Nugent, *Life Work of Thomas L. Nugent,* 166.
15. James B. Weaver, *Call to Action* (Des Moines, 1892), 267.
16. Lloyd, *Wealth Against Commonwealth,* 6, 495, 496.
17. *Ibid.,* 497, 499, 497, 503, 509, 522.
18. *Ibid.,* 531, 532.
19. Weaver, *Call to Action,* 445.
20. Lloyd, *Wealth Against Commonwealth,* 534.
21. *Ibid.,* 534–535.
22. Populists could not accept the validity of an egoistic principle of human conduct because its historical derivation from a greengrocer's world practically insured its irrelevance in modern times. They were mindful that such a world and their own world of the small producer were similar; however, the former was patently out of step with industrial realities, while the latter, by affirming the social dimensions of individual satisfaction and human freedom, sought the democratic control of industry. Populists rejected the idea that egoism was a universal principle; instead they found it to be an apt description of the motivation of upper economic groups. In particular, they saw individual self-interest as the dynamic impulse behind monopolism.

Smith's egoistic principle, especially as the basis of general welfare, had to be opposed if a counterethic of human cooperation was to be established and social protest begun. On practical as well as philosophical grounds, Populists separated the egoistic and less-propertied factors. They could do this because they did not value the property right in absolute terms; instead, they partly viewed it in the context of existing relations of power.

23. *Farmers' Alliance* (Lincoln), May 7, 1891.
24. *Ibid.,* Oct. 22, 1891.
25. *Ibid.,* Mar. 3, 1892.
26. *Alliance-Independent* (Lincoln), Jan. 11, 1894.
27. *Ibid.,* Aug. 11, 1892.
28. The capitalistic basis of Populist economic and political criticism had the effect of creating a framework of structural proximity in which the Populist, Smithian, and contemporary modes of capitalism all shared comparable categories of analysis and organization. This proximity greatly stimulated the Populists' search for clarifying the problems facing American society, particularly the role of government in modern capitalism. Without a sense of immediacy and of their own relevance fostered by such a condition, it is doubtful that the specificity of their criticism and the astonishing breadth of their concerns would have been achieved.

In the American setting, the capitalistic basis of Populist thought had the unexpected advantage of providing a sharper analytical focus: It became less difficult to confront Adam Smith (and to widen the criticism of market operations to include fragmented social relations) than to confront a total Lockean political culture in which the property right had been given the sanction of democracy. The Populists' effort to differentiate competitive capitalism from laissez-faire was the critical step in meeting the larger ideological challenge of democratizing the existing capitalist mode. Yet Populists did not succeed to the same degree in modifying the Lockean universe of property, except in questioning both the unlimited accumulation of capital and the superior rights and rationality of the propertyholder.

Still, if Populism had been a socialist movement, the salience of the controversy I have been exploring—the intracapitalist differences that informed Populists' economic and moral challenge, including their enriched conception of the law and a doctrine of public rights—would have been absent. Abstracted from capitalism, Populism would be incomprehensible; within capitalism, it gave promise of generating an exciting modal alternative.

29. Nugent, *Life Work of Thomas L. Nugent,* 236.

30. Lloyd, *Wealth Against Commonwealth,* 506.

Essay on Sources

The documental core of this book is a small group of Populist writings that I briefly treat in chapters 1 and 2. A detailed explication of text of these sources can be found in my book, *The Just Polity* (Urbana: University of Illinois Press, 1987). See James H. Davis, *A Political Revelation* (Dallas: Advance Publishing Co., 1894); Ignatius Donnelly [Edmund Boisgilbert, *pseud.*], *Caesar's Column* (Chicago: F. J. Schulte and Co., 1890); Donnelly, *Doctor Huguet* (Chicago: F. J. Schulte and Co., 1891); Donnelly, *The Golden Bottle* (New York: D. D. Merrill Co., 1892); W. Scott Morgan, *History of the Wheel and Alliance, and the Impending Revolution* (Fort Scott, Kan.: J. H. Rice and Sons, 1889); Catherine Nugent, ed., *Life Work of Thomas L. Nugent* (Stephenville, Tex.: Catherine Nugent, 1896); William A. Peffer, *The Farmer's Side, His Troubles and Their Remedy* (New York: D. Appleton and Co., 1891); Thomas E. Watson, *The People's Party Campaign Book* (Author's edition: [Thomson, Ga., 1892]); and James B. Weaver, *A Call to Action* (Des Moines: Iowa Printing Co., 1892). I also drew material from the Topeka *Advocate* (Kansas State Historical Society), the Lincoln *Farmers' Alliance* (Nebraska Historical Society), and the Atlanta *People's Party Paper* (Library of Congress), as well as Henry D. Lloyd, *Wealth Against Commonwealth* (New York: Harper and Brothers, 1894).

The following short list of secondary works provides an introduction to the literature about Populism and its historical setting. The studies range in quality, but each has value to the specialist. Peter H. Argersinger, *Populism and Politics* (Lexington: University of Kentucky Press, 1974); Alex M. Arnett, *The Populist Movement in Georgia* (New York: Columbia University Press, 1922); Michael J. Brodhead, *Persevering Populist* (Reno: University of Nevada Press, 1969); Robert P. Brooks, *The Agrarian Revolution in Georgia, 1865–1912* (Madison: University of Wisconsin Press, 1914); Allan G. Bogue, *From Prairie to Corn Belt* (Chicago: University of Chicago Press, 1963); O. Gene Clanton, *Kansas Populism* (Lawrence: University of

Kansas Press, 1969); Chester McArthur Destler, *American Radicalism, 1865–1901* (New London: Connecticut College Press, 1946), and *Henry Demarest Lloyd and the Empire of Reform* (Philadelphia: University of Pennsylvania Press, 1963); Robert F. Durden, *The Climax of Populism* (Lexington: University of Kentucky Press, 1965); Charles L. Flynn, Jr., *White Land, Black Labor* (Baton Rouge: Louisiana State University Press, 1983); Lawrence Goodwyn, *Democratic Promise* (New York: Oxford University Press, 1976); Sheldon Hackney, *Populism to Progressivism in Alabama* (Princeton: Princeton University Press, 1969); Steven Hahn, *The Roots of Southern Populism* (New York: Oxford University Press, 1983); William I. Hair, *Bourbonism and Agrarian Protest* (Baton Rouge: Louisiana State University Press, 1969); John D. Hicks, *The Populist Revolt* (Minneapolis: University of Minnesota Press, 1931); Stanley L. Jones, *The Presidential Election of 1896* (Madison: University of Wisconsin Press, 1964); J. Morgan Kousser, *The Shaping of Southern Politics* (New Haven: Yale University Press, 1974); Robert C. McMath, *Populist Vanguard* (Chapel Hill: University of North Carolina Press, 1975); Roscoe C. Martin, *The People's Party in Texas* (Austin: University of Texas Press, 1933); Stuart Noblin, *Leonidas LaFayette Polk* (Chapel Hill: University of North Carolina Press, 1949); Walter T. K. Nugent, *The Tolerant Populists* (Chicago: University of Chicago Press, 1963); Bruce Palmer, *"Man Over Money"* (Chapel Hill: University of North Carolina Press, 1980); Stanley B. Parsons, *The Populist Context* (Westport: Greenwood Press, 1973); Norman Pollack, *The Populist Response to Industrial America* (Cambridge: Harvard University Press, 1962); Martin Ridge, *Ignatius Donnelly* (Chicago: University of Chicago Press, 1962); William W. Rogers, *The One-Gallused Rebellion* (Baton Rouge: Louisiana State University Press, 1970); Fred A. Shannon, *The Farmer's Last Frontier* (New York: Farrar and Rinehart, 1945); Barton C. Shaw, *The Wool-Hat Boys* (Baton Rouge: Louisiana State University Press, 1984); Vernon L. Wharton, *The Negro in Mississippi, 1865–1890* (Chapel Hill: University of North Carolina Press, 1947); C. Vann Woodward, *Tom Watson, Agrarian Rebel* (New York: Macmillan, 1938), and *Origins of the New South* (Baton Rouge: Louisiana State University Press, 1951); and James E. Wright, *The Politics of Populism* (New Haven: Yale University Press, 1974). See also, Norman Pollack, *The Populist Mind* (Indianapolis: Bobbs-Merrill, 1967), for an extensive collection of Populist documents.

Beginning with chapter 3, I have had to rely on my own wits; there are no specific, known guides for a theoretical study of this kind. Essentially, the evidence was for the reader's convenience: to stir confidence in the findings and pay lip service to scholarly conventions. But I had a social theory of Populism to develop and, behind that goal, theories that would explore the possibilities of democratic modernization in America, the role of social epistemology in the cultural absorption of protest ideologies and movements, and, in whatever ways this might be manifested, the nature of capitalism as a political and social system.

Further evidence from Populism would have been helpful, but it was not essential. And in my construction of an informal political typology of Populism, I relied, of course, on my reading of primary sources carrying over decades. Rather, I wanted to move *from* Populism to the universe of Populist ideas, and then to the national political culture and social structure using the Populist experience to illumine their meaning. As a first step, I simply built on the opportunities afforded by my method—an explication of text. This was part of a continuing effort, begun in *The Just Polity,* to foster the interaction between evidence and interpretation and thereby create the analytical basis for generating new ideas. Evidence helps to particularize theory; in this case, the factual material focused the investigation so that modernization and capitalism would remain central, have specific content, *and* elevate Populism as a tool for comparative study. The confidence I seek to inspire in the reader is not a false confidence. Its purpose is to encourage the flow of reason from known data to what is unknown, or at least to what has not been approached in this exact manner before. Somehow, footnotes provide a source of comfort to the historian, but by the time one reaches chapter 7, it is clear that one cannot cite books that have not been written, about questions that have not been asked. Therefore, I refrained from further citations, preferring instead to let my thoughts stand alone.

It is easy to supply a list (short or long) about Populism, just as it is easy to continue the presentation of evidence almost indefinitely. But it is presumptuous, and perhaps meaningless, to supply lists about capitalism and modernization. Where does one begin, but more, at the other extreme, where does one find concrete discussions of either topic specifically in relation to Populism? At some point, the historian must make his or her own connections. Capitalism and modernization are part of practically every historian's field of study, especially for those who have come of professional age during the last thirty years. They have become part of one's intellectual baggage, regardless of the area of specialization. (A medievalist is as much involved in the historical transformation from feudalism to capitalism as is any modernist, although he also possesses the greater advantage of being able to read Marc Bloch with greater sensitivity.)

In short, my bibliography on these topics is equivalent to my intellectual autobiography: Marx, Locke, Smith, Mill, Weber, Schumpeter are not names or milestones, but lively and living minds to be engaged, wrestled with, and questioned. In the post-World War Two era, there are a host of others, highly qualified, but less challenging or sparkling, ranging from Althusser to Galbraith. In diminished form, the topic of epistemology is also all about, defining the new cultural age. But I cannot, with a clear conscience, list Benjamin Lee Whorf or Noam Chomsky for having provided guidance to my ideas on introjection, cultural mediation, property consciousness, or Populists' devotion to the American construct because, of course, they were working on technical problems concerning the linguistic foundations of knowledge, not the ideological accommodation of social groups or the influence of a propertied culture on thought. In retrospect, perhaps Marx's *Economic-Philosophic Manuscripts* and *German Ideology* have been more relevant to my purposes in this area.

There is, however, a second step in my analysis, which takes me beyond the use of Populist sources as a basis for making extrapolations from Populism to capitalism and modernization. And here, a list of books *is* in order because these works directly provide the bridge from history to theory in the present study. I have relied on certain writers, drawn from diverse fields, to advance my understanding of social structure, political development, and human freedom and/or alienation. They frequently reflect diverse purposes, viewpoints, and systems of analysis. My challenge has been to move from Populism to a broader range of issues, in the process creating an original synthesis of these often quite disparate works. The second step, although it still depends on the evidence, is the construction of an independent framework of interpretation.

There are really several brief lists involved here. To help define democratic possibilities in the nineteenth century as they applied to America, I have relied on four writers (in addition to Lloyd): Emerson, Thoreau, William James, and Louis Sullivan. I have been especially moved by Sullivan's *Kindergarten Chats* as an unsurpassed description of American democracy. To this American Quartet I would also add William Graham Sumner as an indispensable counterforce; his essays sharply articulate an antipodal element inhering in American social thought and reveal the conflict with democratic—and Populist—humanism. Sumner was the outstanding conservative theorist of the age.

Second, I have a favorite core of writings, to which I recur periodically for intellectual stimulation and refreshment. Perhaps because of their ideological and substantive disagreements, these works constantly encourage me to enlarge the scope of my interpretation so that I can integrate their separate ideas and germinal insights. Each book has contributed to the present study, however indirect their influence on specific points of history may have been, because singly and collectively they constitute the preliminary basis for my mental development: Paul A. Baran, *The Political Economy of Growth* (New York: Monthly Revew Press, 1957); Robert A. Brady, *The Spirit and Structure of German Fascism* (New York: Viking Press, 1937); Louis Hartz, *The Liberal Tradition in America* (New York: Harcourt, Brace and World,

1955); C. B. Macpherson, *The Political Theory of Possessive Individualism* (Oxford: Clarendon Press, 1962); Herbert Marcuse, *Eros and Civilization* (Boston: Beacon Press, 1955); F. O. Matthiessen, *American Renaissance* (New York: Oxford University Press, 1941); Barrington Moore, *Social Origins of Dictatorship and Democracy* (Boston: Beacon Press, 1966); Franz Neumann, *Behemoth* (New York: Oxford University Press, 1944); Fritz Pappenheim, *The Alienation of Modern Man* (New York: Monthly Review Press, 1959); E. P. Thompson, *The Making of the English Working Class* (London: Victor Gollancz, 1963); and Thorstein Veblen, *The Theory of the Leisure Class* (New York: Macmillan Company, 1899).

The third group of writings has helped me to "fine-tune" my analysis in chapters 3 through 7: Maurice Dobb, *Studies in the Development of Capitalism* (New York: International Publishers, 1947), for his discussion of mercantilism; Elie Halevy, *The Growth of Philosophic Radicalism* (Boston: Beacon Press, 1955), for his analysis of Adam Smith; Gabriel Kolko, *The Triumph of Conservatism* (Glencoe, Ill.: Free Press, 1963), for his theory of the framework of interpenetration between government and business; N. Gordon Levin, *Woodrow Wilson and World Politics* (New York: Oxford University Press, 1968), for his seminal reading of the contours and premises of the liberal mind; Masao Maruyama, *Thought and Behaviour in Modern Japanese Politics* (London: Oxford University Press, 1963), for his insights into the relationships between political stabilization, counterrevolution, and advanced systems of capitalism; Robert G. McCloskey, *American Conservatism in the Age of Enterprise* (Cambridge: Harvard University Press, 1951), for his perceptive analysis of American social thought in the latter nineteenth century; and Nicos Poulantzas, *Political Power and Social Classes* (London: NLB and Sheed and Ward, 1973), for his discussion of the capitalist state as an integrative force in cementing the class structure.

Finally, John Rawls, *A Theory of Justice* (Cambridge: Harvard University Press, 1971), and Charles E. Lindblom, *Politics and Markets* (New York: Basic Books, 1977), both of which are major works, treat democracy and capitalism, respectively, in ways that suggest a rough correspondence to the ideas of Populists themselves. The levels of analysis between these books and Populist writings is, of course, very different, but the comparisons are instructive in alerting one to nuances of the philosophical and economic positions set forth by Populism. Neither author had Populism in mind when he constructed his interpretation.

Lindblom analyzes market-oriented systems in far greater depth than did Populist writers, and his strength is in clarifying the historical variations and degrees of structural complexity of these systems. He is most useful for an understanding of the Populist variant of capitalism, however, in his matter-of-fact treatment of the interpenetration of business and government. He speaks of a "dual leadership," emphasizes the public functions of private decision makers, and points out the restriction of the scope of polyarchy. He even implies that the business system has been abstracted from (that is, placed outside the reach of) the political process. In effect, he tends to confirm Populists' own criticism of monopolism and the politicization of property.

Yet Lindblom differs from Populists about the meaning of the trends he is analyzing. He uses business performance as the explanation for the drive toward a structural collaboration with government, and he emphasizes industrial, rather than capitalist, imperatives in his assessment of the strengths and weaknesses of market-oriented societies. Populists saw a very different set of factors operating in modal economic behavior. For them, the drive toward a structural collaboration was evidence of the formation of a class state; the interpenetration of business and government had less to do with the criterion of business performance than with the assertion of private sovereignty and power. Moreover, the significant role they assigned to industrialism did not blind them to the particularities of capitalism. Above all, they persisted in treating economics as operating within a framework of ethics. This was previously Lindblom's strong suit, but an antecedent ethical standard is not important to *Politics and Markets*.

Rawls analyzes fundamental political concepts rigorously and, against the trend of twentieth-century philosophy, with social compassion. He has encountered gratuitous criticism for this. Yet his ideas have a greater affinity with the position of Locke than either he or his conservative critics apparently realize. Rawls is deceptively radical: He writes at length about justice, but he fails to adequately stipulate the conditions of equalitarianism that would be required to satisfy his concept of justice, particularly in its application to the basic structure of society. Rawls clearly recognizes the inadequacy of the principle of utility as the basis for achieving the general welfare. Nevertheless, he seeks to reconcile a framework of social cooperation with economic and social inequalities and to gain mass consent for the political formula of justice if these inequalities could be suspended for the purposes of achieving the good of all. This represents a social accommodation with a structural context antagonistic to justice. At least, several writers we have discussed, such as Doster and Lloyd, would have thought so. They insisted that privilege in all its guises was incompatible with the principle of justice, whether or not mass consent followed. Justice was an objective standard; the people could at times be deceived.

To Rawls, this is no doubt Hegelian mystification. But the problem raised by his analysis is that, although he can reject or modify the principle of utility, he will not—and, for reasons of logical consistency, perhaps cannot—question the principle of individual self-interest. Moreover, by assuming at the outset "the absence of strong and lasting benevolent impulses," he reinforces the dependence of his argument on individual self-interest. The source of entrapment is the connection between rationality and self-interest, both of which have been culturally defined to reflect the contemporary system. As a result, he appears to have harmonized the concept of justice with prevailing Western capitalist thought, rather than to have placed strong pressures on the institutions and values responsible for creating differences of power and wealth.

Rawls shares with Populists the implicit approval of the property right as a boundary of cultural and structural democratization; but Lloyd, for one, was dissatisfied by this limitation, as his formulation of the concept of "other-self interest" attests. Both writers adopt the linguistic categories of capitalism. Yet Lloyd demonstrates resilience about the concept of self-interest and seeks to move beyond it, while Rawls proceeds still further with the economic premises of (presumed) rational choice. For example, his emphasis on the contractual framework becomes a substitute for, rather than the basis of, the substantive content of justice. By presenting his theory of justice as part of his theory of rational choice, he uses the principle of rationality to strengthen the position of individual self-interest and subordinates justice, perhaps even to the point of denying its intrinsic value. Justice founders on the rocks of Pareto optimality.

If Populists had been aware of such a concept, they would not have favored it. They also saw the importance of choice and presumed that they were rational in doing so. But for them, this was a clear question of *moral* choice as constituting the basis of freedom, rather than rational choice as constituting the basis of justice. Their usage of freedom denied the abstract meaning of justice and made it applicable to a *transformed* political economy of democratic capitalism. They would have identified Rawls's concept of justice, because of its formal quality, as a symptom of the materialization of democracy. Populists expected more from both democracy and justice. They expected that the result would be human freedom.

Index